Christian Attitudes
Toward
War and Peace

THE CHILDREN'S TRUCE

PEACE: "I'M GLAD THAT THEY, AT LEAST, HAVE THEIR CHRISTMAS UNSPOILED."

"PUNCH" ON CHRISTMAS, 1914

ROLAND H. BAINTON

Christian Attitudes
Toward
War and Peace

A Historical Survey
and Critical Re-evaluation

Abingdon Press

Nashville

CHRISTIAN ATTITUDES TOWARD WAR AND PEACE

ISBN 0-687-07027-9

Library of Congress Catalog Card Number: 60-12064

MANUFACTURED IN THE UNITED STATES OF AMERICA

To

Cornelius Kruse

<small>COLLEAGUE IN COURSES AND COMRADE IN CAUSES</small>

———

Contents

List of Illustrations

11

Introduction

I N our time when the atomic bomb threatens to end the atomic era, the ethical problems of war and peace cry urgently for re-examination. For the Christian this must mean a restudy of the implications of the Christian gospel. For Christian behavior this will suffice, but as a basis for world peace it is not adequate, because all peoples and religions of the earth are involved. When we seek for an international ethos, the inquiry must be broadened. This question will engage us at the end of this book, but our primary concern is with the stand to be taken by the Christian.

The obvious point of beginning is the New Testament. Yet the New Testament has so little to say specifically on the subject that from its pages can be derived only principles rather than precepts. How those principles are to be applied the Christian must discover for himself in the light of changing circumstances. A knowledge of how they have been applied in the past should be of help in the present because the essential human situation has not altered. Admiral Mahan in his work on sea power declared that a history of naval strategy should begin with the days of sailing vessels, because all the technological advances of modern times have not fundamentally changed the lines which any naval encounter must assume. Similarly the moral problem of killing masses of men to vindicate justice and restore peace is not basically different from what it was in the time of Joshua or Jesus. There is, of course, this difference, that the destructiveness of war is today greater and less discriminating, and this difference may invalidate ancient codes. The study of history may thus prove emancipating if it shows that old rules no longer apply. It may at the same time provide guidance if it discloses a thread of principle running through divergent applications.

For the Christian the New Testament is the natural point of beginning, but there is reason for going back of the New Testament. Otherwise one will not appreciate that which is distinctive in New Testament attitudes. An even more important reason is that when the Christian Church, after three hundred years of abstention from politics, came under Constantine to the assumption of political tasks, the gap in the New Testament ethic at the point of politics was supplied by borrowings from Judaism and the classical world, notably Stoicism. The Christian ethic of war was not specifically Christian, but either Hebrew or Greek with Christian accommodations. For this reason, the present sketch of Christian attitudes commences with the ideals of peace and war in classical antiquity and in the Old Testament.

Broadly speaking, three attitudes to war and peace were to appear in the Christian ethic: pacifism, the just war, and the crusade. Chronologically they emerged in just this order. The early Church was pacifist to the time of Constantine. Then, partly as a result of the close association of Church and state under this emperor and partly by reason of the threat of barbarian invasions, Christians in the fourth and fifth centuries took over from the classical world the doctrine of the just war, whose object should be to vindicate justice and restore peace. The just war had to be fought under the authority of the state and must observe a code of good faith and humanity. The Christian elements added by Augustine were that the motive must be love and that monks and priests were to be exempted. The crusade arose in the high Middle Ages, a holy war fought under the auspices of the Church or of some inspired religious leader, not on behalf of justice conceived in terms of life and property, but on behalf of an ideal, the Christian faith. Since the enemy was without the pale, the code tended to break down.

These three attitudes were not rooted in different views of God and only to a degree in different views of man, because all Christians

14

recognized the depravity of man. The question was how to treat his depravity and the problem came to be an aspect of the relationship of the Church and the world. Pacifism has commonly despaired of the world and dissociated itself either from society altogether, or from political life, and especially from war. The advocates of the just war theory have taken the position that evil can be restrained by the coercive power of the state. The Church should support the state in this endeavor and individual Christians as citizens should fight under the auspices of the state. The crusade belongs to a theocratic view that the Church, even though it be a minority, should impose its will upon a recalcitrant world. Pacifism is thus often associated with withdrawal, the just war with qualified participation, and the crusade with dominance of the Church over the world.

These three views had already taken shape before the close of the Middle Ages. Thereafter they were to reappear in various configurations. In the late Middle Ages pacifism was represented by the sects. In the Renaissance in Italy the just-war theory took on new life among the city-states. At the same time among the humanists there was an extensive propaganda for peace on the basis of a Christian humanist culture. The Reformation precipitated wars of religion, in which the three historic positions reappeared: the just war among the Lutherans and the Anglicans, the crusade in the Reformed Churches, and pacifism among the Anabaptists and later the Quakers. The eighteenth century in theory and in practice resuscitated the humanist peace ideals of the Renaissance. The nineteenth century was an age of comparative peace and great agitation for the elimination of war. The twentieth century has seen two world wars. In this period again, the three historic positions have recurred. The churches in the United States particularly took a crusading attitude toward the First World War; pacifism was prevalent between the two wars; the mood of the Second World War approximated that of the just war.

The atomic bomb has brought bewilderment and division. The bomb has divided the bishops and their flocks. There are suggestions of an emergent pacifism, based not on Christian principles but simply on the desire for survival.

The bulk of this book is devoted to a delineation and an account of the historical emergence and adaptation of these concepts. At the close there is a critical appraisal and a defense of a personal position. Necessarily there is a shift from the objective to the subjective and not so necessarily from the dispassionate to the passionate. But why should not a historian be profoundly concerned over behavior which threatens to bring an end to history?

This book has been over thirty years in the making. Portions have been delivered as lectures. The earlier portion constituted the Ayer Lectures at the Rochester Theological Seminary in April, 1939. The section on the Cromwellian period was given as the Southworth Lecture at the Andover-Newton Theological Seminary in April, 1943. A survey of the whole was presented as the Ker Lectures at the Divinity School of McMaster University, Hamilton, Ontario in October, 1958. Sketches of the whole were delivered before the Washington Conference of Methodist ministers in January, 1959, and before the New York Conference in June, 1959. To these institutions and conferences my gratitude is due.

Chapter 1

Ideals of Peace in Antiquity

INASMUCH as the ethic of the just war in antiquity was conceived in the framework of peace, the concept and ideal of peace
afford the best point of departure. There were some variations in the
meaning of the term among the three peoples of the ancient world
who were chiefly responsible for the formation of our Western tradition, namely the Hebrews, the Greeks, and the Romans. For the
Hebrews, peace was more than the absence of war. *Shalom* signified
well-being and was almost synonymous with prosperity. "Peace be
within thy walls, and prosperity within thy palaces." [1] The imagery
of peace was commonly agricultural. "Thy wife shall be as a fruitful
vine . . . thy children as olive branches . . . peace be upon Israel." [2]
Peace meant security and for that reason the word *shalom* could be a
component in the name of an impregnable fortress, *Yeru'shalom*,
Jerusalem.[3]

Among the Greeks the word *eirené* (from which comes our word
irenic) was derived from a root meaning "linkage." Peace was thus
a state of order and coherence.[4] The difference from the Hebrew
concept was, however, slight; because if peace were not identical
with prosperity, at any rate, peace begot prosperity and was commonly accompanied in artistic representations by the cornucopia.
The mature Greek concept was delineated in these lines of the poet
Philemon:

> Philosophers engage in lengthy quest
> To know the good and where it may be found.

17

Virtue, reason and much else they say.
I learned it digging up the ground.
Peace it is, born of kindliest goddess,
Bestower, dearest Zeus, of every treasure;
Weddings, kindred, children, friends,
Wealth, health, wheat, wine and pleasure.[5]

Among the Romans peace came closer to being simply the absence of war. The word *pax* is derived from the same root as pact—an agreement not to fight—hence the association of *pax* with *tranquilitas, quies, otium* (repose), as well as with *securitas*. Yet with the Romans as well as the Greeks, peace was the bestower of abundance.[6]

For all the people of antiquity peace was a religious concept, most of all for the Hebrews. For them, peace was the gift of Yahweh: "I will give peace in the land, and ye shall lie down, and none shall make you afraid." [7] The Greeks and the Romans personified and deified peace, which of course the Hebrews could not do, because of their monotheism. The pagans had gods for all of man's major concerns, for peace as well as for war—Eirené and Pax for the one, Ares and Mars for the other. Altars were erected by the Greeks to Eirené and by the Romans to Pax, adorned with a bas relief of Terra Mater with fruit in her lap, children on her knees, and sheep and oxen at her feet. Some deities, once warlike, grew peaceful. Hercules developed from the Goliath of the Dorians to be suffering servant of humanity, enduring colossal labors to free the world of monsters and befriend mankind. Athena, the protectress of Athens, appeared at first armed with helmet, lance, and shield, but with the cultural development of the city she became the patroness of learning. The fluttered owl of her battles was transformed into the sedate symbol of wisdom, and her favored tree, the olive, gave its branches as a sign of peace. Even Niké, the goddess of victory, enlarged her scope to sponsor any contest whether of sport or art. She would hand not only arms to the warrior, but also the lyre to the musician. Such refined deities were able to pass as mythological symbols into Christian culture, whereas the other gods of the pagan pantheon were relegated to demonology.[8]

Peace was deemed desirable by all the peoples of antiquity in varying degrees. The Assyrians and their forerunners, the Sumerians, were perhaps exceptions. Certainly they were ruthless in war and gloated over carnage. Their art was great only in portraying the dying agonies of men and of beasts. But even they practiced war thus barbarously only in order to ward off attacks from without and to quell revolts from within their empire. In any case, they were exceptional. Nothing comparable is to be found in ancient art to the "stele of the vultures" feeding on the carrion of the vanquished.[9]

THE STELE OF THE VULTURES, EARLIER THAN 2000 B.C. AND PERHAPS AS EARLY AS 2500 B.C.

Among the Greeks, the Spartans trained the ruling oligarchy for war and militarized the state, but they were exceptional among the Greeks. Perhaps in the days of the invasions, war may have been glorified by the Hellenes. The early Homeric poems exhibit profusion of gore: brains spattered, bowels protruding, eyes spurting from their sockets. Such descriptions are not the proof that men enjoyed what they were doing, however. A modern historian has said: "[The Greeks] fought for land; they fought for trade; they fought to gratify the vanity or ambition of leaders or kings and they fought to gratify their own pride; they fought through fear and they fought for revenge. They never fought, I think, because they liked fighting." [10] Such a statement concedes that the Greeks were not willing to forego any of these objectives for the sake of peace, but it does assert that they would have preferred to achieve them without fighting, and particularly, that they did not enjoy fighting for the fun of fighting. Nor was war their normal condition; it occurred chiefly at the time of the harvest when neighboring states sought to steal one another's crops. A modern historian declares "that in spite of their many wars, they never regarded warfare as anything but a tragic interruption of ordinary life." [11]

The Romans manifestly built their empire by war, but considered peace their greatest achievement. The Hebrews were responsible for the idea of the crusade, which will engage us later; but they too exalted peace above war throughout most of their history.

Peace in the Age of Gold

All the peoples of antiquity with the exception of the Assyrians had the myth of a one-time warless world in a lost age of gold, whose recovery was the object of desire and endeavor. In the Greco-Roman form of the myth peace was not so much the bestowal of abundance as itself the result of abundance. In the age of gold, the earth freely yielded her increase without the toil of man; hence, there was no need for private property, no temptation to introduce slavery, and no reason for recourse to war. Peace in this idealistic state obtained even between men and animals; the lion and the lamb lay down together. War resulted from a fall of man. In the Hebrew story the disobedience of Adam and Eve introduced enmity between the serpent and the seed of the woman, while the murder of Abel by Cain started bloodshed among mankind.

The first appearance of the myth in Greek literature was in the poem of Hesiod, who portrayed the golden age of Cronos when men dwelt in ease, prosperity, and peace. There ensued a progressive deterioration through the ages of silver and bronze to the present age of iron in which families were at odds, oaths were disregarded, and might had come to be regarded as right.[12]

The Stoics fitted the myth into their picture of the rational order of the cosmos broken by a fall. Aratus, a disciple of Zeno, portrayed the good old time when men "did not yet understand war or vituperative dispute or the din of battle, but lived simply." In the degenerate age of bronze the evil sword was forged, the plow ox eaten, and justice took her flight to dwell among the stars.[13]

Chrysippus had a rational explanation of the fall in that the gods introduced war to keep down the population.[14] He verged on the suggestion that peace is bound to be her own undoing because the very plenty which she provides breeds too many men.

In Roman literature Ovid popularized the theme with no rationalistic explanations to tarnish his nostalgia for the Hesiodic idyl. Witness these lines:

> When towns were not by moats begirt,
> Nor swords forged, nor helmets wrought,
> Nor trumpets straight, nor twisted horns,
> Men slept secure with soldiers naught.[15]

The concept of the golden age of peace was not without practical import because of the belief that it could be restored. The Hebrews were confident that the bliss of Eden would return in the Messianic age to be inaugurated by a Prince of Peace, of whose "government and peace there shall be no end." The wicked would be slain by the breath of his lips and men would beat their swords into plowshares. The bow would be broken, the spear cut in sunder, and the chariot burned in the fire. Villages would have no walls, no gates, no bars.[16]

The plenty which peace bestows was to be restored. "He will make her wilderness like Eden, and her desert like the garden of the Lord." Peace would obtain again between men and the animals. "The wolf also shall dwell with the lamb, and the leopard shall lie down with the kid." Yahweh declared, "And in that day will I make a covenant for them with the beasts of the field, and with the fowls of heaven, and with the creeping things of the ground: and I will break the bow and the sword and the battle out of the earth, and will make them to lie down safely." [17]

Among the Gentiles the picture of the golden age could convey less comfort to those who held a cyclical view of history, for though peace might come again, so also would war. Scipio Africanus, when he committed Carthage to the flames, wept not out of pity for the fifty thousand survivors whom he was about to enslave, but only from the reflection that the revolving wheel of time would at long last bring the same fate to Rome.[18] Not all of the pagans were of this mind, however: Virgil's *Fourth Eclogue* combines Greek primitivism, Roman imperialism, and Hebrew messianism. Even before the accession of Augustus, this poet announced that a child would be born at whose coming a race would descend from heaven to restore the age of gold. Certainly no historical determinism impeded the efforts of the Stoics to ameliorate the social evils of their day, including war.

The Critique of Wars

The wars of antiquity elicited criticism, which though voiced only by the minority is not unimportant, because it was later incorporated into the writings of the Christian fathers. Even the Homeric poems exhibited weariness of war. "Were not the Trojans insatiate of battle," sang the poet, "Menelaus would enjoy sleep, love, song and dance." [19] Odysseus observed vexation of heart in him who, absent from his wife, must spend a single month in a benched ship.[20] At times the men of Homer were on the verge of composing their differences when the gods intervened to drive them to their doom. Aeschylus derided the Trojan war. To be sure, said he, Menelaus was bereft of Helen, but every soldier who sailed for vengeance left behind a brooding wife to whom Ares would return urns and ashes. The epitaph would read "hero fallen in action," but the secret comment would be "for another man's wife." [21] Euripides in *The Daughters of Troy* retold the story from the standpoint of the enemy and caused Andromache to say, on learning that the Greeks would dash her child against the rocks through fear of rearing the son of a hero, that the Hellenes were barbarians.[22]

Though the war against Persia was celebrated by Aeschylus, who fought at Salamis, his poem concluded with the lament of the mother of Xerxes.[23] Aristophanes scoffed at the Athenian war party in the Peloponnesian conflict. In the drama entitled *Peace*, this goddess had been thrown into a pit by the demon of war. The

22

Greek cities were summoned to her help and were scathed by the dramatist because of their obstructionist assistance.

Alexander, whose conquest actually fostered cosmopolitanism, was nonetheless berated in the silver age of Latin literature for his brutality and ambition. Seneca compared Alexander to a beast rending more than he could devour.[24] Juvenal observed that one globe was too small for Alexander, yet in the end a sarcophagus sufficed.[25] Quintus Curtius had a Scythian ambassador tell Alexander that he who boasted to have come against brigands was himself a brigand.[26]

The conquests of Rome likewise were scathed by the vanquished. The Gauls lamented that their land was prostrate beneath the victor's ax.[27] The Britons said, "The Romans are robbers of the world. After denuding the land, they rifle the sea. They are rapacious toward the rich and domineering toward the poor, satiated neither by the East nor by the West. Pillage, massacre and plunder they grace with the name of empire and where they make a desert, call it peace." [28] Orosius the Spaniard considered the ravages of the Goths in the early fourth century to be but flea bites compared to the Roman conquest of Spain when the natives killed their wives and children and cut their own throats rather than linger amid carnage and famine.[29] The conquered Greeks complained, "What manner of men are the Romans? Are they not shepherds who, unable because of base blood to secure wives, seized them by violence? who established their city by parricide and sprinkled the foundations of their walls with the blood of a brother?" [30] Among the Romans themselves Horace discovered a virus of corruption in the Roman blood stream, because the city had been founded on the fratricide of Remus by Romulus.[31] Sallust traced the degeneration of Rome to the demolition of Carthage.[32]

The civil wars of Rome were deemed by some to be particularly monstrous. After the death of Nero in A.D. 69 his generals fought over the succession for a year. During this struggle Tacitus recorded that a Spaniard enrolled on one side, leaving at home a son who later enlisted on the other. The lad unwittingly struck down his father and, recognizing the dying man, embraced him and prayed not to be abhorred for his parricide, since the blame should rest with the state. The soldiers watched as the son performed the last rites for his father, while down the line went cries of stupor, grief, and execration of this most cruel war. It was in this same conflict that Musonius the Cynic went among the ranks deriding the war.[33] Perhaps he addressed the men in the words of one of his surviving fragments. "Is not the world the common fatherland of all men? I am a citizen of the city of God." [34]

War as Scourge

In addition to the critique of particular wars there was criticism of war in general. Pindar summed it up when he said: "Sweet is war to him who knows it not." [35] The terror of war was described by Aeschylus as he portrayed the anguish of a siege:

> Groaning within: without
> A net is spread,
> Gripping the towers about.
> Man strikes man dead;
> And inarticulately
> Like beasts in dread,
> Mother and infant cry,
> And blood runs red.
> Running, they rob, they fly.[36]

The costliness of war was recognized by Pindar, who said: "Even by the feeble a city may be shaken to its foundation, but to set it up again is a sore struggle." [37] The unpredictability of the outcome in war, the folly of hastening death which comes in any case inevitably and quickly, are recurrent themes in the passages about to be cited.

The irrationality of war was seen in that it strikes those most entitled to live—the young and the weak. Herodotus caused Croesus to excuse himself in the following words for having started a war: "No one is so foolish as to prefer war to peace in which instead of sons burying their fathers, fathers bury their sons, but the gods willed it so." [38] Aristophanes observed the hardship that war inflicted upon women whose youth withered while the men were absent on the field.

GREEK WARFARE, A DETAIL FROM AN ATHENIAN VASE

In the drama *Lysistrata,* the women conspired on both sides to end the conflict by refusing all relations with their husbands until peace should be concluded. The magistrate complained of the impudence of the women:

> "these who have nothing to do with the war . . .

LYSISTRATA: Nothing to do with it, wretch that you are!

> We are the people who feel it the keenliest,
>   doubly on us the affliction is cast;
> Where are the sons that we sent to your battle-fields?

MAGISTRATE: Silence! a truce to the ills that are past.

LYSISTRATA: Then in the glory and grace of our womanhood,
>   all in the May and the morning of life,

> Lo, we are sitting forlorn and disconsolate,
>   what has a soldier to do with a wife?

> We might endure it, but ah! for the younger ones,
>   still in their maiden apartments they stay.

> Waiting the husband that never approaches them,
> watching the years that are gliding away.

MAGISTRATE: Men, I suppose, have their youth everlastingly.

LYSISTRATA: Nay, but it isn't the same with a man:

> Grey though he be when he comes from the battlefield,
> still if he wishes to marry, he can." [39]

That war is irrational because it is counter to the very grain of the universe was a theme particularly congenial to the Stoics, who believed reason to be immanent in the universe as a principle of harmony and cohesion. The heavenly bodies, said Dion of Prusa, move in harmony. The sun at night graciously gives way to the weaker stars and to the moon and even by day suffers himself to be eclipsed or beclouded. The stars in turn preserve their orbits without collision. Likewise in the lower world the birds nest beside the birds. The ants assist the ants and the bees do not quarrel over the same flower.[40] The theme of peace among animals derived from a remark by Aristotle, that at least animals of the same species exhibit friendship toward each other.[41] How preposterous then, argued his successors, that men, being of the same species and endowed also with conscious reason, should exhibit less amity toward their kind than serpents! Juvenal wrote in this vein:

Wild beasts are more merciful to beasts spotted like themselves. When did the stronger lion ever attack the weaker? In what wood did a boar expire under the tusks of a larger boar? The fierce tigress of India dwells in perpetual peace with her fellow; bears live in harmony with bears. Men formerly made only hoes, harrows, spades and plowshares but now, having learned to forge the deadly blade on the impious anvil, are not content merely with killing someone but act as if a man's breast, arms and face were a kind of food.[42]

Ways to Peace

A number of ways for achieving peace were proposed, and in a measure practiced, alike by the Gentiles and the Jews in antiquity. The approach of the Gentiles was primarily pragmatic. The elimination of the economic causes of war engaged Xenophon who addressed himself to the economics of peace and considered how Athens might renounce her empire without impoverishing her citizens. Athens might then at least eliminate wars of her own making if she could solve the problem of production and finance.[43]

Another way to peace was by way of concession. The *Pax Romana* was actually on occasion preserved in this fashion. The barbarians were not always repelled, but were admitted into the empire by a policy of controlled immigration. Constantine settled some 200,000 Sarmatians. A writer under the empire advocated peace by purchase: a subsidy should be given to the barbarians that they might be friendly and serve as buffers against more remote tribes. The policy was phrased in the words placed in the mouth of a prince who said, "I share my wealth with my enemies. The barbarians on my frontier were perpetually raiding my territory. Now I control them with money and instead of invading, they serve as a patrol against more troublesome barbarians beyond." [44]

A parallel existed in Hebrew thought, in the retouching of the stories of the patriarchs by later writers opposed to the extermination of the Canaanites. Writers of this school portrayed Abraham as sojourning many days peacefully among the Philistines, though of course in his day there were no Philistines in the land.[45] The spirit of the gloss was more fully revealed in Abraham's treatment of Lot, for when strife arose between the herdsmen of the two, Abraham proposed that they separate and suffered Lot to take the plain of Jordan, well watered as the garden of the Lord.[46]

Mediation and Magnanimity

If a dispute admitted of no resolution by agreement, mediation was the next recourse. If that failed, war should not so be waged as to preclude peace. These points are the subject of the next chapter.

For the avoidance of a future war no means was more expedient than magnanimity in the making of a peace. The Greeks and the Romans alike exhibited on occasion a generous spirit. The ideal was well expressed in an address in the Sicilian assembly when the aged

Nikolaos sought to dissuade his countrymen from severity toward the vanquished Athenians:

> Let no one accuse me of softness toward Athens. Have I not lost two sons in the war? How do I envy those who died gloriously for their country leaving me to a childless old age. Nevertheless mercy should be extended to Athens, partly on the grounds of law since the common usage of the Greeks forbids the slaughter of the vanquished, and partly on the grounds of humanity. To crush a bruised reed is to despise the common weakness of mankind. Why did the ancients set up their trophies in wood rather than in stone? That the memory of their victories might be short. Let Athens, who first erected an altar to Mercy, find mercy in the city of Syracuse. In the fluctuations of Fortune the victor of today may be the vanquished of tomorrow and how can he expect to find mercy if he refuse it? Magnanimity will be the best way to establish peace and make the Athenians ashamed of their unjust war. Recall their contributions to Greek culture and the common loss which will be sustained in the destruction of their citizens . . . forget not the common soldier who has not to reason why and above all let humanity be exercised toward those of the same stock.[47]

Here one finds a blending of Panhellenism and humanitarianism plus the prudential consideration that magnanimity is the best way to insure an enduring peace.

Pacifism

Again there were a few in antiquity who sought peace by a renunciation of politics and war.

Withdrawal from the state is evidenced by the Essenes who lived in segregated communities. Among the Greeks the Cyreniacs and the Epicureans eschewed political entanglements. Said a Cyreniac, "Where I thrive; there is my country." [48] Another declared that reason is opposed to sacrifice for the sake of fools. One's country is the world.[49] The Epicureans esteemed military exploits as the plague.[50] Lucretius besought glamorous Venus to enchant Mars to leave Rome in peace.[51]

A stronger motive for withdrawal was found in the disparagement of the body. One finds this in some measure later in Christian monasticism. Tendencies in this direction in pagan antiquity issued in the Neoplatonism of Plotinus. His political theory was ambiguous. He had been a soldier, but perhaps before he became a sage. Certainly he disparaged civic virtue and said that the savior of a state might be a rascal.[52] He suggested to the Emperor Gallienus the reconstruction of a ruined city in Campania as the seat of a platonic republic.[53] But he recognized that not all men should or would adopt the road of philosophy. In that case peace by withdrawal becomes the privilege or the vocation of the few.

Peace by poverty was the way of the Cyreniacs who avoided war by renouncing all that for which men fight. Said one of their members, "May neither I nor any friend of mine have need of silver or gold, for from the desire of these things, all human evils spring— factions and wars and conspiracies and murders." [54] Diogenes, when he saw a boy drinking from his hands, smashed his own cup saying, "How long have I carried superfluous baggage?" [55] He who had so little, was able, when the Greeks were at war, to move in a perpetual armistice.

Pacifism based on a belief in metempsychosis was ascribed to Pythagoreans whose leader according to Seneca inspired men with the fear of killing animals lest inadvertently they harm a parent.[56] Empedocles said expressly that in killing an animal one might be putting to death the very parent to whom one prayed.[57] Such opinions were extended to a repudiation of war by Pythagoreans who, "felt repugnance to killing living things as unlawful and contrary to nature and they considered it even more unrighteous to kill a man. For that reason they have given up making war. For war is the author and contriver of murders." [58] Actually we have no record of any concerted Pythagorean opposition to war.

There are passages in Seneca and Marcus Aurelius with a pacifist ring. Said Seneca:

We punish murders and what shall we say of wars and massacres which we laud because they destroy whole nations? . . . That which would be visited with death if done privately is vaunted when committed publically. . . . Shameful it is that men, the mildest breed, should delight in mutual bloodshed, even handing on their wars to their children, whereas animals devoid of reason are at peace. . . . Man who is sacred to man is even killed for sport.

In his book on natural history Seneca said that the winds were not designed to waft men to battle and death without burial. "Fools, what are you seeking? Death which is everywhere?" [59]

Marcus Aurelius likewise derided military bombast. "A spider," said he, "prides itself on capturing a fly; one man on catching a hare, another on netting a sprat, another on taking wild boars, another bears, another Sarmatians. Are they not all brigands?" [60]

Yet Seneca was the prime minister of Nero, and Marcus wrote his meditations in the camp defending the empire against the barbarians.

The thought of the Hebrews was so deeply religious that human devices for achieving peace were seldom proposed. Peace is a gift of God. Man fulfills the covenant; God bestows peace. A condition of peace is righteousness, but the point is not plain whether the righteous will enjoy peace because unrighteousness by its very nature is productive of strife, or that the righteous will be rewarded with the gift of peace. "[Those who] shed innocent blood have made them crooked paths: whosoever goeth therein shall not know peace." "There is no peace for the wicked." "The work of righteousness shall be peace; and the effect of righteousness quietness and assurance." Only when righteousness and peace have kissed each other will the Lord speak peace unto His people.[61]

Another condition of peace is trust in God, not in the strength of man: "Rely not on Assyria against those tails of smoking firebrands Pekah and Rezin. Lean not upon Babylon against Assyria. Trust not to Egypt nor to horses and chariots. The Egyptians are men not God; horses are flesh not spirit." "In returning and rest shall ye be saved, in quietness and in confidence shall be your strength." [62]

Another road to peace was much more prudential. When Israel was captive in Babylon, Jeremiah recognized the futility of rebellion. He advised acquiescence in the peace of Babylon[63] and even when help from Egypt was forthcoming, counseled against such an alliance. His advice may have been nothing more than political sagacity.

There is finally in Israel a suggestion of a redemptive pacificism which by suffering may usher in peace. This is the picture of the suffering servant of the Lord in the book of Second Isaiah.[64] The servant is a governor who "shall bring forth judgment to the Gentiles. . . . He shall not fail nor be discouraged, till he have set judgment in the earth." He is a shepherd "a bruised reed shall he not break and the smoking flax shall he not quench." He was despised and rejected of men and though he had done no violence "he made his grave with the wicked." The Lord will vindicate him because he poured out his soul unto death. Immortality appears to be his reward and the meaning of his suffering is that "with his stripes we are healed." Does this mean simply that we are reconciled to God or that we are so transformed by his example and by God's mercy that we shall be at peace among ourselves, and will this mean anything for the peace of the world?

For a mind so religious as that of the Hebrew the answer could scarcely be any other than that man must do justice, love mercy, walk humbly, and leave to God the bestowal of his peace.

Peace by Conquest

Actual peace on a wide scale was achieved in antiquity only by conquest. All of the arbitration among the Greeks did not stop wars, which were terminated only when Philip of Macedon deprived them of their freedom. On the death of his son Alexander, the Greeks revolted for liberty to destroy each other and continued their conflicts until peace was again imposed by the Romans.

The enthusiasm with which the *Pax Romana* was greeted is evidence alike of war-weariness and peace-mindedness. When Augustus triumphed over his last rival and closed the gates of the temple of Janus as a sign of peace, men hailed its advent as the return of the age of gold. Virgil saw in Augustus that figure of divine descent who should bring again to Latium the sway of Saturn. On willing subjects he would bestow the laws of Rome and confer on every race the ways of peace.[65] Blessed then was he who tended his own field, unwilling

31

to wreck a city in order that he might drink from a jeweled cup or sleep on Tyrian purple.[66]

The poets of the Augustan age took up the strain. Horace rejoiced in the return of faith, honor without shame, and peace. Tibullus prayed that love might walk unharmed upon the earth.[67] Propertius portrayed the soldier's wife cursing him who first made the trumpet out of bones. She rejoiced in her husband's triumphs only because they brought him home:

> Love is a god of peace,
> And peace is by lovers adored.
> Naked thou goest, oh fool,
> To ferry the Stygian ford,
> Equal to walk among shades,
> Be thou vanquished or be thou a lord.[68]

Praises of the *Pax Romana* continued to resound throughout the years. Toward the close of the second century Aelius Aristides rejoiced that the world had laid aside its ancient dress of steel. Cities no longer required an acropolis, and the name of Rome applied not to a city but to a race. Those who were formerly at war now lived as tranquilly as noiselessly gliding water.[69] On the eve of the barbarian debacle Claudian exulted that one might travel "to the drear recesses of the world" and yet find there a fatherland. "Whether we drink of the Rhine or the Orontes, we are all one people. Of Rome's sway there will be no end." [70]

Chapter 2

The Classical Origins of the Just War

THE idea of the just war arose in the context of the ideas of peace already described. The object of such a war was the vindication of justice and the restoration of peace; of necessity, therefore, peace had to be esteemed as an ideal, and recourse to war as a very last resort after mediation had failed. The war should be so conducted as not to preclude the restoration of an enduring peace. Hence, the conduct of war would have to be restrained by a code.

The resolution of disputes by mediation if possible, and if not, then by limited war, presupposed certain practical conditions which were fulfilled by the Greek city-states. The first was a relative equality of power; the lion does not arbitrate with the lamb. Rome was a lion, Israel a lamb. Rome would not submit her own disputes to arbitration, though willing to enforce it upon her subjects. Israel was not in a position to ask for arbitration with Rome, nor for that matter with Egypt or Assyria. The Greek cities, however, were independent sovereign states of approximately equal strength. To be sure, Athens first led, then Sparta, then Thebes, but the discrepancy of power was at no time so great as that between Assyria and Israel or between Rome and Spain. In the case of the Greeks, with forces so well matched that neither an easy victory nor certain defeat could be predicted, wisdom pointed to mediation rather than to the arbitrament of a long and indecisive conflict.

If war did come, and if the opportunity through some freak of fortune was afforded of liquidating the foe, why not be forever rid of the menacing assailant? What considerations dictated restraint? They might be prudential: that a state would fare better with friendly competitors than with sullen vassals or encircling waste lands. Such mundane wisdom would scarcely have prevailed, save for the belief that other Greek states had their worth and their right to live. Some sense of kinship was essential if fratricide were to be avoided among the peoples of a civilization divided into independent political units.

The Greeks were in a position to develop such a sense by reason of a common language—despite dialects—and a common culture. Though these of themselves did not unite them at the outset, and at the Battle of Plataea some fifteen thousand Greeks are estimated to have fought on the side of Persia, growing awareness of the menace of the common foe at length generated the sense of a common interest and a fellow feeling. The Persian Wars first prompted the distinction between Hellene and barbarian. Athens presumably inaugurated the Panhellenic propaganda and Herodotus disclosed its character when in the seventh book he commenced to use the term "barbarian" opprobriously in contrast to "Hellene." In the mouth of a Persian he placed the observation that "The Greeks are wont to wage wars against each other through sheer perversity. . . . Now surely, since they are of one speech they should compose their differences by any means rather than battle." [1]

Obviously Panhellenism had its limitations as a restraint upon war, because it could only apply to Hellenes. If the scope of the restraint were to be extended, the range of kinship must be enlarged. Stray Sophists and Cynics anticipated this development. Antiphon asserted that by nature all men are equal—Greek and barbarian alike.[2] Diogenes, when asked whence he came, replied, "I am a *cosmopolites, a citizen of the world,*" [3] by which he really meant not so much that he belonged to the world as that he did not belong to any particular state. The great growth of genuine cosmopolitanism came partly as a result of the conquests and the program of Alexander the Great, who has been hailed in our own day as the first to essay the unification of mankind.[4] In his own time, Alexander was lauded by Plutarch because by arms he had imposed what the word had been unable to effect: in the bowl of friendship he had mingled the lives and customs of men; the terms Greek and barbarian had reference henceforth not to peoples but rather to the cultivated and to the uncouth.[5] Such a statement, however, is a trifle extravagant, because Alexander undertook only to blend the Greeks and the Persians. His successors went farther in their effort to disseminate Hellenism throughout the whole of what is now called the Middle East. The attempt was never altogether successful. The Copt, the Syrian, the Armenian, and the Jew were never thoroughly assimilated and the Byzantine Empire was eventually to disintegrate through the resurgence of these peoples. Nevertheless, many persons came to think of themselves as belonging to a world vastly greater than the cities of their birth. The poet Meleager in the century before Christ wrote this epitaph:

> Attic was I born in Syrian Gadara,
> Nurtured in island Tyre, the Hellene Muse employed.
> What wonder, friend, that I should hail from Syria!
> One world our country, mortals gendered by the void.[6]

Coincidentally Stoicism provided a philosophical basis for a cosmopolitanism embracing all mankind. Since all men participate in the rational order of the universe they are able to comprehend the structure of their world and to order their affairs accordingly. The basis for world unity here is obviously intellectual rather than biological and does not of necessity insure unity, for the Stoic could not deny that some men do not behave reasonably. There are fools as well as wise men and fools may have to be coerced.

A Hebrew parallel to Stoic universalism is to be found in the extension of God's covenant to include more peoples than Israel. Strictly speaking this was not cosmopolitanism in which all the world is one city, but literally a syn-agogism, a going up together to the mount of the Lord. The breakdown of Jewish particularism consisted, not in a vague diffusion of cosmic fellowship, but in making others the heirs of the same promise. Yahweh's exclusive concern for Israel disappeared. He had brought the Philistines from Caphtor and the Syrians from Kir, just as he had brought Israel from Egypt.[7] "In that day shall Israel be the third with Egypt and with Assyria, even a blessing in the midst of the land: whom the Lord of hosts shall bless, saying, Blessed be Egypt my people, and Assyria the work of my hands, and Israel mine inheritance." [8] But the promises were still to Israel and through her "the people that walked in darkness have seen a great light." [9] Obviously here also there was still a line of cleavage between the children of the Covenant, however much enlarged, and the Gentiles, not of the flesh indeed but of the spirit.

Mediation

Among peoples who looked upon themselves as akin, war was considered a hideous extremity. Attempts at mediation must come first, and among the Greeks they did. Their record of successful arbitration is remarkable, for during the years from 798 B.C. to 740 B.C. eighty-one cases occurred, with frequency increasing toward the end of the period. Not all were voluntary, nor did the sum of them prevent the Greeks from mutual decimation. Nevertheless the record is impressive.[10] In various other ways the Greeks obviated conflicts; the Olympian games, the Amphictyonic councils, and the Delphic oracle all contributed.

The Olympic games served as a focus for Panhellenism. Here all the Greeks came together peaceably. Elis, the city of the games, was to enjoy perpetual immunity from war, nor could any of the participating states engage in hostilities during the time of the festival. At such assemblies treaties were made and local rivalries satisfied by sport.[11]

The Amphictyonic councils were assemblies for political purposes, of which the most famous was the Delphic. Members swore not to demolish any towns of the association and not to cut off running water in peace or in war. Any members violating the rule should be punished by the destruction of their cities. The league had teeth. The council served repeatedly as a court of arbitration, though it could not be characterized as a permanent court of international justice.

The Delphic oracle was consulted alike by Hellene and barbarian. Apollo the god of light and humanity, responded to all save the cruel, as for example the Milesians, who were refused a response because they had not expiated their excesses in the civil wars. Here was a form of excommunication. An order to a city to take down and bury an impaled head was obeyed. Athens was refused a response for failure to pay a fine to the Eleans. She complied. Again, having expelled the Delians in 422 B.C., she restored them at the behest of the god. The oracle both recommended arbitration and acted as an arbitrator.[12]

Peace the Object of War

If all other means of adjusting a difference had failed and war ensued, then it should be waged with an eye to the restoration of peace. Such was the view of Plato who, without using the expression, first gave formulation to the code which came to be called that of the "just war." [13] He could not employ this expression because his rules were intended to apply only among the Hellenes whose conflicts he would not dignify by the name of war. Rather, they were factions or feuds; such conflicts should be conducted always with an eye to reconciliation. The conquered were not to be enslaved; by the same token they were not to be exterminated.[14] Plato's word was not a utopian counsel, but had already been actually exemplified in the contests of the Greeks. At the close of the Peloponnesian War, Lysander the Spartan had caught the Athenian fleet at anchor while the crew were foraging. Only a remnant escaped to bear the news. No man in Athens slept that night, fearing that Sparta would raze the city and enslave the populace. The Corinthian and Theban allies of the victor recommended such a course, but Sparta declined to efface the glory of Greece and did no more than raze the walls to the music of flute girls.[15]

On a notable occasion Rome did not treat her vanquished foe in this magnanimous fashion. Carthage was destroyed. Significant, however, was the protest which preceded and the condemnation which followed the demolition. The circumstance was that Carthage, having been disarmed after the first Punic War, rearmed herself in contravention of the treaty in order that she might defend herself against the Numidian Massinissa. Rome saw here a threat to herself and Cato reiterated: *Carthago delenda est*. Scipio Nasica opposed on prudential grounds, arguing that Rome's western dependencies—such as Spain—would be less submissive if relieved of the menace of invasion by another great power; and Rome herself would succumb to dissension if not united by the fear of a rival.[16] His advice went unheeded. Carthage was levelled and her people enslaved. When subsequently Rome was rent by civil wars, later Romans reproached the ruthlessness of their sires.

Limited Violence

Since according to Plato the object of the Hellenic feud was the restoration of peace, the amount of violence should be restricted to the minimum necessary to obtain satisfaction from the enemy. The houses of the Greeks should not be burned. The land should not be scorched. Only the annual harvest might be confiscated. The sensibilities of the foe were not to be outraged by despoiling the dead of anything but weapons, nor by erecting trophies of victory in temples. Indiscriminate destruction would harm the innocent because in any conflict the whole population, consisting of men, women, and children should never be regarded as an enemy. Those really responsible for the quarrel would always be few.[17] Plato was here verging on the distinction between the combatant and the noncombatant, but used rather the terminology of the guilty and the innocent and did not suggest that they could be segregated during the course of the conflict. His warning was simply against indiscriminate violence in which all alike would suffer.

Justice and Natural Law

The restoration of peace was indeed the object of the just war, but it was called just primarily because its first object was the vindication of justice. Only thereafter would peace be proper. If justice, then, were the object, the concept of justice demanded definition, and nothing very precise was proposed. Plato defined justice as "giving to each his due." What then was his due? The answer, rather assumed than expressed, was conceived in terms of a static society resting on the basis of social inequality.[18] That was why Aristotle could apply the term, a "just war"—and he first coined the expression—to a war whose object was to enslave those designed by nature for servitude but who resisted their proper assignment in the social scale.[19] Between states justice meant the inviolability of harvests and the integrity of boundaries. It meant that each state should be content with what it had. Such a formula obviously had to be expanded or circumvented by casuistry if it were to cover wars of imperialism.

The concept of justice received a deeper base and a wider scope when incorporated into the system of natural law, a universal morality binding upon all peoples. The concept of natural law has had a venerable history. It was adopted and adapted by the Christian Church to undergird the political ethic alike of the Scholastic theologians and of the Protestant reformers. It was to enjoy an enormous vogue in the age of the enlightenment. Though obscured in the nineteenth century by the romantic movement, it continues today in large measure to provide the presuppositions of the Western democracies. In content it is vague and therein may lie, in part, the secret of its popularity. To be applied it must be rendered concrete, and concretion produces divergent interpretations. Its value lies in the assumption that a universal moral code exists. Such a faith inspires the quest in our day for an international ethos.

In antiquity the theory of the law of nature assumed shape in response to the divorce by the Sophists of law from nature. Some of them affirmed that by nature all men are equal, by law they have been made unequal. Other Sophists declared that by nature the strong should rule, whether they be strong individually or collectively; laws were held to be the conspiracy of the weak to deprive the strong of their natural due. Nature was held to justify the strong in recourse to ruthlessness for the recovery of their right. Against such unabashed brutality, Socrates steadfastly set his face. Better, said he, to suffer wrong than to inflict it.[20] Plato agreed. Law and nature were not thus to be divided; they were reassociated as the law of nature.

Precisely what was the law of nature? The answer depended on how the source of nature and the nature of nature were conceived. If nature were rooted in the transcendental, as in Plato's realm of ideas, or if nature were the will of the God of Israel, then the law of nature could be viewed as a fundamental norm for the laws of the state by which they could be corrected if at variance with the standard. If nature were a cosmic, rational principle immanent in the universe, as the Stoics claimed, then again it had a force far beyond statutes. But if nature were only that which is empirically observed to be universal in human experience, it might serve indeed to correct a particular constitution, but could not support a radical transformation of the social structure of the ancient world—for this reason Aristotle's law of nature was conservative.

Apart from the question of the source and sanction for nature, there was the problem of the nature of nature. Some defined it as the intrinsic, the core after the accidental had been stripped away. Others understood nature in terms of origins, as that which was there at the commencement; these therefore evaluated human institutions in terms of primitivism, as to whether they conformed to the conditions of the golden age without property, slavery, or war. Here plainly was a very radical concept which served well to justify the revolt of the Gracchi and the republican opposition to the empire. This radical natural law was blunted through the idea of the fall of man which necessitated an accommodation. The distinction between two varieties of natural law—the one radical, corresponding to the age of gold, the other conservative, corresponding to the behavior of fallen man—was first clearly formulated by the Roman jurist Ulpian in the second century of our era. Both varieties were to reappear in Christian social thought.[21]

Despite all these attenuations, natural law was conceived as a universal and self-vindicating morality. Applied to war, the concept meant that this institution must be judged in a wide ethical context, in terms of a law which enjoyed at least the weight of universal usage, and was commonly believed to enjoy a religious or a cosmic sanction. Yet in spite of all these imposing speculations, justice in antiquity was usually construed quite simply as the rectification of injury to life and goods, and this was deemed a proper ground for war.

Roman Adaptations: The State

When the notion of the just war was taken over by the Romans certain modifications were introduced by reason of the altered circumstances. Cicero was to transform the just war into a code for conquerors—an ethic for empire. His life span encompassed the last days of the republic and the beginning of the Roman Empire in the first century of the Christian era. Behind him lay the extension of Rome's sway well-nigh to the confines of the then known world. His version of the just war contained certain elements derived from old Roman practice.[22] To be just, said he, a war must be conducted by the state. A soldier not inducted by oath could not legally serve. This formula excluded the possibility of a revolution against the government. Cicero went so far as virtually to personify the state when he said that individuals die but the state should live forever.[23] One state, he continued, should not make war upon another without a formal declaration of hostilities. This stipulation was in accord with Roman practice which required that the *Fetiales,* a college of priests, should first deliver an ultimatum, allowing thirty days for a reply. If satisfaction were not given hostilities would be solemnly announced to the enemy. These *Fetiales* presided also over truces and treaties.[24]

In all dealings with the enemy the code required that good faith be observed and every oath fulfilled, whether sworn by the citizen or by the state. The classical example was the case of Regulus, a Roman prisoner at Carthage, who was released on oath to return, so that he might go to Rome and plead for a negotiated peace. Instead he informed the senate of the depleted state of Carthage and urged implacable prosecution of the war. Then, faithful to his promise, he went back to Carthage to die of torture.

Cicero, like Plato, distinguished between the guilty and the innocent among the enemy, but he did not specify that noncombatants were to be spared. His greatest concern was with the treatment of the vanquished, because only a liberal peace was a sound basis for the building of an empire. Reviewing the history of Rome until his time, he rendered the verdict that she had conquered the world by means of the just war and the generous peace.[25] Her enemies after defeat were incorporated unless they had been barbarous like Carthage. (Cicero justified her demolition.) Through incorporation the vanquished enjoyed all the benefits of Roman civilization.

In war and peace the conduct of rulers and peoples should be guided by the principle of *humanitas*.[26] This ideal had been elaborated by a Greek Stoic, Panaitios, who joined the circle of Scipio Africanus; the *philanthropia* of Panaitios became the *humanitas* of Cicero. The concept was based upon that which is congruous with the nature of man, himself a being endowed with excellence and dignity inspiring reverence. Decorum, civility, and refinement are becoming to him and should govern his deportment. In his dealings with others he should exhibit benevolence, magnanimity, and mercy. Harmony and concord should prevail in his society. Pompey exemplified the ideal, in that after conquering the pirates he did not crucify them but settled them inland where they might satisfy their needs without gratifying their habits. (One of Virgil's finest descriptions of nature was inspired by the garden of an ex-pirate.) Julius Caesar likewise broke with the proscriptions of Sulla and instead erected a temple to Clemency, sculptured as a goddess holding the hand of Julius the Conqueror. Such was the ideal in war and peace of those who established the *Pax Romana*.

Old Testament Parallels

These concepts were the more readily appropriated later by Christian writers because certain parallels were to be discovered in the Old Testament. Natural law had its counterpart in the covenant between Yahweh and his people. His will was seen as a universal morality binding not only upon Israel but upon all peoples. It came close to the Greek logos, pervading the universe, for the covenant was even with the beasts, as well as with day and night and even with the very stars. It was graven on hearts like the unwritten law of the Greeks. "I will put my law in their inward parts and and in their

42

hearts I will write it." [27] The covenant was vindicated by Yahweh who could use even the very Assyrians as the rod of his anger.

An obvious parallel was to be found between the golden age of the Stoics and the Garden of Eden, and in both myths there was the notion of a fall.

A code of war was elaborated in Deuteronomy 20. Enemy cities within the confines of Israel were subject to extermination, but if they were situated beyond the borders and would submit, they were to be incorporated as tributaries. If they refused to submit, only the males were to be put to the sword. Women, children, cattle, and goods were not subject to the ban, but might be enjoyed as spoils. Even if the city lay within the confines of Israel, though the people were to be killed, the fruit trees should be spared.

Another rule of warfare became prominent in the Maccabean struggle—the Jews would not fight on the Sabbath.[28] When consequently they were butchered, the rule was relaxed until it prohibited attacks but not defense upon that day. The Romans, discovering no resistance on the Sabbath desisted from warfare until the morrow and spent the intervening time in erecting earth works with which the Jews did not interfere but adhered to their scruples to their own hurt.

Chapter 3

The Origins of the Crusading Idea
In the Old Testament

THE crusade differed from the just war primarily in its intensely religious quality. The just war, to be sure, was not devoid of religion, and to disregard its conditions would be to incur the displeasure of the gods, but it was fought for mundane objectives, albeit with a religious sanction, whereas the crusade was God's war. As such it could scarcely have originated in antiquity save among the Jews.

The crusade stemmed out of the holy war which sought to ensure the favor of Yahweh by observing the conditions conducive to his good pleasure. An inspired religious leader sent out pieces of flesh to summon the tribes as yet only loosely consolidated. The men volunteered. They were dedicated to the Lord together with their weapons. Sacrifices were offered and a religious leader inquired as to the will of Yahweh. Then came the announcement to the people that their God had already delivered the enemy into their hands, that Yahweh was with them on the field of battle; later the ark came to be the sign of his presence. As the ark advanced, Moses cried "Rise up, Lord, and let thine enemies be scattered." [1]

One instance of a primitive holy war is recorded in the song of Deborah, who was awakened by Yahweh into a frenzy of religious ecstasy and fanned the fever of war, visiting curses on Reuben who abode in the sheep fold and Asher who remained in the ships. Without their help the mighty Sisera was brought low.[2]

The crusade went beyond the holy war in the respect that it was fought not so much with God's help as on God's behalf, not for a human goal which God might bless but for a divine cause which God might command. The sincerity of the warriors was evidenced by the consecration of the booty to the Lord. The power of God was made manifest by the fewness and the weakness of the troops. The leadership of God was revealed in that the war was inaugurated not by a government organized with reference to earthly security but by a God-filled leader, the mouthpiece of the Lord.

Before the period of the Maccabees one may doubt whether a crusade ever really took place in Israel. The conquest of the land is held by some archaeologists to have been rather a gradual infiltration punctuated by conflict.[3] The nomadic invaders had first pastured their flocks on the hillsides. If molested by lowlanders they would annex a city as a precaution. When they were fairly well established, a serious rival appeared in that the Philistines, coming by way of the sea, gained a footing on the coastal plain. In order to hold ground against them, the Israelites began to develop those institutions congenial to the just war, namely national consolidation, monarchical government, and military defense. Saul, the first king, had a bodyguard,[4] and David had his pretorians, the Gibborim, six hundred in number.[5] Solomon had a regular standing army with 1,400 chariots and 12,000 horsemen.[6] The primary role of the farmers thereafter was not to wield the sword but to pay the taxes. Prophets ceased to be the inspired instigators of war and became instead the chaplains of kings, still with the function of inquiring as to Yahweh's pleasure.

The establishment of the monarchy made possible the fulfillment of the condition of the just war that it be waged under the auspices of the ruler. The citizen served at the behest of the king rather than volunteered in response to the summons of the prophet. The conservatives interpreted these changes as defection from Yahweh. Samuel warned the people that the king "will take your sons, . . . for his chariots, and to be his horsemen. . . . And will set them to plow his ground, and reap his harvest, and to make his instruments of war, and instruments of his chariots. . . . And he will take the tenth of your seed, and of your vineyards, and give to his officers, and

45

to his servants." [7] The census of the land ordered by David in order to learn the military potential was undertaken against the advice of his captain Joab. When the numbering was done, David's heart smote him, because the Lord was sore displeased and visited the land with a pestilence in which there died seventy thousand men.[8]

Then arose a much more serious question in which David the statesman acted in the material interest of the nation against the scruples of the devout—particularly of the ardent prophets. The question was what should be done with the Canaanites who still dwelt in the land. They had not been exterminated. The Book of Judges explained that they had been left to give Israel exercise in war.[9] There they were, and their presence was a sore offense because they seduced Israel from the worship of Yahweh. The Book of Judges confessed with dismay to fraternization and corruption: "The children of Israel dwelt among the Canaanites, Hittites, and Amorites, and Perizzites, and Hivites,, and Jebusites: and they took their daughters to be their wives, and gave their daughters to their sons, and served their gods." [10]

The Purists called for their extermination. Saul thought to slay the "Gibeonites . . . the remnant of the Amorites." [11] Prophets like Elijah and Micah were for a root and branch extermination because the Canaanites worshiped local fertility deities—the Baalim and Ashtaroth, male and female—with drunken orgies and sexual excesses. Elijah smote four hundred of the priests of Baal.[12] Jehu beheaded seventy of the sons of Ahab and destroyed "Baal out of Israel." [13]

David saw the folly of weakening the land by wiping out so many of the inhabitants, and even made expiation to the Gibeonites by turning over to them seven of Saul's sons to be hanged.[14] Hosea discountenanced the violence of Jehu and predicted that Yahweh would avenge the blood of Jezreel upon his house.[15]

The Crusade Proper

In the course of these controversies the implacables formulated the policy of a genuine religious crusade against the Canaanites, on behalf of the faith of Israel. They were not concerned as to all the features of the holy war and were not necessarily averse to having the king as leader, but felt that an aggressive war should be undertaken to purify Israel of the abomination. The program was anachronistically placed into the mouth of Moses, as though he were instructing the people prior to the conquest of the land. The book of Deuteronomy records his alleged instruction:

When the Lord thy God shall bring thee into the land whither thou goest to possess it, and hath cast out many nations before thee, the Hittites, and the Girgashites, and the Amorites, and the Canaanites, and the Perizzites, and the Hivites, and the Jebusites, seven nations greater and mightier than thou: And when the Lord thy God shall deliver them before thee; thou shalt smite them, and utterly destroy them; thou shalt make no covenant with them, nor show mercy unto them.

Thou shalt surely smite . . . that [faithless] city with the edge of the sword . . . and all that is therein, and the cattle thereof . . . [thou] shalt burn with fire the city . . . and it shall be an heap for ever.[16]

The Deuteronomists then constructed the account of the conquest and in the books of Numbers, Joshua, and Judges represented their ideal as having been actualized in the taking of the land. An exceedingly important point in their rationale was that Israel had invaded at the behest of Yahweh and advanced under the protection of his outstretched arm.

A change in the character ascribed to Yahweh is observable in the course of these developments. We have already noted that Yahweh was the giver of peace. That he should also be the author of war need not surprise us because in a monotheistic system the one God has to do everything. Functions cannot be distributed among the gods of peace and the gods of war. Yahweh gives peace, and Yahweh gives war. Yahweh bestows victory, and Yahweh may inflict defeat as a chastisement.

Historically speaking, his warlike characteristics were magnified in the course of the descriptions of the conquest. Originally Yahweh appears to have been regarded as the deity of natural catastrophe—

of sirocco, hail, earthquake, and pestilence. If he fought, it was through the instruments of nature: the sea closed upon Pharaoh; the ground clave asunder to devour Korah; the sun stood still upon Gibeon and the moon in the valley of Ajalon until Joshua was avenged of the Amorites; the stars in their courses fought against Sisera.[17] Later Yahweh acquired the characteristics of a man of war. In the Song of Moses he was disclosed as whetting his glittering sword and as declaring "I will make mine arrows drunk with blood, and my sword shall devour flesh." [18] The army of Gideon was reduced by 22,000 leaving only three hundred men, that at the blowing of the trumpet the Lord might set the sword of every man in the enemy camp against his neighbor.[19] David slew Goliath with a pebble. Jael smote Sisera with a tent pin.[20] At the sound of the trumpets the walls of Jericho came tumbling down.[21] Not by the conscript armies of kings, but by the weak instruments of the Lord of Hosts were his enemies put to confusion.

The disinterestedness of the warriors was evidenced in the observance of the ban, which entailed the destruction of everything among the enemy which the victor might have retained and enjoyed. Israel had vowed a vow unto the Lord and said, "if thou wilt indeed deliver this people into my hand, then I will utterly destroy their cities." [22] When Achan laid hand upon the spoils and took for himself a goodly Babylonian mantle and silver and gold, the anger of the Lord was kindled against the children of Israel and could not be appeased until Achan was stoned, together with his sons and daughters, his oxen and his sheep and his tent.[23] Though Saul slew the Gibeonites, yet he offended by saving some of the booty devoted to Yahweh, and Samuel had to expiate the offense by hewing Agag in pieces before the Lord.[24] As for the Israelites at Jericho, they "utterly destroyed all that was in the city, both man and woman, young and old, and ox, and sheep, and ass with the edge of the sword." [25] Ai was taken by strategem and twelve thousand men and women wiped out. And Joshua "burnt Ai, and made it an heap for ever, even a desolation unto this day. And the king of Ai he hanged on a tree until eventide." The summary of several exploits was that Joshua "smote all the country of the hills and of the south, and of the vale, and of the springs, and all their kings: he left none remaining, but utterly destroyed all that breathed, as the Lord God of Israel commanded." [26] One observes how ill fared the code for humane conduct required by the just war when the conflict became a crusade. War is more humane when God is left out of it.

The Problem of Defeat

Not only was the program of the crusading exterminists not realized, but Yahweh even permitted the great empires of the East to swoop down upon his people. "The Assyrian came down like a wolf on the fold." Hezekiah entrenched himself in Jerusalem. Whereas the biblical account says that the host of Sennacherib was smitten by the Lord and withdrew, the Assyrian records reveal that Sennacherib actually overran the land, captured forty-six villages and carried off 200,000 men, besides the cattle, and caged Hezekiah in Jerusalem. All the king's horses and all the king's men had been of no avail. Manasseh, the son of Hezekiah, at first submitted, then resisted and was deported. His successor Josiah, more as prophet than king, revived the Deuteronomic ideal and rebuilt the army, presumably on the basis of voluntary recruitment.[27] Political resistance to Assyria appeared feasible, because of the emergence of Babylon as a rival. When Egypt then rallied to the support of Assyria, Josiah assayed to impede the passage of Pharaoh's army, but was defeated and killed at Megiddo in 609 B.C. Thenceforth Israel was to be a subject people.

How could such defeat be explained? Had not Josiah fulfilled the Word of the Lord in relying on no standing army, nor on alliances with Egypt and Assyria? He had withstood them both, but Yahweh had performed no miracle and the king had been brought back "in a chariot dead from Megiddo." [28] Long since, the Assyrian Rabshekah had taunted the men on the walls of Jerusalem with the folly of trusting to their God. "Where," he jeered, "are the gods of Hamath and Arpad? Where are the gods of Sepharvaim? Who are they among all the gods of these lands that have delivered their land out of my hand that Yahweh should deliver Jerusalem?"

Yahweh did not deliver Jerusalem. Later he even suffered his people to be taken captive to Babylon. Yet such events did not shatter faith nor prove the futility of crusades. Defeat was explained as chastisement. Israel stood in covenant relationship with Yahweh, who would perform what he had sworn, but only provided that Israel observed his precepts to do them. The moral, then, was that Israel should rend her heart and not her garments.

Though Israel strove to obey, the chastisement of the Lord was grievously prolonged. Surely she had received double for all her sins. Not so much resignation before the Lord as bitterness against the enslaver began to invade the hearts of many, who predicted vengeance upon the foe. "Oh daughter of Babylon, who art to be destroyed; happy shall he be, that rewardeth thee as thou hast served us. Happy shall he be, that taketh and dasheth thy little ones against the stones." Babylon shall be as Sodom and Gomorrah. "The wolves shall cry in their castles and jackals in their pleasant places." Why did Yahweh delay? Nineveh he had laid waste; why not Babylon? Could it be that he was impeded by foes in the heavenly places whom he must first overthrow before vindicating his people on earth? Lucifer had ascended to heaven and exalted his throne above the stars of God. He had shaken kingdoms and overthrown cities and would not loose his prisoners to their home.[29] Likewise Gog of Magog was more than an earthly adversary. The conflict had assumed cosmic proportions and only after an apocalyptic denouement would the Redeemer succor his people. This is a transfer of the crusading idea to the heavenly places. The result of this shift may be quietism with everything left to God. Yet frequently those who believe in an apocalyptic war are ready if the opportunity comes to initiate it by earthly effort.

Resurgence of the Crusade

Unexpectedly, in the case of Israel, there came at long last another chance for a crusade on earth. It was in the days of the division of

Alexander's empire, when the Seleucids controlled Palestine. They desired to promote the blending of cultures and looked with favor on the Hellenizing of Judaism. Many of the Jews were not averse. They saw no infidelity to Yahweh in treating Melkart as his colleague. "Let us go and make a covenant with the heathen who are round about us," said they. "For since we departed from them, we have had much sorrow." [30] The Hellenizers were ready to abandon circumcision and the Sabbath. Jason, the high priest of Yahweh, sent a present to the sacrifices of Hercules of Tyre, and all of this without any thought of abandoning the Temple and the Law.[31] Rigorist Jews would not tolerate such fraternization, however. The struggle was at first between Jews and was peaceful until at Jerusalem insubordination was penalized by the forbidding of circumcision and the requirement of sacrifices to the heathen gods alongside of Yahweh. When a Jew complied, the Maccabees flared up and slew the apostate. The days of Deborah and Gideon then returned: Judith slaying Holofernes was the new Jael. The covenant again became the oath which the Lord swore unto the fathers to destroy the host of their enemies. Bands of frenzied enthusiasts, sometimes without armor and sword, trusting in the God, who turned the Red Sea waters, leaped like lions upon the defilers of their laws, and the Lord came down from heaven once more to the field of battle, discomfiting their enemies before their faces. Resisting cities were fired when taken and all males put to the sword. Those who took refuge in temples were burned together with the sanctuaries, while the Maccabean warriors sang psalms and hymns as they went through the land. The crusade had returned.

The Christian Church for centuries was unaware of the stages in the historical development of the rise, fall, and, revival of the crusading ideal, and the early Fathers never so much as suspected that the wars of the conquest of Canaan might have been only the romancing of reformers whose program was never attained. The books of Deuteronomy, Numbers, Joshua, Judges, and Maccabees were taken over into the Christian canon of Scripture. Thereafter the wars of Yahweh might be allegorized but they could not be omitted; not until the rise of modern biblical criticism did anyone suggest that they had never occurred. The architects of the Christian crusade, therefore, drew their warrant from the books of the conquest and of the Maccabean revolt.

Chapter 4

War and Peace in the New Testament

THE three attitudes to warfare already delineated in antiquity were to reappear in Christian thinking with modifications. The crusade curiously received the least alteration—because it was so thoroughly religious. The just war of pagan origin was baptized by sprinkling. But the pacifism of antiquity was subjected to the most drastic revision because it became a program of action. Prior to the advent of Christianity there is no record of anyone suffering death for a refusal of military service. The Stoics had not lived in accord with the pattern of the golden age of no slavery, no property, and no war. The Christians did reject war, however, and of these three only war. Private property was freely shared but not abandoned by Christians, and slavery was ameliorated but not abrogated. War alone was repudiated until the time of Constantine, for until then no extant Christian writing countenanced Christian participation in warfare.

Christian Attitudes

The rejection of military service on the part of the early church was not however derived from any explicit prohibition in the New Testament. The attitude of the Gospels to the soldiers' calling was neutral. The centurion was commended for his faith rather than for his profession, but was not called upon to abandon his profession. The pacifism of the early church was derived not from a New Testament legalism, but from an effort to apply what was taken to be

53

the mind of Christ. Christianity brought to social problems, not a detailed code of ethics or a new political theory, but a new scale of values. The quality of Christian love transcended the highest in Judaism and Hellenism. Christian *agapé* was utterly other-regarding love. There was an approximation of *agapé* in the Old Testament— in the love of David for Absalom, of Hosea for Gomer, and of Yahweh for Israel; but love there was attenuated by legalism, inasmuch as the Lord bestowed his favor upon those who remembered his precepts to do them. The characteristic Greek word for love was *eros*, a lofty aspiration for union with the beautiful and the good by which the self was fulfilled and transformed. It tended to inspire rather composure than compassion, for even Seneca regarded sympathy as a disease of the soul,[1] and Marcus Aurelius counseled compassion only on the ground that injury is unworthy of notice since it cannot foul the inner shrine.[2] Juvenal grounded the tenderness betokened by tears upon reverence for the nature of man as capable of divine things.[3] But Christian love was directed toward the prodigals of the world. It was a love which sought the wayward and stooped to suffer and to share.

The whole scale of the classical virtues was thereby altered. Martial valour disappeared from the pages of the New Testament. Cicero would have said "By valour Moses refused to be called the son of Pharaoh's daughter." In the New Testament the victory which overcomes the world is faith.[4] Many Hebrew concepts were transformed. The covenant, which God swore to the fathers to destroy their enemies from before their face[5] became in the mouth of Jesus "the new testament in my blood." [6] The apocalyptic doomsday of Judaism, when God would annihilate the enemies of Israel, became the day when wrath would be pronounced upon those who had not clothed the naked.[7]

The distinctive quality of Christianity was nowhere more evident than in its transformation of the concept of peace.[8] In the New Testament peace was still well-being and security, but the physical characteristics disappeared. The Kingdom of God consisted not in food and drink but in righteousness and peace. The recovery of Eden was not a return to toilless bliss, but the restoration of the image of God in fallen man. Peace was victory, as with the Greeks, but it was victory over the powers of darkness.[9] Peace in the New Testament had of course a certain negative aspect. It was naturally the absence of its opposite, but the opposite was not only war but contention. Christians were exhorted to display lowliness, meekness, longsuffering, and forbearance, "endeavoring to keep the unity of the Spirit in the bond of peace." [10] Peace was more deeply religious than even among the Hebrews, because it was not in the first instance the cessation of hostilities between nations.[11] It was peace with God, a rare note in the Old Testament.[12] "Being justified by faith, we have peace with God." [13] Enmity was thereby broken down between man and man, for the peace of God proclaimed by Christ made the Gentiles fellow citizens with the saints.[14] He who was at peace [15] was able to bestow peace.[16] The Christian peace was creative and dynamic, accompanied not by the cornucopia but by joy, life, hope, and power. "Now the God of hope fill you with all joy and peace in believing, that ye may abound in hope, in the power of the Holy Ghost." [17] Because Christians were peacemakers, they would be called the sons of God.[18]

These attitudes were plainly not irrelevant to the issues of peace and war. The more specifically political problems, however, were not posed, let alone answered, in the New Testament.

The Political Situation

During the first century A.D. three political situations confronted Christians. The first was that of the early period in Palestine, when the question was whether Judea should revolt against Rome. The answer of Christians was clearly "No." The second was that of the Pauline missionary journeys in the Gentile world, when Christians could avail themselves of the *Pax Romana* for the dissemination of the gospel and when they enjoyed the protection of the Roman state against violent Jewish interference. The question then might have been whether Christians could take arms in defense of the Roman peace, but to our knowledge the question was not raised. A decision was, however, necessary as to whether the Christian might avail himself of the protection of the Roman government. The answer in this instance was affirmative, but war was not here involved. The third situation emerged after the death of Paul, when the Roman government began to persecute the Christians. Then the book of Revelation reverted to the imagery of the Jewish apocalyptic war in which Babylon, symbolizing Rome drunk on the blood of the saints, should in one hour be made desolate. War on earth was not suggested for Rome's extinction, however. It would have been futile, but had a Christian then been asked whether he would defend Rome, his reply might well have been in the negative.

Texts for the Crusade

Despite all the ambiguities in the New Testament, every one of the subsequent Christian attitudes to war and peace has relied on New Testament texts. Support for the crusade has found its most congenial passage to be Jesus' cleansing of the temple with a whip of cords, a detail mentioned only in John's gospel.[19] Here was undeniably an instance of fiery indignation against the profanation of the sacred, but the whip of cords, if genuine, was no hand grenade, and the success of Jesus in routing the hucksters was scarcely due to physical prowess. For what was one man, even with strands of rope, against such a company? They must have dispersed because they were cowed by a wrath which they recognized as right.

Another crusading text is the pronouncement, "I came not to send peace, but a sword." [20] Evidently here the word "sword" was used metaphorically, because in the parallel passage in Luke we read instead the word "division." [21] More puzzling is another favorite crusading passage, "he that hath no sword, let him sell his garment, and buy one." [22] The difficulty here is that the verse has a double focus. It is placed in the midst of directions for a new missionary journey where Jesus' followers would no longer be freely entertained. Hence he that had a purse was advised to take it. Then follows this text. The immediate sequel was the scene in the garden where one of the disciples smote the High Priest's servant and was rebuked on the ground that they who take the sword will perish by the sword.[23] One is tempted to feel that the deed of violence arose from the misunderstanding of a metaphor. If, however, the passage is to be taken literally, it does not go beyond permission to imitate the Essenes, who forbade the manufacture of arms in their communities but allowed their members when on journeys to carry arms against brigands. Such a practice was obviously not nonresistance, but neither was it international war—let alone a crusade.

Texts for the Just War

The concept of the just war has been validated by reference to those passages in the Gospels and the Pauline writings which in some measure endorse civil government. Among the words of Jesus the classic text has been "Render to Caesar the things that are Caesar's." [24] This pronouncement was actually a rejoinder to a question posed by the Herodians and Pharisees on the propriety of paying tribute. A more incriminating question could not have been contrived. Palestine was an occupied country. The tribute was a device of exploitation and therefore the symbol of imperialism. To facilitate the collection of the tax at the very time when Christ was born a census had been instituted by Augustus. Three parties had developed in Judaism with reference to the occupation and the tribute. The Herodians were ready to fraternize; the Zealots to rebel. They had in fact done so at the time of the census, under the leadership of Judas of Galilee, but the insurgents had been crushed and crucified. The Pharisees would neither fraternize nor rebel, but would keep the law and await God's vindication. They quarreled with Jesus over his interpretation of the law and his claim to divine authority. For that reason they were willing to join with the Herodians in the captious question, embarrassing to Jesus however answered. If he said that the tribute should not be paid he could be denounced to the Roman authorities as a new Judas of Galilee; but if he counseled payment, he would lose face with the numerous Zealots.

The reply of Jesus was adroit. He asked to be shown a specific coin, a denarius.[25] This was a silver coin minted outside of Palestine. The time was the reign of Tiberius. His denarius bore a bust of the emperor crowned with laurel as the sign of his future divinity and bore the inscription "Augustus son of the divine Augustus." On the reverse was the title *Pontifex Maximus* and sometimes an image of the emperor's mother seated upon the

A COIN OF TIBERIUS *
A.D. 22

throne of divinity. The emperor was thus celebrated as the head of the pagan religion and as the divine son of divine parents. The coins were Rome's best device for popularizing in the provinces the cult of the deified ruler. The Jews would have none of it, however, and when Pilate introduced in Jerusalem military standards bearing symbols of the imperial cult, the Jews made such a stout protest that he yielded. Purists were equally averse to the coins and later, during the revolt of Akiba, hammered them flat and stamped them afresh with Hebrew characters. But many of the Jews, while adamant as to the Roman standards, were pliant in regard to the coins. Jesus accordingly asked to be shown a denarius and inquired whose head and inscription it bore. His questioners answered simply "Caesar's." His reply might be paraphrased, "If then you trifle with your scruples and carry the tainted coins, give back to Caesar what he has given to you, but remember your prime allegiance is to God." No wonder Mark commented "and they were amazed at him"!

Jesus had parried skillfully, but what was his own position? The point of his words might have been that neither were the coins to be carried nor the tribute to be paid; but we do know that Jesus paid tribute, for so Peter informed the tax collectors.[26] We may infer that Jesus was traduced before the Romans as a Zealot, otherwise they would not have crucified him; but equally we may assume that he was not a Zealot, for otherwise his countrymen would not have pre-

* Ti[berivs] Caesar Divi Aug[vsti] F[ilivs] Avgvst[vs] Imp[erator] VIII. On the reverse: *Pontif[ex] Maxim[vs]*. The shape is irregular because the coin has been clipped to steal metal.

ferred Barabbas. To derive from these few conclusions a complete political philosophy, however, is to make vast assumptions. Payment might have been regarded simply as submission under tyranny rather than as the endorsement of a regime. When the Devil offered Christ all the kingdoms of the world, our Lord apparently agreed that they were under Satan's control.

The apostle Paul was more explicit than the Gospels with regard to the role and authority of the state. In the famous passage in Romans 13 he said "Let every soul be subject unto the higher powers. . . . The powers that be are ordained of God . . . [the ruler] beareth not the sword in vain: for he is a minister of God. . . . Wherefore ye must needs be subject . . . for conscience sake. . . . Pay tribute also." [27]

This passage in later ages received three interpretations. The first was that the coercive power of the state was ordained by God because of sin and should be administered by sinners. The saints should submit to all commands not contrary to conscience but should not collaborate. So said the Anabaptists in the age of the Reformation. The second position was that the state was indeed ordained because of sin; but Christians, though they would not need the state for themselves, should nevertheless assume political responsibilities, because otherwise in a nominally Christian society the state would collapse without their help. So said Luther. The third view was that the state was ordained not only because of sin but also to foster righteousness and faith. Such had been the view of the Old Testament theocracy, and it was espoused again by Calvin.

In the New Testament these positions did not clearly emerge, but there were suggestions of all three. The first might be inferred from the sharp differentiation of the Church from the world. The Church was called the new Israel of God,[28] and Christians were described as an elect race, a royal priesthood, a holy nation.[29] Christ purchased "us to God by [his] blood out of every kindred, and tongue, and people, and nation; and hath made us unto our God kings and priests: and we shall reign on the earth." [30] The Church encompassed the earth,[31] but more than the earth, for her membership included the immortal dead,[32] and her head was the Risen Lord.[33] Her citizenship was in heaven.[34] She could not, therefore, identify herself with any earthly community and must stand in some measure aloof. "Come out from among them, and be ye separate." [35] The world was rejected because it was transitory. Christians were but strangers and pilgrims seeking an abiding city.[36] Marcus Aurelius confessed one world, one God, one reason, and one truth.[37] Paul could not confess one world because the world passes away. He confessed one Lord, one faith, and one baptism.[38] The world was rejected because it was evil. "From whence come wars and fightings among you? come they not hence, even of your lusts that war in your members? . . . ye fight and war . . . know ye not that the friendship of the world is enmity with God?" [39] Paul enjoined Christians not to appeal to the Roman courts. Such injunctions and affirmations disclosed an aloofness from social participation and political involvement.

On the other hand, Paul did accept an escort of soldiers to conduct him from Jerusalem to Caesarea, and one might infer that he would have been willing to serve in a police capacity. A passage in II Thessalonians has been interpreted as an indorsement of the police action of the Roman government. It is the passage in which Paul was discouraging extravagant expectations with regard to the nearness of the Lord's coming, because first a man of sin must be revealed who would set himself forth in the temple as God. This would not take place immediately, however, because of a power which restrained. Now who was the man of sin and what the power that restrained? Early commentators identified the man of sin with the deified Roman emperor and the power that restrained with the Roman empire. The point was obviously not that the empire was restraining the emperor, but that the empire was restraining all the forces of chaos which would be let loose in the final debacle. The empire in other words was a force for order. Whether this interpretation was actually Paul's meaning cannot be positively determined; his words might be so understood and would then lend countenance to the assumption by Christians of political tasks. Whether they might go to the length of war would still be debatable.

The third view—that the state and particularly the Roman empire had positive functions in God's plan—was to play a great role in the age of Constantine, but in the New Testament there were only premonitory hints. The Lukan writings were the most favorable to the Roman government, which they portrayed as the protector of the faith against Jewish and pagan turbulence. The pronouncement that God must be obeyed rather than man was addressed only to the Jewish authorities. Luke alone observed the synchronism between the gospel and the empire, that Christ was born under Augustus Caesar [40] and that John the Baptist began his ministry under Tiberius.[41] In matters military Luke was also the most favorable. Only he had the soldiers come to John the Baptist [42] and he alone told the story of the king who prepared for war.[43] Luke omitted the injunction, "Put up the sword," [44] and only he recounted the enigmatic statement about buying the sword. The nuances of Luke point to the Constantinian view that Christianity and the Roman empire were conjoint works of God for the advancement of his kingdom.[45]

Pacifist Texts

Pacifism has been supported out of the New Testament chiefly by texts found in the Sermon on the Mount: "Resist not evil, turn the other cheek, go the second mile, love your enemies." [46] Several of these sayings demand a word of explanation. The first one reads in full "whosoever shall smite thee on thy right cheek." Among the Jews of that day a slap on the right cheek was not a case of assault but an extreme insult administered with the back of the hand. The point here was not that one should not defend one's life, but that one should not resent indignity.[47] The injunction to go the second mile had reference to impressment for service by the government: if required to carry the mails for a mile, go two. Far from resisting Rome, Jesus thus counseled service in excess of the levy. The meaning of "love your enemy" has been debated as to whether the enemy was public or private. The text is preceded by the statement "Ye have heard that it hath been said, Thou shalt love thy neighbor, and hate thine enemy." Now no Jew had ever said that a private Jewish enemy should be hated. The reference must therefore have been to the public enemy who was to be loved. The remaining text, "Resist not evil," is clear enough.

Taken together, these texts enjoined so great a degree of submissiveness that many devices have been employed to obviate their apparent intent. One method has been to take them in a theological rather than in an ethical sense. These precepts are said to have been enjoined because they cannot be kept. They demand the imitation of God and the imitation of God is impossible. Thus reason some modern theologians; but the Jew of Jesus' day did not consider the imitation of God to be impossible, for did not the book of Leviticus say "Ye shall be holy: for I the Lord your God am holy"? [48]

Another proposal for obviating the apparent meaning of these texts is to refer them not to outward acts but to an inner disposition of the heart. These precepts plainly tell us to love our enemies but do not say that we may not constrain or kill. The distinction is not without point, but inwardness cannot be used as the sole clue to the ethic of the Sermon on the Mount. The command not to look upon a woman to lust after her called indeed for an inward disposition, but not for a disposition at variance with outward behavior.

Some interpreters have restricted these precepts in another way: namely at the point of the time to which they apply. The method is twofold, referring either to the short time prior to the Lord's coming or to the indefinite period after his return. In the first instance we have an *ad interim* ethic. The injunctions are then binding only until the coming of the Son of Man within the lifetime of Jesus' own generation. This was practically to say "give away your cloak because there will never be another winter." Yet in the Sermon on the Mount such a motive was never assigned. Rather the appeal was to the imitation of God. One must bear in mind also that the expectation of a coming divine intervention did not of necessity make for pacifism. In Judaism it served rather to inspire messianic war. More than the temporal factor is required to explain why the messianism of Jesus repudiated armed revolution.[49]

The second variant of the temporal device posits a *post interim* ethic. The assumption is that the precepts on nonresistance were not expected to go into effect until after the coming of the Son of Man, when the whole structure of society would be altered and such submissiveness would then become feasible. Paul certainly did not so interpret Jesus. He exclaimed "Now it is high time to awake out of sleep . . . The night is far spent . . . let us walk honestly *as in the day*." [50] Observe that the day had not yet come. Before it arrived Christians were even then enjoined to walk honestly.

The failure of the eschatological hope is offered by some in our own day as a reason for discarding Jesus' precepts on nonresistance. We are reminded that even in the Gospels God is portrayed as exercising great severity at the last judgment. Since that day is a long way off, however, we are in the meantime to act on God's behalf and practice a like severity. If this view be defended as constituting the mind of the New Testament, it forgets that we are there called upon to imitate the mercy but not the wrath of God. "Be ye therefore merciful as your Father also is merciful." "Dearly beloved, avenge not yourselves . . . vengeance is mine; I will repay, saith the Lord." [51]

The Catholic Church has done better than Protestantism in taking these sayings at face value, though it has avoided their universal application by relegating them to the monastery. Restricted in scope, they remain intact as to meaning.

One other mode of delimiting these precepts has greater validity than the rest. It is the way of constricting the circumstances under which they apply. One observes that nowhere in the Sermon on the Mount is there any confrontation with the problem of protection. Throughout it is said, if one take away *thy* cloak, if anyone compel *thee* to go a mile, if anyone strike *thee*, and so on. The question was not so much posed as to what the Good Samaritan should have done had he arrived a little earlier while the thieves were still on the spot. Should he have gone no further than to deliver the sort of denunciation which we find in the New Testament against extortioners and devourers of widow's houses? The answer can be derived only from New Testament principles. There are no specific precepts.

Peacemaking

The pacifism of the New Testament centers on the yielding spirit rather than on plans or philosophies of world peace as in the classical tradition. But the pacifism of the New Testament is not exhausted by counsels of submission. There is a positive role for the peacemaker. The beatitude, "Blessed are the peacemakers: for they shall be called the children of God" is an extremely striking saying, if one bears in mind that in the Roman Empire of that day the only persons elsewhere to be called Sons of God because they were peacemakers were the Roman emperors, the upholders of the *Pax Romana*. The very same Greek word for peacemaker, *eirenépoios*, is to be found upon the emperors' coins.[52] Of this Jesus was presumably unaware, yet how amazing it is that a wandering Galilean rabbi, talking to a handful of fishermen, should have committed to them the role ascribed to emperors! Perhaps unwittingly he was saying that the peace of Rome had provided only an external framework which Galilean peasants must make real by setting within it the peace of God.

The meek in the New Testament were to be anything but mild in their conflict with demonic foes, "the spiritual forces of evil in the heavenly sphere." [53] The New Testament begins with the proclamation of peace on earth and ends with the announcement of war in heaven. Paul delighted to dwell on the Christian's battle, and his epistles abound in military imagery. "We do live in the flesh but we do not make war as does the flesh; the weapons of our warfare are not the weapons of the flesh, but divinely strong to demolish fortresses, to cast down reasoning, and every rampart erected against the knowledge of God, to take prisoner every conception for obedience to Christ and to courtmartial every insurbordination." [54] Even Christian love could be described as a breastplate,[55] and the spirit as a sword and faith as a shield.[56] The use of military metaphors was a part of the Romanizing of the gospel. The Oriental understood what it was to bear the cross. The Roman responded better if told "to fight the good fight." [57] More than once, wrote James Moffatt, we feel that the early Christians were sensible of the paradox and even delighted in the use of such language. To state the gospel of peace in terms of war-fare was a telling as well as an intelligible method of self-expression. To say that their faith was "the victory that conquers the world" or that by bearing persecution and suffering, they were "more than conquerors" was to put a new edge on language. Besides, the principles of these early Christians were so well known that these militant terms could be employed without the slightest risk of misconception.[58]

We may conclude that the Christian religion makes in some respects for the reduction and in other respects for the intensification of strife. Many of the cleavages which divide men are removed. There is no longer Jew nor Greek, circumcision nor uncircumcision, Hellene nor barbarian, bond nor free. A racial war, a cultural war, a national war, a servile war, are unthinkable if Christianity be taken seriously. But there are new divisions. The believer stands over against the unbeliever, and Paul's anathema upon any who should preach another gospel foreshadows, however dimly, the wars of orthodoxy. There is also the distinction between the elect and the non-elect. It may coincide with the other cleavage, though not necessarily at a given moment, because the Saul who persecutes the faith today may tomorrow become Paul, the apostle and martyr. But if any way is discovered for the identification of the elect and the nonelect, then they may be set against each other even in military array.

Chapter 5

The Pacifism of the Early Church

THE three Christian positions with regard to war, already briefly delineated, matured in chronological sequence, moving from pacifism to the just war to the crusade. The age of persecution down to the time of Constantine was the age of pacifism to the degree that during this period no Christian author to our knowledge approved of Christian participation in battle. The position of the Church was not absolutist, however. There were some Christians in the army and they were not on that account excluded from communion.

This period will receive a more detailed and documented treatment than many of those which follow, because the early Church is frequently regarded as the best qualified to interpret the mind of the New Testament. The history of the Church is viewed by many as a progressive fall from a state of primitive purity, punctuated by reformations which seek a return to pristine excellence. The first church fathers are thus held to have been the best commentators, and if the early Church was pacifist then pacifism is the Christian position.

This conclusion is not to be assumed too blithely, for one recalls that slavery was abolished only by the conscience of the nineteenth, not by that of the first, second, or third centuries. There were, to be sure, attenuating circumstances in the early period. Slavery in the ancient world was not so inhumane as in the modern and has in fact been called an enforced induction into Roman civilization. The acceptance of slavery by the apostle Paul was colored by his belief that in view of the shortness of the time it mattered little whether one were bond or free. Yet when the time proved not to be short the church fathers were not alert in revising their ethic.

There is a sense, however, in which the thought of these fathers was closer to the New Testament than to that of succeeding periods, namely, that they operated almost exclusively with New Testament concepts without drawing so heavily as did later generations on classical and Old Testament themes. If at times a classical motif was borrowed, it was radically transformed in the process. For example, the Cynic cult of poverty reappears in several of the fathers; not with the intent of achieving emancipation from the fickleness of fortune nor with the thought of promoting peace, but rather as a daily discipline in preparation for possible martyrdom.

The second reason for treating the stand of the early Church in detail is in order to take account of controversy. Precisely because of the high evaluation placed upon primitive practice the attempt has been made by every confession to interpret the facts in favor of its own ethic. For example, Catholics today usually strive to bring the position of the early Church into line with the later Thomistic formulation, by ascribing the pacifism to nonpacifist considerations. The fathers are said to have objected to military service because of the danger of idolatry in the army or because of aversion to Rome, the persecutor. If there was genuine pacifism, it was due to heresy. Protestant nonpacifists frequently assign eschatology as the reason for the early Christian abstention from warfare. Pacifists, on the other hand, explain the nonexcommunication of soldiers by the early congregations on the ground that these soldiers were engaged in police rather than military duties.[1] These various contentions are not to be dismissed simply because they support the views of those who propose them. Some may be right.

Abstention from Military Service

The best point of departure is a consideration of the factual questions, whether and how many Christians were in the army prior to Constantine. From the end of the New Testament period to the decade A.D. 170-80 there is no evidence whatever of Christians in the army. The subject of military service obviously was not at that time controverted. The reason may have been either that participation was assumed or that abstention was taken for granted. The latter is more probable. The expansion of Christianity had taken place chiefly among civilians in the urban centers. Few as yet were converted while in the army. Converts not already in the ranks had many reasons against volunteering, and they were not subject to conscription. As slaves or freedmen many were ineligible. The danger of idolatry in the army was greater than in civilian life. Add to these considerations the rigorism of the Church which throughout the second century would not readmit to communion penitents guilty of apostasy, adultery, or bloodshed, and the likelihood appears greater that the Church withheld its members from military service than that they were permitted to serve without a single reproach or penalty.

The decade A.D. 170-80 affords two pieces of evidence pointing in opposite directions. The first is the reproach of Celsus, the pagan critic of Christianity: "If all men were to do the same as you, there would be nothing to prevent the king from being left in utter solitude and desertion and the forces of the empire would fall into the hands of the wildest and most lawless barbarians." [2] Such words are so explicit as to warrant the assumption that Celsus knew of no Christians who would accept military service. But he was mistaken. In the very decade in which he wrote, we have our first testimony of Christians in the army, in the so-called Thundering Legion under Marcus Aurelius in the year A.D. 173. From that day forward the evidence of Christians in the ranks increases. Tertullian in his *Apology*, written in A.D. 197, refuted the charge of misanthropy leveled against the Christians by pointing to their presence in the palace, the senate, the forum, and the *army*.[3] His stern rebuke in the *De Corona* (A.D. 211) to voluntary enlistment is a witness to the practice which he condemned.[4] During the persecution of Decius in A.D. 250, we have a reference in Cyprian to two soldier martyrs.[5] The number of Christians in the army must have increased during the latter part of the third century, because even before the great persecution of A.D. 303-4 Galerius sought to weed Christians out of his forces.[6] When the storm broke the brethren in the ranks suffered the first shock.[7] A number of soldier Christians died for their faith, not for casting off their weapons.[8] How numerous were the Christians in the army at the commencement of the fourth century we have no means of knowing. The historian Cadoux has conjectured that they must have been relatively few because no sovereign would readily deprive himself of a tenth or even of a twentieth of his military power.[9]

The inscriptions referring to Christian soldiers offer very little assistance. Leclercq compiled a list of 176, chiefly from Latin sources. He pointed out that these figures were minimal because the sources had not been fully exploited and because many early Christians did not see fit to record any profession. A more serious difficulty for the present purpose is that the inscriptions in most instances cannot be dated with sufficient precision to assign them with confidence to the pre-Constantinian period. Out of Leclercq's total only six belong incontestably to the age of persecution; two belong to the second century, and four to the third.[10] To this number Cadoux added another couple, making a total of eight.[11] These inscriptions do, however, witness to something more than the mere existence of eight Christian soldiers. The inscriptions are epitaphs and as such prove that the Christian communities where these men were buried did not prohibit the recording of the military profession upon their tombs.

Our data, albeit scanty, permit of more geographical classification than has hitherto been attempted. The results indicate that pacifism best flourished within the interior of the *Pax Romana* and was less prevalent in the frontier provinces menaced by the barbarians. The section most disinclined to military service appears to have been the Hellenistic East. Such may be inferred in a general way from the testimony of Celsus, whose provenance we do not know, but who wrote in Greek. Origen of Alexandria, replying to him in A.D. 248, revealed that in the territory of his acquaintance the situation had not altered. "We do not fight under the emperor," he testified, "although he require it." [12] Origen through his travels was able to speak not only for Egypt, but also for Palestine, Greece, and Asia Minor.

The situation must have been on the point of change at the time of his death in A.D. 251, because we have one inscription from Phrygia disclosing Christian soldiers about the middle of the century.[13]

In northern Africa there is evidence alike of acceptance and rejection of military service. Tertullian, who is our witness for the presence of Christians in the army, also affirmed that many upon conversion withdrew from military service.[14] Cyprian, as we have seen, mentioned two soldier martyrs, yet close to the grave of Cyprian was buried a youth, Maximilianus, executed for his conscientious objection to wearing the soldier's badge.[15]

Of the pre-Constantinian inscriptions mentioning Christian soldiers, one is from Besançon, one from Phrygia, and six from Rome —the Church notorious for its leniency toward offenders. Rome under Callistus first let down the bars in granting forgiveness to sexual offenders (A.D. 220) and under Cornelius to apostates (A.D. 250). We cannot be certain, but the assumption is plausible that Rome may have been ahead of other Christian communities in relaxing opposition to the military profession.

The most indisputable and persistent tradition of Christian sanction for participation in warfare comes from the eastern provinces. The Thundering Legion, which contained Christian soldiers in A.D. 173, was recruited in the province of Melitene in southern Armenia. In that same district, early in the fourth century when a persecuting emperor attempted to enforce idolatry, the Armenian Christians took up arms and defeated him.[16] In Syria, Abgar IX, the king of Edessa (A.D. 179-216), was converted to Christianity in A.D. 202 and for the remainder of his reign made this religion the official cult of Osrhoene. The Constantinian revolution was thus anticipated on the eastern fringe of the empire by fully a century. We can scarcely suppose that the ruler of a frontier province would have embraced the faith if by so doing he deprived himself of military resources. In Palmyra in A.D. 278 Paul of Samosata was the first Christian bishop to hold the post of civil magistrate and to employ a bodyguard.[17] In the fourth century Bishop James of Nisibis inspired the defense against the Persians by calling upon the name of the Lord, who sent clouds of mosquitoes and gnats to tickle the trunks of the enemy's elephants and the nostrils of his horses.[18] These examples indicate a continuous tradition of military service on the part of Christians on the eastern frontier.

The Constantinian revolution was anticipated in this region in another respect. When the state favored the Church and the Church sanctioned warfare, a cleavage took place within the Church itself and the more rigorous spirits adopted a strenuously ascetic and even a monastic life, repudiating military service. Syrian Christianity in the third century already had its solitaries dedicated to chastity and abstinence from wine and flesh.[19] In such circles we find also a rejection of military service. Tatian as early as the second century was a forerunner. His provenance is commonly thought to have been Mesopotamia. He was an ascetic and a founder of the Encratites. Military service appears in a list of his aversions: "I have no desire to rule. I crave not riches. I decline military command. I hate fornication." [20] The Bardesanic Book of the Laws, composed in Syriac early in the third century, by way of disproving astrology pointed out approvingly that among the people known as the Seres Mars the planet of war had not sufficient power to "compel a man to shed the blood of his brother with an iron weapon." [21] A case of the rejection of military service by Christians in the region of Mesopotamia is recorded in the closing years of the fourth century, when a large number of soldiers, having been converted while on garrison duty, "threw off the belt of military service." [22] Even if the story be legendary, it testifies to an aversion to participation in warfare on the part of its author, writing on the eastern frontier in the early fourth century.

The evidence, then, for Christians in the armed forces before the time of Constantine adds up to this: until the decade A.D. 170-80 we are devoid of evidence; from then on the references to Christian soldiers increase. The numbers cannot be computed. The greatest objection to military service appears to have been in the Hellenistic East. The Christians in northern Africa were divided. The Roman church in the late second and third centuries did not forbid epitaphs recording the military profession. The eastern frontier reveals the most extensive Christian participation in warfare, though concurrently we find there a protest against it among groups tending to ascetic and monastic ideals.

The attitude of ecclesiastical writers toward military service on the part of Christians during the same period shows a correlation with the data on actual practice. The period in which we have no evidence of Christians in the ranks is also the period in which there is no specific prohibition of such service. The pronouncements of the Fathers up to A.D. 180 are general. Athenagoras said that Christians "do not strike back, do not go to law when robbed; they give to them that ask of them and love their neighbors as themselves." [23] Justin Martyr was more specific: "We who were filled with war and mutual slaughter and every wickedness have each of us in all the world changed our weapons of war . . . swords into plows and spears into agricultural implements." [24] "We who formerly murdered one another now not only do not make war upon our enemies, but that we may not lie or deceive our judges, we gladly die confessing Christ." [25]

The period from A.D. 180 until the time of Constantine exhibits both in the East and West a number of more or less explicit condemnations of military service. In the East we have already observed the witness of Celsus and Origen to total abstinence for the period up to A.D. 250. Clement of Alexandria was less precise. When his plea for an equal code of conduct for women and for men met the objection that women, unlike men, are not trained for war, he preserved the equality by denying to men also military exercises.[26] "In peace, not in war, we are trained. War needs great preparation but peace and love, quiet sisters, require no arms nor extensive outlay." [27] Various peoples incite the passions of war by martial music; Christians employ only the Word of God, the instrument of peace.[28] "If the loud trumpet summons soldiers to war, shall not Christ with a strain of peace to the ends of the earth gather up his soldiers of peace? A bloodless army he has assembled by blood and by the word, to give to them the Kingdom of Heaven. The trumpet of Christ is his gospel. He has sounded, we have heard. Let us then put on the armor of peace." [29] Irenaeus, despite his residence in Gaul, may be reckoned by origin, language, and ideas to the East. He referred the prophecy of beating swords into plowshares to the Christians who do not know how to fight, but when struck offer the other cheek.[30]

In the West, Tertullian was the most unambiguous when he said that "Christ in disarming Peter ungirt every soldier." [31] In his *Apology* he averred that Christians were sufficiently numerous to offer successful resistance to persecuting emperors did they not count it better to be slain than to slay.[32] Elsewhere he inquired, "Shall the Son of peace, for whom it is unlawful to go to law, be engaged in battle?" [33] Minucius Felix said that Christians cannot bear to see a man killed.[34] Cyprian remarked that homicide is considered a crime when committed by individuals, a virtue when carried on publicly.[35] God, however, designed iron for tilling, not for killing.[36] Arnobius, in a work composed A.D. 304-10, assumed that the tranquillity of the *Pax Romana* was the result of the peaceableness of Christians:

For since we in such numbers have learned from the precepts and laws of Christ not to repay evil with evil, to endure injury rather than to inflict it, to shed our own blood rather than to stain our hands and conscience with the blood of another, the ungrateful world now long owes to Christ this blessing that savage ferocity has been softened and hostile hands have refrained from the blood of a kindred creature.[37]

Lactantius, writing A.D. 304-5, asserted: "God in prohibiting killing discountenances not only brigandage, which is contrary to human laws, but also that which men regard as legal. Participation in warfare therefore will not be legitimate to a just man whose military service is justice itself." [38] Thus all of the outstanding writers of the East and the West repudiated participation in warfare for Christians.

On what grounds? Some modern interpreters assert that the primary reason was the danger of idolatry in military service. The danger was real. The cult of the deified emperor was particularly prevalent in the camps. Officers were called upon to sacrifice; privates participated at least by their attendance.[39] Origen listed idolatry and robbery as sins common in the army.[40] On the other hand, Tertullian indicated that the problem was not so acute for the private soldier, who was not called upon actually to perform a sacrifice.[41] Moreover one cannot well understand how the Church could have permitted its members—as it did—to remain in the service even in peacetime in the pre-Constantinian period, if idolatry had been unavoidable.

Attitude to Rome

A further reason commonly adduced for the aversion of Christians to military service in the age of persecution was their hostility to Rome as a persecuting power. Why should they fight for the maintenance of an empire which threw them to the beasts? The situation at this point was complex.

All of the attitudes to Rome implicit in the New Testament became more explicit in the next century. The main line continued to be that of Paul in Romans and II Thessalonians. The antipathy of Revelation reappeared only in the writings of Commodianus, who would have welcomed a Gothic invasion for the overthrow of Rome.[42] The favorable attitudes of the Lukan writings were more pronounced in Melito of Sardis,[43] and other Asiatic bishops, who looked on Rome and Christianity as two conjoint works of God for the benefit of mankind. But these voices were a minority until the time of Constantine.[44] The fathers in the main followed the view of Paul that the deification of the emperor was to be resisted to the death, but that the empire was to be regarded as a force restraining disorder.[45]

The Patristic judgment upon the empire was qualified. The Christians neither condoned its sins nor despised its benefits. The Church addressed to Rome all the imprecations of the conquered, together with the encomia of the panegyrists.[46] Christian apologists, in order to parry the charge of calamity-bringing so often leveled against their religion, quarried in the classical literature which recorded and bemoaned Roman decadence. Tertullian and Minucius Felix [47] took over from Horace the contention that the fratricide of Romulus

74

had injected a virus of corruption into the Roman blood stream, while Lactantius[48] borrowed from Sallust the theme that Rome by destroying Carthage lost the stimulus of rivalry and fell a prey to dissension, cruelty, ambition, pursuit of luxury, and debauchery. The process by which Roman rule had been acquired was subjected to scathing denunciation. Rome grew great, averred Tertullian, not by religion, but by wars which always injure religion.[49] Lactantius was scornful of the Roman "just war," since entirely in accord with its rules Rome had subjugated the world.[50]

At the same time, the early Church did not follow the book of Revelation in identifying Rome with Antichrist.[51] The blessings of the Roman peace were appreciated. Irenaeus rejoiced that the roads were free from brigands and the seas from pirates.[52] Tertullian was glad that Carthage enjoyed tranquillity.[53] Origen saw in the Roman peace a providential provision for the dissemination of the gospel.[54] Christians did not wish to see the empire overthrown. Their opposition to war cannot therefore be explained on the grounds of hostility to the empire.

Eschatology

Some modern interpreters would say that the ground for early antimilitarism was indeed not hostility but rather indifference, because of the belief that the empire would pass away with the imminent coming of the Lord. In the period when pacifism was prevalent in the early Church, however, the expectation of the Lord's speedy return was long since waning. Even at the beginning of the second century Christians were asking, "Where is the promise of his coming, for since the fathers fell asleep all things continue as they were?" [55] In the second century the Montanists, who sought to keep alive the eschatological hope, were repudiated by the Church at large. Tertullian however joined them, and the attempt has been made to ascribe his pacifism to their eschatology. The proper interpretation hinges on the chronology of his writings. The common Catholic view is that when Tertullian wrote the *Apologia* in A.D. 197

he was a Catholic and not a pacifist. When he wrote the *De Idolatria,* however, he had become a Montanist and was therefore a pacifist. The argument is faulty at two points. In the first place the *Apologia* is not nonpacifist. Tertullian, in order to refute the charge of social aloofness, did indeed say that there were Christians in the army, but in the same tract declared that Christians were sufficiently numerous to resist persecution by force of arms were it not that they would rather be slain than slay. The other error lies in circuitous reasoning in the dating of the *De Idolatria;* if pacifism must of necessity be Montanist, then the pacifist *De Idolatria* must be dated in the Montanist period. As Harnack rightly pointed out, rigorism as such was not Montanism. On literary grounds he placed the tract prior to Tertullian's conversion to Montanism in A.D. 202.[56]

In the third century we discover that among pacifist authors the eschatological hope had already diminished. Some blunted the subversiveness of the expectation of the return of the Lord by advancing the date. Hippolytus placed it three hundred years ahead of his time and Lactantius, writing a century later and using the same chronology, had still two hundred years to go. The Alexandrians, Clement and Origen, achieved the same end by a spiritualization of the entire concept.[57] Still more significant is the shift in the Christian perspective from hope to fear of the consummation because it would be preceded by calamities. Christians could not quite make up their minds whether to pray "Come quickly, Lord Jesus," or to pray for the "delay of the end." Even Tertullian, whose pacificism has been attributed to his expectation of the imminent advent, found himself praying at times *pro mora finis.*[58]

Belief in the limited duration of earthly society was, in fact, by no means so significant for the political and social thought of the early Church as was the universal subjection of the temporal to the eternal. On earth Christians were but pilgrims and strangers.[59] A reason more definitely assignable for their unwillingness to take up arms against their persecutors, though they could have done so, was their certainty of vindication in the life to come.[60]

Love Versus Bloodshed

Yet they were not indifferent or irresponsible toward life in the present. Living as strangers, they yet more than fulfilled the laws of their community. The primary ground of their aversion was the conviction of its incompatibility with love. The quality of love set forth by Jesus and by Paul had not been lost in the early Church. Tertullian asked, "If we are enjoined to love our enemies, whom have we to hate? If injured we are forbidden to retaliate. Who then can suffer injury at our hands?" [61] Clement of Alexandria said to the heathen: "If you enroll as one of God's people, heaven is your country and God your lawgiver. And what are his laws? . . . Thou shalt not kill. . . . Thou shalt love thy neighbor as thyself. To him that strikes thee on the one cheek, turn also the other." [62] Cyprian reminded his brethren of Paul's hymn of love, "And what more—that you should not curse; that you should not seek again your goods when taken from you; when buffeted you should turn the other cheek; and forgive not seven times but seventy times seven . . . That you should love your enemies and pray for your adversaries and persecutors?" [63] Dionysius of Alexanderia declared: "Love is ever on the alert to do good even to him who is unwilling to receive it." [64] Tertullian called love of enemies the "principal precept." [65] Justin inquired: "If you love merely those that love you, what do you that is *new?*" [66]

Concretely, the early Church saw an incompatibility between love and killing. In later times the attitude and the act were harmonized on the ground that the destruction of the body does not entail the annihilation of the soul. The early Church had an aversion to bloodshed, however. To some extent this was due to the Western text of the Apostolic Decrees, recorded in Acts 15. The Eastern text which came to prevail enacted abstention from "things sacrificed to idols and from blood and from things strangled and from fornication." [67] In this context blood was taken to mean the eating of blood. The Western text, as known to a long series of Latin authors from Tertullian to Augustine, read: "To abstain from things sacrificed to idols, from fornication, and from blood," plus the Golden Rule. In that context blood was taken to mean bloodshed. Whichever text is historically correct, and many scholars regard the Western as the more defensible, the form containing bloodshed was early and widely received. It was applied alike to murder, capital punishment, and killing in war. On the basis of this verse Tertullian formulated the three irremissible sins as idolatry, adultery, and homicide.[68] Augustine testified that many regarded these three as *crimina mortifera*.[69] This is not to say of course that the aversion to *effusio sanguinis* rested solely upon the Western form of this text. The Easterners equally shrank from bloodshed.

Examples of opposition to killing are extant from various sections of the empire. In the West, Tertullian declared that the Christian would rather be killed than kill.[70] For Minucius Felix, "It is not right for us either to see or hear a man being killed." [71] Cyprian lamented that the world was wet with bloodshed and homicide esteemed a virtue if practiced publicly.[72] Arnobius thought it better to pour out one's own blood than to stain one's hands and conscience with the blood of another.[73] Lactantius declared that when God forbade killing he forbade not only brigandage but also that which is regarded as legal among men.[74] Vitricius described his rejection of military service in the words, *arma sanguinis obiecisti*.[75] In the East Athenagoras said that the Christian cannot bear to see a man put to death even justly.[76] Origen averred that "God did not deem it becoming to his own divine legislation to allow the killing of any man whatever." [77] The Canons of Hippolytus enacted that "a soldier of civil authority must be taught not to kill men and to refuse to do so if he is commanded." [78] Even after the objection to warfare was abandoned by the Church, the aversion to bloodshed remained. Basil the Great wrote: "Killing in war was differentiated by our fathers from murder . . . nevertheless perhaps it would be well that those whose hands are unclean abstain from communion for three years." [79] In Syria the Bardesanic Book of the Laws asserted that Mars cannot compel a man "to shed the blood of his brother." [80]

Police Function Sanctioned

That the objection to war lay in the scruple against killing rather than in social indifference is borne out by the willingness of a number of early Christian writers to sanction even military service provided it were restricted to police functions and did not entail bloodshed. A soldier might serve for a lifetime without killing in an empire at peace where the army was vested with the functions of a police force. For example, in the city of Rome fire protection and the keeping of the peace were assigned to a military unit known as the *Vigiles*.[81] We have evidence of Christian participation in two branches of the service devoted primarily to police work. The *beneficiarii* were troops assigned to the governors of provinces as aids in the administration of their territories; [82] several Christian epitaphs record this title.[83] While these inscriptions cannot be dated as distinctly pre-Constantinian, we do have the testimony of Tertullian in A.D. 211 to Christian association with this branch.[84] A number of undated inscriptions also describe certain Christians as *protectores, protectores domestici,* or simply *domestici*.[85] These titles in the late third century were conferred on those who previously had been denominated centurions. Their functions included the guarding of the emperor's person, the custody of prisoners, care of public transport and the mails, supervision of ordinance, and even secretarial duty—the two latter both in military and civilian administration.[86] An example of the type of service sanctioned for Christians even in Alexandria in the late third century is found in the case of Philoromus, a layman who served as a judge attended by a military guard.[87]

In view of the diversified functions of Roman soldiers, there were Christians who did not condemn military service as such, but only the taking of life. The Canons of Hippolytus in the early third century required—as noted above—that "a soldier of the civil authority must be taught not to kill men and to refuse to do so if he is commanded." [88] The injunction has greatly puzzled historians, who could not well understand how a Christian could be a soldier at all if he were under obligation not to kill. A recognition of the distinction between wartime and peacetime service is apparent in writings of Tertullian who, however, rejected both. He inquired: "How will a Christian take part in war, nay, how will he serve even in peace?" [89]

The understanding of a passage in Clement of Alexandria is clarified by this distinction between types of service. The translation by Butterworth in the Loeb Library is as follows: "Were you a soldier on campaign when the knowledge of God laid hold on you? Then listen to the commander who signals righteousness." [90] Plainly Clement did not call upon the Christian convert to leave the ranks. The nature of the restriction laid upon him depends in part on the interpretation of the word "commander." Some of the translators take it to mean an earthly general issuing orders in a just war. Combès, for example, translates: *"La foi chretienne t'a saisi dans le metier des armes, obeis au capitaine qui t'ordonne des choses justes."* [91] Eppstein represents Clement as treating "the soldier's profession on a level with any other legitimate calling." [92] Such an interpretation is difficult to square with the above citations from Clement in condemnation of warfare. The present passage needs to be interpreted in its context. It is the third in a series. The two preceding are these: "Till the ground, we say, if you are a husbandman; but recognize God in your husbandry. Sail the sea, you who love seafaring; but ever call upon the heavenly pilot." Then comes this passage. Can we suppose that Clement, having mentioned God in the first and the heavenly pilot in the second couplet, should be talking about an earthly commander in the third, particularly since in another passage he referred to "our great General, the Word, the Commander-in-Chief of the universe"? [93] He was saying that if a soldier were converted while in the army he might remain, but he became subject to a divine commander. Plainly there is here no express statement that police functions alone were permissible to a Christian, but such an interpretation would harmonize this passage with those from Clement in which warfare was condemned.

The distinction of police service likewise makes sense of the baffling canon of the Council of Arles, which in A.D. 314, decreed that those who laid down their arms *in peace* should abstain from communion: *De his qui arma proiciunt in pace placuit abstineri eos a communione* (Canon III) .[94] The injunction has given great difficulty for commentators, partly because it appears so completely to reverse the previous position of the Church. The words *in pace* are particuarly troublesome. Most scholars have referred them to the peace of the Church. The meaning then is that a Christian may leave the army under a persecuting emperor, but not under a tolerating sovereign like Constantine. Such is certainly not the natural sense of the words. The normal antithesis to *in pace* is *in bello*. The meaning then is that the Christian is not to lay down his arms in time of peace, when he may be called upon only for police duty, but he is still at liberty to withdraw in case of war. This interpretation is strengthened by the example of Martin of Tours, who on conversion remained in the army for two years, until an actual battle was imminent, and only then declined longer to serve. This was in the year A.D. 336.[95] We may say, then, that ecclesiastical authors before Constantine condemned Christian participation in warfare, though not necessarily military service in time of peace.

Varieties of Pacifism

All varieties of early Christian pacifism had in common an emphasis on love and an aversion to killing. Within this set of assumptions there were varieties. The first may be called legalistic and eschatological. Tertullian was its representative. His legalism was more significant than his eschatology, as we have noticed, though the latter was undeniably present. "Shall the son of peace," he demanded, "be engaged in battle when for him it is *unlawful* to go to war?" [96] Tertullian did not inquire as to the social consequences of abstention. Not for the Christian to ask whether the barbarians would overcome the empire. The Christian must obey Christ and leave to him the outcome. Vindication would be meted out at the last judgment. Observe that this eschatology looked forward not to a millennial reign of Christ on earth but only to a reversal in the life to come.

A second variety of pacifism was a combination of Christian love with Gnostic repugnance to the physical, a position which is not Christian. Marcion represented this view in conjunction with Christian elements. In the name of Christian love he rejected the God of the Old Testament together with all his wars. Had not Yahweh sent the flood upon mankind, consumed Sodom and Gomorrah with fire, plagued the Egyptians, hardened Pharaoh's beart, blessed the murderer Moses and the ruthless conqueror Joshua, burned the priests of Baal, and brought bears to devour the children who mocked Elisha? Paul said, "Let not the sun go down upon your wrath." But Joshua had kept the sun up till his wrath went down.[97]

These passages in the Old Testament were very troublesome for the pacifist church fathers. Doubly so because Christians in the army appealed to these examples for their own justification.[98] The fathers had two methods of disposing of such texts. The first was chronological. War belonged to a former historical dispensation. In this way Tertullian took care of the *lex talionis*. [99] Origen said that wars had been necessary for the preservation of the Jewish state, but since such wars were no longer allowed, God had suffered the dissolution of that state.[100] The other escape was by way of allegory and to this Origen normally had recourse, declaring that the disciples of the peaceful Christ would never have been permitted to read the historical books of the Old Testament unless the horrible wars there recounted were to be spiritually understood.[101]

Marcion's pacifism arose, however, from a deeper root than the incongruity between New Testament love and Old Testament terror. He was Gnostic in his adverse judgment as to the goodness of life in the body. The world, said he, is fundamentally bad because it contains wars, flies, fleas, and fevers.[102] The body which is subject to their torments should not be allowed to continue as a prison for the spirit. For that reason marriage was rejected.[103] In view of this theory one might assume that the killing of the body would have been regarded as advantageous, but presumably the objection was to the carnal character of a struggle between body and body. This type of pacificism was not Christian.

The third type of pacifism might be called pragmatic or redemptive. It took cognizance of life on earth and of social consequences and responsibilities, but objected to war in part because there was a more excellent way. The most outstanding representative of this type was Origen. The problem was set for him very pointedly by Celsus who claimed that Christians should either assume the full burden of citizenship or else cease to have children and withdraw from the world.[104] The Church was eventually to agree with Celsus, in that it allowed some Christians to take the one course and some the other. But Origen did not agree and argued that Christians might reject war and yet remain in society, because their prayers and their disciplined lives were of more service than soldiers to kings, since wars are fomented by demons who inspire the violation of oaths and disturb the peace.[105] "Men fight," said he, "sometimes because of hunger and more frequently because of avarice, the lust of power, an insane craving for vain glory and absence of a tranquil disposition." [106] The greatest warfare, in other words, is not with human enemies but with those spiritual forces which make men into enemies.

Christian warfare should supplant political warfare. Implicit in the concept of Christian warfare was a parallelism between the Church and the state. Both had similar objectives—justice and peace —but the Church had a better and more effective way of bringing them to pass. The state had created the external peace of the *Pax Romana*. The Church must give to it reality by overcoming dissension within. Even the barbarian foe without could be tamed by the persuasiveness of the Winsome Word which is Christ.[107] Irenaeus looked upon the Church as the restoration of the lost paradise.[108] Justin Martyr believed that the Church rather than the empire was the force restraining the powers of chaos.[109] For these reasons Origen considered office in the Church more challenging than office in the empire.[110]

What then of the empire? Did it also have a place? In view of Romans 13, no Christian could deny that the empire was ordained of God, but the view that it was ordained because of sin and should be left to sinners was the position of Tertullian. Nothing, said he, is more alien to the Christian than political life.[111] Origen compared the state to a chain gang composed of criminals engaged in useful work.[112] Two levels of ethical conduct were here implicitly recognized, in which the lower had also its rules. Even convicts might have a code. For those who fought courage was better than cowardice. Hence Tertullian, the pacifist, prayed that the imperial armies might be *brave*.[113] Humane conduct in war was superior to cruelty, and Clement of Alexandria commended the humanity of the code of war in Deuteronomy 20.[114] Origen proposed that if men fight they should imitate the bees in observing the rules of the just war.[115] At one point Origen hinted a solution of this double ethic by way of a functional division of society according to which pagan emperors and their armies should fight while all Christians, like the pagan priests, should be exempt in order to pray.[116] Origen was not far-removed from the position of his contemporary Plotinus, that the sage should abstain from conflict, whereas common folk might participate. The Christian Church was in the end to find a vocational resolution by way of monasticism, involving a division of function not between the Church and the world, nor between the Church and the state, but between differing levels within the Church itself. Eusebius, writing in A.D. 313, posited two grades of Christian conduct, the first for the laity who might participate in pure marriages, in just wars, in farming, in trade, and in civic pursuits; and the second for the clergy, requiring celibacy, poverty, aloofness from the world, and complete dedication to God.[117] But with Eusebius we are already in the age of Constantine.

Chapter 6

The Theory of the Just War
In the Christian Roman Empire

THE accession of Constantine terminated the pacifist period in church history. A change apparently so abrupt prompts a doubt whether the earlier pacifism had actually been as widespread and profound as here portrayed. One must realize, however, that the transition was not achieved by the single battle of the Milvian Bridge. Constantine attained sway over the entire empire only after twenty years of civil war in which Christianity was itself an issue. There were at one time seven contestants for the purple, each with a policy of persecution or toleration. Inevitably the hopes, prayers, and frequently also the arms of Christians gravitated to their champion, and when Constantine with the standard of the cross discomfited the enemies of the faith, he was hailed as the Lord's Anointed. He could the more readily be accepted by the Church because already in the popular mind a fusion was taking place between Rome and Christianity as over against the barbarian and the pagan. The alignment was rendered plausible by the provenance of the great persecutors of the third and fourth centuries, who had come from the half-barbarian provinces in the Danubian area: Maximinus Thrax, Decius, Diocletian—in a measure, Galerius, and Maximinus Daza. A Christian author saw in Galerius a "barbarity foreign to Roman blood," and Constantine was lauded not only as the champion of the faith but as the restorer of Rome.[1]

At the same time one cannot but marvel that neither the emperor nor the Church felt an impropriety in placing the cross upon the military *labarum*. Constantine tacitly ranged himself in the succession of the martyrs in that he was the first emperor to bestow upon himself the title Victor. This designation, which the pagans gave only

THE VICTORY OF CONSTANTINE AT THE MILVIAN BRIDGE
THE CIRCLE IN THE SKY HAS THE GREEK WORDS "BY THIS SIGN CONQUER"
IN THE FORM OF A CROSS

to the gods and the Christians only to the martyrs, was assumed by the Christian emperor on the ground that what the martyrs had commenced with their blood, he had completed with his sword.[2]

The Christian Peace and the Roman Peace

Christian authors could the more easily look upon the empire and the Church as partners because Constantine had restored the *Pax Romana*. The minority view of Melito and the Asiatic bishops in the second century that Rome and Christianity were conjoint works of God became under Constantine the prevailing position. The theologians recognized that the empire had pacified the world, established universal communication, and made possible the proclamation of the gospel to all nations. Christianity, they claimed, had coincidently tamed belligerent peoples by overcoming the demons which incited them to war. The Roman peace and the Christian peace thus supported each other, and the prophecy that swords should be beaten into plowshares had received fulfillment in the *Pax Romana*. Christ by these Christians was turned into a Roman citizen and Augustus well-nigh made into a Christian. The religion of the one God and the empire of one ruler were recognized as having been made for each other. Polytheism was a religion appropriate for a congeries of city-states perpetually in strife, but monotheism and universal monarchy were congruous, and to the confession of one faith, one lord, and one baptism could now be added that of one empire and one emperor.

These themes were struck by Eusebius of Caesarea in his *Oration on Constantine*, in which the Stoic ideals of harmony and concord were held to have been realized by the partnership of the Roman Empire and the Christian religion, so that the human race from East to West appeared as a well-ordered and united family and that ancient oracle was fulfilled that "Nation should not take up sword against nation, neither should they learn war anymore." [3]

The Eastern theologians echoed the strain. Diodor of Tarsus declared that through Christianity and Rome God had caused wars to cease to the ends of the earth and had mingled cities and peoples through the preaching of the city of God.[4] Chrysostom more realistically saw the fulfillment of the prophesies of Isaiah in that the greater part of the world was at peace with only a few soldiers doing the fighting for the others.[5]

The theme was not confined to the Easterners. Jerome, who might be reckoned both to the East and to the West, saw realized in the *Pax Romana* all the pacific hopes of the Old Testament and of the New—spears beaten into pruning hooks, the beatitude on the peacemakers, the dream of every man under his own vine and fig tree.[6] Ambrose wrote in a similar vein[7] and Orosius made the Redeemer of the world into a Roman citizen by virtue of his birth during the time of the census, when the gates of Janus were closed and the world rejoiced in the most blessed tranquillity of peace.[8]

The classical expression of the fusion of the *Pax Romana* and the *Pax Christiana* is found in the lines of Prudentius:

> When God desired that men asunder rent
> By tongue and dress should own a single sway,
> With gentle bonds of concord were they drawn
> Till love of piety all hearts conjoined . . .
> Mortals by rage of Bellona embroiled,
> Wild armed hands inflicting mutual wounds
> By God were curbed and taught the laws of Rome,
> Joined by one right, one name, one brotherhood . . .
> Triumph on triumph gave to Rome the earth,
> And laid the road on which the Lord should tread . . .
> And now, O Christ, a world prepared takes Thee,
> Linked by the common bond of Rome and Peace.[9]

Pacifism: Its Collapse and Survival

The practice of early Christianity was so far reversed by the early fifth century that under Theodosius II those polluted by pagan rites were excluded from the army—only Christians could serve.[10] Most surprising is the bearing of arms on occasion even by the clergy. We have already noticed the case of Bishop Jacob of Nisibis, who, while not himself in arms, yet inspired the war against Sapor.[11] Synesius of Cyrene organized the defense of his island against barbarian inroads. He was not yet a bishop, but he recorded the exploits of clerics in the fray. An unarmed deacon, leading hastily recruited peasants, on sighting the enemy picked up a stone, leapt upon one of the foe, and struck him dead. To the valor of this deacon Synesius attributed the victory.[12] Clerical participation was, however, unusual and long after lay service was sanctioned, clerical service was censured.[13]

The debacle of the earlier pacifism was not absolute, and some instances of refusal of military service are to be found among Christians in this period. We have noted the case of Martin of Tours who stayed in the army only until a battle was imminent, then refused longer to serve, saying, "I am a soldier of Christ; I cannot fight." To prove his sincerity he offered on the morrow to face the barbarian foes with no arms save a cross. The conclusion of peace without battle saved him from the ordeal and he was allowed to retire from the ranks.[14]

A similar example was recorded by Paulinus of Nola in the case of a soldier who on conversion immediately refused further service on the ground, as he said, that he had exchanged the weapons of iron for the weapon of Christ. Paulinus tells us that he was saved from decapitation because the executioner was stricken blind.[15]

The prime transmitters of the nonmilitary tradition of the early Church were the monks.[16] They accepted the dilemma set by Celsus that either Christians should accept full political responsibilities or else give up having families.[17] Their withdrawal from society at large necessarily entailed withdrawal also from the army. The emperor Valens in A.D. 376, we are told, struck against these monks by forcing them into military service. Into the deserts of Egypt "he sent tribunes and soldiers that the saints and true soldiers of God should be subject to persecution under another name." [18] Chrysostom interpreted monastic pacifism as vocational. "If you consider war," he wrote, "then the monk fights with demons and having conquered is crowned by Christ. Kings fight with barbarians. Inasmuch as demons are more fearful than barbarians, the victory of the monks is more glorious. The monk fights for the religion and true worship of God . . . the king to capture booty, being inspired by envy and the lust of power." [19]

Curiously the pagan emperor Julian the Apostate continued to regard Christianity as inculcating pacifism and partly for that reason rejected it. Scornfully he inquired of the Alexandrians whether their city owed her greatness to the precepts of the odious Galileans and not rather to the prowess of their founder, Alexander the Great.[20]

The Just War: View of Ambrose

A Christian ethic of war appears first to have been formulated by St. Ambrose and then more fully by St. Augustine. The former presumably had never entertained any scruples against military service, because he had been the pretorian prefect of northern Italy before being impressed into the bishopric of Milan. The justification of

Christian participation in war was rendered easier for him because the defense of the empire coincided in his mind with the defense of the faith. The barbarians were Arians. The Danubian provinces which offered so weak a resistance to the invaders were also Arian. Ambrose regarded the whole incursion as a proof of the divine wrath because of the spread of unbelief. "From Thrace, Dacia, Moesia, and all Valeria of the Pannonians we hear blasphemy preached and barbarians invading. . . . How could the Roman state be safe with such defenders? . . . Plainly those who violate the faith cannot be secure. . . . Not eagles and birds must lead the army but thy name and religion, O Jesus." [21]

· The accommodation of Christianity and military service was facilitated for Ambrose by borrowings from Stoicism and the Old Testament. His tract *On the Duties of the Clergy* was a free reworking of Cicero's *De Officiis,* taking over the concept of the just war in which the suppliant was to be spared and good faith observed with the enemy. From the Old Testament Ambrose enthusiastically appropriated many examples of military prowess. "Moses feared not to undertake terrible wars for his people's sake, nor was he afraid of the arms of the mightiest kings, nor affrighted by the savagery of barbarian nations." Abraham's recovery of his captured son-in-law was more glorious by arms than had it been by ransom, and Judas Maccabeus did well to repel aggression on the Sabbath day.

Christian pacifism was relegated by Ambrose to the private and clerical sphere. The question of Carneades whether a wise man would give up a plank to another in a shipwreck was thus answered: "I do not think a Christian, a just and wise man, ought to save his own life by the death of another; just as when he meets with an armed robber he cannot return blows lest in defending his life he should stain his love toward his neighbor." As for clerics, "The thought of warlike matters seems to be foreign to the duty of our office, for we have our thoughts fixed more on the duty of the soul than on that of the body, nor is it our business to look to arms but rather to the forces of peace." [22]

Ambrose furnished two of the ingredients of the Christian theory of the just war: that the conduct of the war should be just and that monks and priests should abstain.

The View of Augustine

What Ambrose thus roughly sketched Augustine amplified. His background and outlook were very different. Augustine was an African with a deep sense of the wrongs of the conquered. He was at the same time a Roman, speaking Latin not Punic. He was the heir of classical antiquity, quoting Cicero even while berating him. Yet Augustine was a Christian, and the Sermon on the Mount had burned into his heart. He was steeped in the writings of the age of persecution and thought of the Church as the remnant of the persecuted. He was at the same time a member of the Church catholic, coextensive with the empire and allied with the state. Such a man could not find an easy solution to the problem of the relation of Christianity to society and more particularly to war and peace.

His view of man was much more somber than that which had prompted the pragmatic pacifism of Origen. Augustine had abandoned his belief in the possibility of Christian perfection on earth. Once he had said that the precepts of the Sermon on the Mount should be perfectly obeyed as "we believe them to have been fulfilled by the apostles." [23] Later he said that they should "be obeyed as perfectly as they were fulfilled by the apostles," meaning that even the apostles had not realized them to the full.[24]

With the passing of the hope of Christian perfection was coupled the vanishing of the dream of peace on earth. Swords never had been beaten into plowshares and never would. "Such security is never given to a people that it should not dread invasions hostile to its life." [25] On our earthly pilgrimage we pant after peace, yet are involved in constant strife—with the pagan, with the heretic, with the bad Catholic, and even with the brother in the same household. One may grow weary and exclaim, "Why should I eat out my life in contention? I will return within myself." But even there one will find that the flesh lusts against the spirit.[26] Peace will not come until this corruptible puts on incorruption, and then only for the redeemed, because hell is the perpetuation of unresolved conflicts.[27] Perfect peace is reserved for heaven, where there shall be no hunger nor thirst nor provocation of enemies.[28]

The inwardness of Augustine's ethic served to justify outward violence, because right and wrong were seen to reside not in acts but in attitudes. Such a distinction had proved very useful in explaining the apparently unchristian deportment of the patriarchs of the Old Testament. Elijah, for example, was warranted in calling down fire from heaven because at the same time he had love in his heart, whereas the disciples were rebuked for wishing to do the like against the Samaritans because the wish was prompted by vengeful intent.[29] Killing and love could the more readily be squared by Augustine because in his judgment life in the body is not of extreme importance. What matters is eternal salvation. The destruction of the body may actually be of benefit to the soul of the sinner.[30]

Another respect in which Augustine differed from Origen was in his view of the Church, which could not be set so easily over against the world as embodying a different spirit and employing a different technique. According to Augustine the Church is not a society of the saints, and the Church on earth is not to be equated with the Church in heaven composed only of the elect. The Church below is the field in which the tares grow together with the wheat until the harvest.[31] So long as the "City of God is a stranger in the world, she has in her communion, bound to her by the sacraments, some who shall not eternally dwell in the lot of the saints." [32] The difference between the Church and the world is therefore obscured, because the world is partly mixed with the Church.

Augustine assigned to the Church a larger role in the fashioning of society, because the duration of that society was extended by the projection of the Lord's return into an indefinite future. The Church, despite her imperfections, was to be a directive force in the coming order. Hence the thrones of the book of Revelation were located on earth, and the Church was deemed even now to have commenced her reign. Like Eusebius, Augustine envisaged a partnership of Church and empire, but the leadership should lie with the Church.

The thought of Eusebius pointed to the Caesaropapism of the East, whereas that of Augustine looked toward the papal theocracy of the West.

The Barbarian Invasion

With these presuppositions and their vast implications Augustine confronted the concrete situation of the barbarian invasion which had advanced since the day of Ambrose from the heretical fringe of the empire to the orthodox core. The inroads could no longer be explained as a divine chastisement visited upon heresy within the empire. Augustine was challenged by the pagan taunts that God had suffered this collapse not because of heresy but because of Christianity itself. There was the more urgent question of whether the inroads should be resisted by Christian generals.

On this second point Augustine was in no doubt. Africa was on the verge of invasion by the Vandals; only the Roman legions stood in the way. At that juncture Boniface, the Roman general in Africa, having lost his wife, desired to retire and become a monk. "Not now," pleaded Augustine. "The monks indeed occupy a higher place before God, but you should not aspire to their blessedness before the proper time. You must first be exercised in patience in your calling. The monks will pray for you against your invisible enemies. You must fight for them against the barbarians, their visible foes." [33]

The larger question remained as to why God had suffered Rome, the eternal, to be taken by Alaric in A.D. 411. Augustine answered with a philosophy of history according to which states both rise and fall through their vices. Virtues indeed of a sort they have, and Rome would never have succeeded without self-discipline,[34] but all of her virtues were tainted. The very good faith of Regulus was elicited only because of his implacability toward Carthage.[35] The state itself was created good, grounded on the God-implanted desire of man for association, but the fratricide of Cain introduced corruption. The state survived even though unjust, for justice is not necessary for its being, as Cicero held, but only for its well-being. A robber band has the essential characteristics of a state, and states have been in the main

93

robber bands.[36] By way of illustration Augustine moved down the years chronicling the sins of states. Even the Hebrews, he held, achieved their victories not by their virtues but by the vices of their foes.[37] Rome, founded on fratricide, grew by the rape of the Sabines and deteriorated through the destruction of Carthage. All of the earlier theories of Roman decadence were thus worked into a scheme of progressive decline.[38] The establishment of the empire evoked in Augustine no enthusiasm. By him the emperor Augustus was slighted [39] and the *Pax Romana* was not lauded as a preparation for the gospel,[40] let alone as the fulfillment of the prediction that swords should be beaten into plowshares.[41] What then of the cultural benefits of the Roman empire? What of the one language, the bond of peace? Yes, agreed Augustine, but by how many wars, how much slaughter, how much *bloodshed* was this unity obtained? As for the benefits conferred by the Roman government, are there no senators in countries which have never heard of Rome? How much better if the dubious benefits had been conferred with the consent of the nations? Talk not of glorious victories. Look at naked deeds—the lust of dominion with which Sallust reproached mankind. If a gladiator fought with his father in the arena, should we not all be shocked? Is it less shocking that a daughter nation should fight with her mother? Why glory in the greatness of an empire built up by dark fear, cruel lust, and blood, which, whether shed in civil or in foreign war, still is human blood? Well did Pompeius Trogus trace the cycle of robber empires from Assyria to Rome.[42] So wrote Augustine and the imprecations of the vanquished reverberate through his pages.

The deduction properly to be drawn from all this would appear to be that Rome was but receiving at the hands of the barbarians the treatment which she had inflicted upon others, and that she should therefore be left to suffer retribution at the hand of the Lord. This was not Augustine's conclusion, however, because he was able to discover in Rome's history a break in the nexus of corruption. It took place, not when Augustus became emperor and established the Roman peace, but when Constantine was converted. If the ruler of an empire be Christian, there is then a possibility of justice in the state. Augustine had asserted that "great states without justice are nothing but robbery on a large scale." Pagan states were bound to fit this description, but Christian states, or at least states with Christian rulers, might be just. If then an emperor upheld the true faith, let his sway increase. The objection to large states consequently disappeared, and Augustine could praise God for the notable victories of Constantine and Theodosius.[43]

His argument at this point would seem to be wrecked. His explanation of the barbarian invasion as retribution for the crimes of pagan Rome scarcely explained why expiation should be made by Christian Rome, but Augustine really did not care too much about the argument. The rise and fall of nations was not of ultimate concern. Eternity could not be promised to Rome nor to any institution upon earth, for nothing is eternal save the kingdom of Heaven. Earthly life does not greatly matter.[44] We may be stripped of our goods but cannot be deprived of heavenly treasures. Women may be raped in the body but cannot be polluted in the spirit. Men may be killed, but those who destroy the body have nothing more they can do to the soul.[45] There is basically then no need to explain why God should suffer one empire to fall or another to rise.

This philosophy might lead to a complete disregard for temporal concerns—to a Neoplatonic withdrawal of the sage from the strife. Augustine as a Christian could not be so unconcerned, however. When all was said and done, the empire stood for order against barbarian chaos. The empire was Christian. The Church was able to give guidance. Some semblance of justice might be realized. Therefore the empire was to be defended and Christians might fight.

The Code of War

Now let us consider Augustine's code of war. It was the code of Plato and Cicero, with Christian additions. The war, Augustine agreed, must be just as to its intent—which is to restore peace. To Boniface Augustine wrote, "Peace should be the object of your desire. War should be waged only as a necessity and waged only that through it God may deliver men from that necessity and preserve them in peace. For peace is not to be sought in order to kindle war, but war is to be waged in order to obtain peace. Therefore even in the course of war you should cherish the spirit of a peace maker." If injustice can be corrected without bloodshed, how much greater the victory! A higher glory it is to stay war than to slay men. Even those who fight seek peace through blood.[46]

Although perfect peace on earth is impossible, the hope of approximate peace was not abandoned by Augustine. Even the peace of Babylon was for him a relative good. All the classical arguments in favor of peace were revived, since peace is that principle of cohesion without which even robber bands would disintegrate. Peace is the concord exhibited in the harmony of the universe. Peace is the gregariousness evident among animals of the same kind. Does not the tigress gently purr over her cubs? The kite solitary in soaring for prey yet seeks a mate, builds a nest, and maintains a domestic alliance as peacefully as he can. How much more powerful are the laws of man's nature which move him to preserve peace with all men, so much as in him lies? [47]

An object of the just war is to vindicate justice. The specific quality of justice in Augustine's thought was somewhat vague. This was his formula: "Those wars may be defined as just which avenge injuries." [48] What sort of injuries? An attack on the existence of the state, Augustine held, was ordinarily an injury to be repulsed by war, but not under all circumstances. Cicero had said that the state might defend its safety and honor. Augustine pointed out that the two might conflict, as in the case of the Saguntines who were able to preserve honor only at the price of their national existence.[49] Honor is to be preferred to safety, but ordinarily the divine law permits self-defense to states.[50] Other injuries to be forcibly rectified included failure to make amends and refusal to grant passage.[51]

The war must be just in its disposition, which is Christian love, and this is not incompatible with killing, because love and non-resistance are inward dispositions. Augustine said:

If it is supposed that God could not enjoin warfare because in after times it was said by the Lord Jesus Christ, "I say unto you, Resist not evil . . . ," the answer is that what is here required is not a bodily action but an inward disposition. . . . Moses in putting to death sinners was moved not by cruelty but by love. So also was Paul when he committed the offender to Satan for the destruction of his flesh.[52] Love does not preclude a benevolent severity,[53] nor that correction which compassion itself dictates. No one indeed is fit to inflict punishment save the one who has first overcome hate in his heart. The love of enemies admits of no dispensation,[54] but love does not exclude wars of mercy waged by the good.[55]

The war must be just as to its auspices. It is to be waged only under the authority of the ruler. The taking of the sword which the Lord condemned referred to the use of the sword by another than the constituted authority.[56] On the prince rests the responsibility for determining when the sword may be used. The common soldier should leave the decision to his lord and obey even an infidel emperor like Julian the Apostate.[57]

The conduct of the war must be just. The rules were taken from classical antiquity. Faith must be kept with the enemy. There should be no wanton violence, profanation of temples, looting, massacre, or conflagration. Vengeance, atrocities, and reprisals were excluded, though ambush was allowed.[58]

Augustine believed that in point of fact Christianity had mitigated the asperities of warfare. The very barbarians now invading the empire, said he, exhibited the influence of Christianity in that they spared the refugees in the churches. When in pagan antiquity had a like regard been shown for temples? The novelty in the recent sack of Rome lay in the gentleness of the invaders. He was blind, said Augustine, who did not see that this was to be attributed to the name of Christ and to the Christian temper.[59]

Finally, Augustine classified Christians as Ambrose had done. Only those in public authority may take life. The private citizen may not defend himself because he cannot do so without passion, self-assertion, and a loss of love. The law which permits killing to the ordinary citizen to prevent robbery or rape is an unjust law.[60] "As to killing others to defend one's own life I do not approve of this, unless one happen to be a soldier or a public functionary acting not for himself, but in defense of others or of the city in which he resides." [61]

The religious, the secular clergy, and the monks must not engage in warfare at all. The monks are bound to go the full length in practicing the counsels of perfection insofar as that is possible on earth. For them there is no marriage, no private property, no war. The monastery is a foretaste of the Jerusalem that is above.

Augustine thus gathered up the strands of Hebrew, classical, and Christian antiquity. Like the prophets, he believed in a transcendent and righteous God who would guarantee permanence to no human institution. Like the apocalyptics, he despaired of the present order, though unlike them he centered his hope not so much upon a divine intervention in the historic process as upon a new order beyond the grave. For that reason he had no hope for entire peace on earth, yet regarded peace as an ideal and appropriated the classical arguments in its favor. He sought to restrain war by the rules of the *justum bellum* and the dispositions of the Sermon on the Mount. The Roman empire, especially under a Christian sovereign, was regarded as an institution to be preserved, though the process by which it had arisen was excoriated with all the rancor of the conquered peoples. These elements, diverse in origin, were synthesized in a graded ethic. The distinctive points in Augustine's theory were these: that love should be the motive in war, and that justice should lie on one side only.

There is one other point distinctive of Augustine's view of all the coercive activities of the state: namely, a mournful mood. The judge may employ torture to determine guilt, but the suspect may not after all be guilty, in which case the innocent has been punished in order to avoid punishing the innocent. "If then," inquired Augustine, "such darkness shrouds social life will the wise judge take his seat on the bench? That he will. For human society, which he cannot rightly abandon, constrains him to do his duty. He will take his seat and cry 'From my necessities deliver Thou me.'" [62]

What Augustine said of the judge he would have said equally of the general.

The position of Augustine here delineated is of extreme importance because it continues to this day in all essentials to be the ethic of the Roman Catholic Church and of the major Protestant bodies. Whether, assuming the premises, this ethic is valid for our time, is a problem to engage us later. Whether it was sound even in Augustine's day may detain us here for a moment.

Augustine assumed that a just war can be just on one side only. To him it seemed obvious that the cause of Rome was just, that of the barbarians unjust. They were invaders. Not only would they commit injuries to property, life, and honor, but they would disrupt the order maintained by the empire.

We today, who are actually more fully informed than was the Bishop of Hippo as to what was going on all over the empire in his own day, can make out a very good case for the barbarians. They were being pushed westward by hordes from the East. There was room for them in the empire. They had long been infiltrating by a process of controlled immigration. The Roman army in the imperial period had been increasingly recruited from among the barbarians. When Rome was taken by Alaric the Goth, the defender of the capital was Stilicho the Goth. Then arose an old Roman party which sought to purge the Goths within the empire. The spokesman of this group was Synesius, later to be the bishop of Cyrene. He argued before the Emperor Arcadius that the barbarian Germans could not be the watchdogs of the Roman empire, because they were wolf cubs not reared in the laws of Rome. Theodosius ought never to have admitted them. Let them be deported or made into helots. Actually the Gothic general Gainas was assassinated and thirty thousand of his men were butchered; consequently the weakened empire could not cope with barbarian inroads.[63]

An army might not have been needed to cope with invasions had good faith and sagacity prevailed. The above-mentioned Theodosius had stepped in after Rome, through her own treachery, had suffered a severe disaster. Under Valens the Visigoths pressed by the Huns asked permission to settle in the empire with their families, to the number of a million souls. They were for the most part Christian. Fritigern was their leader. The Emperor Valens promised admission. The horde came over the Danube, but instead of being settled was coralled by the forces of Rome and kept alive by a supply of dead dogs. The price for each dog was a child to be sold into slavery. The guard of Fritigern was treacherously murdered by the Romans. The Goths broke loose and ravaged Thrace. Valens met them in battle. The emperor himself perished, together with two thirds of the imperial army. Then it was that the Spanish general Theodosius restored order by honorably granting the settlement promised at the outset.[64]

Had Rome practiced her ancient virtue of *bona fides,* the barbarian invasions might have continued to be a controlled immigration.

When history is written fifteen hundred years later by the descendants of these barbarians, the question becomes even more pertinent as to whether their invasion was "just." The incorporation of their vitality into the classical-Christian tradition led eventually to a great fructification. Augustine's theory of the "just war" was a slogan of conservatism. Yet it is too much to expect that a people will suffer itself to be overrun because out of its collapse will come a new and better order. It is not too much to hope that a people will exercise the wisdom to make voluntarily those adjustments to change which will both avoid collapse and provide for a better order.

Chapter 7

From the Just War to the Crusade and Sectarian Pacifism

THE barbarian invasions disrupted the unity of the Roman Empire. The Church set herself to reconstruct. The task was stupendous, though less formidable than it might have been if the invaders had been as diverse as they were numerous. Politically they were divided, but culturally closer than were many of the sections of the Roman Empire to each other—for example, the Basques and the Copts, or the Berbers and the Armenians. The barbarians had a common tongue, which made it possible for the Saxon Boniface to pass from England to the continent, there to carry on missionary work among the Germanic people. They had common institutions, nor were they altogether ignorant of or alien to Rome, for there had long been contacts, and the barbarians admired the empire which they had overrun. Yet the task was formidable, because there were religious differences and political divisions to be overcome. The barbarians were in part Christian heretics and in part pagans. The Church must convert them to Christianity and to orthodoxy. They were distributed in many independent kingdoms: Visigoths, Ostrogoths, Lombards, Suevi, Vandals, Franks, Saxons, Angles, and Jutes. Nor were they able, once within the confines of the empire, to enjoy tranquillity. What they had done to the Romans other barbarians did to them. For centuries invasions were led and pressures were exerted by the Norsemen, the Slavs, and the Magyars.

The Church, in the light of her recent history, appeared ill-fitted to take the lead in unification, for she had not fulfilled the promise of the early fathers nor the hope of Constantine that she would be the cement of the empire. On the contrary, theological divisions had fused with already existing rifts within the social structure to intensify the cleavages. In the West the Donatist controversy in northern Africa had pitted the Berber and Punic against the Latin elements in the population, and in the East the Christological controversies had set the Copts, Syrians, and Armenians against the Greeks, thus facilitating the eventual disruption of the Byzantine Empire. Yet the Church actually did exert a unifying influence in the West, as also in early Russia. One is tempted to make the generalization that the Church is divisive when the state is strong and cohesive when the state is weak, which is only another way of saying that the Church can unify only on her own terms. When the state is strong and seeks to implement policies or force beliefs which the Church cannot accept, then she is bound to be in opposition. If the state is feeble, however, the Church is able unhampered to give substance to a social entity. It was to be so in the West. There the Church became the architect and molder of our civilization. The Church was heir to the unity of Rome and custodian of the unity of the faith. Through many centuries she sought to convert, tame, and unite the Northern peoples. Her success was Christendom.

With regard to war and peace the Middle Ages began in chaos, with pacifism in recession and the code of the just war violated in practice and strained in theory. The Church struggled to subdue the warlike propensities of the Northern peoples and to allay their feuds through a great peace movement, which curiously was turned into a crusade when the plea for peace at home ended in a summons to war against the infidel abroad. The enterprise did foster the unity of Christendom, but new sources of conflict emerged. Returning crusaders imported heresy into Europe, and the crusade was then revived to crush internal dissension. Even before the crusades, the universal leadership of the Church had been challenged by another claimant to universality, namely, the empire. The continuing clash

between the two great powers of integration, the papacy and the empire, facilitated the rise of city-states and nation-states. Their existence as sovereign political units with a common faith and culture gave a new relevance to the doctrine of the just war, while their centralization of government opened a possibility of making war more deadly when it came.

Adaptation of the Just War

The promotion of peace by the Church in the period following the invasions was more difficult because the invaders had cut their way into the empire by the sword. They were bellicose and utterly devoid of any feeling for the beatitude upon the meek. When these lusty warriors embraced the cross, they regarded it not as a yoke to be placed upon their pugnacity, but as an ensign to lead them in battle. The barbarians militarized Christianity.

Clovis regarded Jesus as the new Yahweh of Hosts. The king had long resisted the entreaties of his wife, Clotilde, to become a Christian, but when pressed in battle with the Alamanni, he ejaculated, "Jesus Christ, whom Clotilde asserts to be the Son of the living God, who art said to bestow victory on those who hope in thee, if thou wilt grant me victory over these mine enemies, I will believe in thee and be baptised in thy name." [1]

The earliest extant German poem in the old Germanic tongue celebrated the exploits of Peter in drawing the sword for his Master.

> Then boiled with wrath
> The swift sword wielder,
> Simon Peter,
> Speechless he,
> Grieved his heart
> That any sought
> To bind his Master,
> Grim the knight faced
> Boldly the servants,
> Shielding his Suzerain,
> Not craven his heart,
> Lightning swift

> Unsheathed his sword,
> Strode to the first foe,
> Smote a strong stroke,
> Clave with the sharp blade,
> On the right side
> The ear from Malchus.[2]

Apart from the bellicosity of these braves, the anarchic situation resulting from the breakdown of government rendered inoperative the theory of the just war, which posited sovereign states under responsible governments. The just war required the authority of the prince, but often enough there was no prince in territories from which the Roman legions had withdrawn, and even after the invaders were settled in the land, Viking raids continued against which no defense was instituted by government. Under such circumstances each defended himself as best he might, on the principle of *vim vi repellere,* that force may be repelled by force. Plainly the injunction of Augustine that the private man should not defend himself was in abeyance.

Another element in the Augustinian code of the just war frequently violated was the requirement that the clergy and the monastics should abstain. The clergy, being the only learned men, were soon drawn into the civil service of the Frankish kingdoms and thereby also into the military. Between the years A.D. 886-908 ten German bishops fell in battle. Around the year A.D. 1000, Bishop Bernward headed the forces of Otto III and fought with a spear containing some nails from the cross of Christ.[3]

Sometimes the clergy conserved the letter while violating the spirit of the code. Witness the case of Christian, the Archbishop of Mainz in 1182, of whom it is recorded that with his own hand he killed in battle nine men with a club rather than a sword because the Church abhors the shedding of blood. The account continues that the Archbishop after the slaughter donned his pontifical robes and said the divine office. Three hundred soldiers, all apostate monks, were in attendance. A choir of nuns sang sweetly *Gaudeamus.* After the mass the Archbishop assembled the abundant booty.[4]

The monastics sometimes forsook their assigned roles; when monasteries were attacked, monks would slip armor over their cowls. Even nuns, whom one would have expected to be restrained by their sex if not by their vows, had recourse to violence, employed on occasion not against barbarian invaders but against ecclesiastical superiors. Chrodield led the nuns of Poitiers in a revolt in which she engaged the aid of a rabble of murderers, vagrants, and sundry lawbreakers, and for two years defied alike the churchmen and the laity of the region.[5]

The Church of course did not approve of such behavior. Defections from the code did not invalidate the code, and churchmen labored valiantly to adapt it to the new conditions. The problem of the authority of the prince could not be solved so long as there was no prince and was not greatly eased when there came to be not one, but a multiplicity of princes in a graded hierarchy. The feudal system ranged from the serfs to the emperor, and everyone in between was both an inferior and a superior to someone else. The theory of the just war was then elaborated by the provision that an inferior ruler could not make war upon a superior ruler; to do so would be rebellion. Neither could a superior make war upon an inferior. The use of armed force in this instance would not be war, but either an exercise of the police power or else tyranny. Only equals could make war upon equals and even for them the question arose whether a baron could declare war on a baron, a duke on a duke, or a count on a count, without securing first the permission of his own superior, and whether the aggrieved could properly initiate hostilities without first seeking redress at the hand of the superior of his opponent.[6] The upshot was that he who wished to fight, fought, and war was less subject to formal restraints. Distinctions of rank were sometimes ludicrously disregarded, as when a cook together with his scullions and dairymaids issued a challenge of war to the Count of Salms. On what trivial pretexts the code was bypassed is evidenced in the case of a lord who declared war on the city of Frankfurt because a young lady of that city had refused to dance with his uncle.[7]

The Church did try to keep war within the framework of law. One way was that of accommodation. The law was modified and adapted. The structure of medieval society was more agrarian than had been that of the Roman Empire. With the invasions and the interruption of commerce, cities had declined. Wealth therefore consisted in land and the produce of land. For this reason, the scholastic theologians, who often discussed the ethic of war, laid the stress not upon the protection of life and honor, as Augustine had done, but upon the protection of property. A decretal of Gratian, for example, affirmed the object of the just war to be the repulse of enemies—this Augustine would have said—and the recovery of stolen goods.[8]

The ultimate sanction for this position was found by the scholastic and the canon lawyers increasingly in the doctrine of natural law rather than in the word of the New Testament; for obviously the injunctions of the gospel to give away the cloak as well as the coat, and the plea of Paul that Christians should not even go to law, preclude the use of war to reclaim one's own. Natural law was pitched on a less exalted plane, particularly when it was itself conceived more in terms of Aristotelian social conservatism than of Stoic radicalism —with its picture of the communistic golden age.[9]

If the object of war was to recover property, the pragmatic consideration entered that war might destroy more property than it recovered. St. Thomas raised the question, not with regard to war but with regard to revolution against a tyrant, and propounded the principle that recourse to arms would be justified only if the foreseeable damage would not exceed the injury sustained by submission.[10] In other words, justice was made to depend upon a fallible forecast. This principle to my knowledge was not extended to war prior to the sixteenth century, when Vittoria said that no war was just which would inflict great damage upon the world at large and upon its Christian population.[11]

The provision that an object of the just war is to recover stolen goods suggests the question, Whose goods? The goods of private citizens would sometimes be the answer, but then again the goods might be the land appertaining to the state. When, then, there were many little states contending with each other, the tendency was to think of them as individuals—in other words, to personify the state as Cicero had long since done. This personification became more than a convenient fiction when supported by the medieval philosophy known as realism, according to which entities called universals really exist. The state is such an entity or universal, and is not simply the aggregate of its component citizens. The maxim that force[12] may be repelled by force may therefore be invoked to preserve the existence of the state as a corporate entity.[13] This theory has been revised in modern times to justify the use of atomic weapons.

The theory of universals presents a threat to individualism, for if individuals are nothing but infiinitesimal concretions of universals, by what right may an individual go counter to such great corporate entities as the Church and the state? Here is the problem of conscience. Among the scholastics Abelard was the first to confront it. A point of departure was to be found in St. Paul's Epistle to the Romans, chapter 14, where he discussed the propriety of eating meat which had been offered to idols. The apostle said, "Let every man be fully persuaded in his own mind." Mature conviction was binding, even though in error, and Paul believed that those who scrupled to eat were in error; nevertheless, they should not eat so long as they scrupled. Abelard on this basis formulated the principle that conscience may be subjectively right while objectively wrong. The erring conscience is obligatory though not exempt from the consequences of error. Then arose the question of a conscientious heretic who would die in the flames rather than recant his faith. Bonaventura justified his punishment by the device of positing three steps in a moral judgment. The first is that of synteresis, meaning man's general moral capacity, which decrees that that which is right ought to be done. Reason then rules a particular course of action to be right and conscience finally requires that this be done. The ruling of conscience is thus dependent upon a prior judgment of reason, and reason may be mistaken. If an individual finds himself conscientiously opposed to the affirmations of the Church, he should consider whether his reason is likely to be right against that of the whole body of the faithful. If he adheres stubbornly to his own view, he may rightly be

107

punished for his obstinacy. On this basis, a heretic may not rightly stand against the Church, nor a conscientious objector against the state.

St. Thomas was more discriminating. For him the great cleavage was between the natural and the supernatural. To the natural he relegated synteresis, reason, and conscience. Faith belongs to the supernatural. Therefore conscience does not apply at all in the realm of faith, and the heretic is without any sort of standing. War belongs to the natural order, however. Here then, conscience does apply. Thus, on a Thomistic basis, conscientious objection to military service has a definite place, as it does to this day in Catholic ethics.[14]

Suppose now that an individual were conscientiously convinced, not that he should abstain from war, but that he should wage war without the sanction of the state and against the head of the state? Here was the problem of the legitimacy of tyrannicide. One observes that the raising of this question was a way of escaping from the static and conservative character of the just-war theory, which aimed as in antiquity at maintenance of the *status quo* and provided no place for revolution. The main form which revolution assumed in the Middle Ages was the attempt to eliminate despotic rulers. The ethic of tyrannicide was much debated, and a warrant for it was discovered in a combination of several traditions. There was the old Germanic view that the chieftain owed fealty to his men as much as they to him. The Old Testament afforded an example in the assassination of Holofernes by Judith, and classical antiquity provided the case of Brutus. Medieval canonists and scholastics invoked ideas of contract grounded in natural law, saying that a ruler who violated the constitution could be driven out like a faithless swinehard.[15] St. Thomas was unable to reach an unequivocal position. He was clear that a usurper might be killed and endorsed the judgment of Cicero sanctioning the assassination of Caesar. A legitimate ruler if a tyrant might be disobeyed, but might he be resisted? In the treatise *De Regno,* Thomas appealed to constitutional theory whereby the ruler, if he violated the covenant, might be deposed by the people. Even so, the resistance must proceed from public authority. Did this mean that some other officers of the state should lead the people in popular insurrection? In his other works, however, Thomas declared that tyrannicide was not allowable.[16]

The Church sought thus to repristinate and by adaptation to conserve the just-war theory as a restraint upon war. But better far would it be if there were no war, and valiant efforts were made for its eradication. The approval of the Church was never bestowed on those clerics and monastics who had taken defense into their own hands. St. Thomas, writing even after the commencement of the crusades, held that the clergy should be excluded from military functions, not so much, however, for ethical as for sacramental reasons. He declared that there are some acts which cannot be performed by the same persons; although participation in warfare is legitimate for the Christian, it is not for the clergy because they serve at the altar. For that reason they may not shed the blood of another, but should be prepared rather to shed their own in imitation of Christ. Various enactments of the period prescribed also that the cleric might not act as a judge. The Fourth Lateran Council, for example, declared in 1215 that those who administered the sacraments of the Saviour might not pronounce sentence of death.[17]

For the laity a moral taint continued to be attached to warfare up to the very threshold of the crusades. Ten years after the Norman conquest some of the participants sought counsel from their bishops as to the appeasement of their consciences for the blood they had shed. A council at Winchester in 1076 enacted that he who had killed a man should do penance for a year. He who did not know whether his wounded assailant had died should do penance for forty days. He who did not know how many he had killed should do penance one day a week throughout his life. All archers should do penance thrice for the space of forty days.[18]

From the Peace of God to the Holy War

If then killing, even in a just war, called for penance, every form of war should be eliminated. How inappropriate in any case that Christian princes should be devouring one another! The great reformatory movement emanating from the monastery of Cluny aimed at the radical Christianizing of society by the purging of the Church, the subordination of the state to the reformed Church, and the enlisting of the laity in the Church's service. To this end Christians should make peace among themselves. Or if fight they would, then their warfare should be restricted by rules much more hampering than those of the traditional code of the just war.

The first half of the eleventh century was marked by a great campaign—mainly in France, but also in Germany—to promote the Peace of God and the Truce of God. The first category limited those involved in war by increasing enormously the category of the exempt. The Council of Narbonne in 1054, for example, decreed that there should be no attack on clerics, monks, nuns, women, pilgrims, merchants, peasants, visitors to councils, churches and their surrounding grounds to thirty feet (provided that they did not house arms), cemeteries and cloisters to sixty feet, the lands of the clergy, shepherds and their flocks, agricultural animals, wagons in the fields, and olive trees.

The Truce of God limited the time for military operations. There should be no fighting from Advent through Epiphany nor from Septuagesima until the eighth day after Pentecost, nor on Sundays, Fridays, and every one of the holy days throughout the year.[19]

The Peace of God and the Truce of God could be combined, and we find elements of both in the oath taken by Robert the Pious (996-1031):

I will not infringe on the Church in any way. I will not hurt a cleric or a monk if unarmed. I will not steal an ox, cow, pig, sheep, goat, ass, or a mare with colt. I will not attack a vilain or vilainesse or servants or merchants for ransom. I will not take a mule or a horse male or female or a colt in pasture from any man from the calends of March to the feast of All Saints unless to recover a debt. I will not burn houses or destroy them unless there is a knight inside. I will not root up vines. I will not attack noble ladies traveling without husband nor their maids, nor widows or nuns unless it is their fault. From the beginning of Lent to the end of Easter I will not attack an unarmed knight.[20]

There were those who took these oaths and did not keep them. What then? How could they be punished? How could they be coerced? Should the enforcement be left to the civil power or should the Church undertake sanctions? Were she to do so, she would encroach upon the traditional role of the state. The lines of demarcation were, however, already obscured. The prince bishop in his own person already combined Church and state. He was a bishop. He was a prince and he had armies. Why should he not then as a bishop call upon the troops which he commanded as a prince in order to enforce the Church's peace? In the eleventh century peace militia were formed in Germany and in France, in which the clergy participated with their church banners. We read that in Germany one such army got out of hand and ravaged the country, so that a count with his forces withstood and defeated the peace fighters, leaving seven hundred of the clergy dead upon the field.[21] In other words a civil ruler assumed his traditional role against the usurpation of the Church. Another example occurred in Italy, where Giovanni de Vincenza, a preaching friar, in 1233 organized a great peace league of the northern Italian cities. Then he became so overweening that the Benedictines of Padua roused their city to resistance. The apostle of peace retaliated with armed forces, was defeated, and retired to a monastery, thus ending his "withered dream."[22]

Implicit in these attempts to enforce the peace was the idea of a crusade, that is to say of a war conducted under the auspices of the Church for a holy cause—the cause of peace. These initial ventures had failed at home. Perhaps they might be more successful if channeled into a war abroad. The great speech of Urban II at the Council of Clermont in 1095, which inaugurated the crusades, commenced with another of the peace speeches so frequent in the French councils of the previous half century. The Pope said:

Oh race of the Franks, we learn that in some of your provinces no one can venture on the road by day or by night without injury or attack by highwaymen, and no one is secure even at home. Let us then re-enact the law of our ancestors known as the Truce of God. And now that you have promised to maintain the peace among yourselves you are obligated to succour your brethren in the East, menaced by an accursed race, utterly alienated from God. The Holy Sepulchre of our Lord is polluted by the filthiness of an unclean nation. Recall the greatness of Charlemagne. O most valiant soldiers, descendants of invincible ancestors, be not degenerate. Let all hatred depart from among you, all quarrels end, all wars cease. Start upon the road to the Holy Sepulchre to wrest that land from the wicked race and subject it to yourselves.[23]

The assembly cried *Deus Vult*. Peace should thus be achieved at home by diverting bellicosity to a foreign adventure.

Here was a war inaugurated by the Church. Service was volunteered rather than exacted by a ruler from his retainers. The code of the just war, which was being elaborated and refined by the secular ideals of chivalry and the Church's ideal of the Truce and the Peace of God, was largely in abeyance in fighting the infidel. Crucifixion, ripping open those who had swallowed coins, mutilation—Bohemond of Antioch sent to the Greek Emperor a whole cargo of noses and thumbs sliced from the Saracens—such exploits the chronicles of the crusades recount without qualm. A favorite text was a verse in Jeremiah "Cursed be he that keepeth back his hand from blood." [24] There was no residue here of the Augustinian mournfulness in combat. The mood was strangely compounded of barbarian lust for combat and Christian zeal for the faith.

Raymond of Agiles has given us the following account of what happened on the capture of Jerusalem:

Some of our men (and this was more merciful) cut off the heads of their enemies; others shot them with arrows, so that they fell from the towers; others tortured them longer by casting them into the flames. Piles of heads, hands, and feet were to be seen in the streets of the city. It was necessary to pick one's way over the bodies of men and horses. But these were small matters compared to what happened at the temple of Solomon, a place where religious services are ordinarily chanted. What happened there? If I tell the truth, it will exceed your powers of belief. So let it suffice to say this much at least, that in the temple and portico of Solomon, men rode in blood up to their knees and the bridle reins. Indeed, it was a just and splendid judgment of God, that this place should be filled with the blood of the unbelievers, when it had suffered so long from their blasphemies.

THE CAPTURE OF JERUSALEM IN 1099 FROM A MINIATURE OF THE THIRTEENTH CENTURY. ON THE LEFT ARE SOLDIERS OF THE FRANKS WITH THE *fleurs de lys* ON THEIR SHIELDS. THE FIGURE IN THE MIDDLE IS OPERATING A CATAPULT. FURTHER TO THE RIGHT FRANKISH SOLDIERS ARE BOOSTING A COMRADE ONTO THE BATTLEMENT OF THE FOE. SAPPERS ARE CRAWLING THROUGH A HOLE UNDER THE TOWER. DEFENDERS STRIKE DOWN WITH A SWORD, EMPTY A JAR OF BOILING OIL, AND HURL A STONE

Now that the city was taken it was worth all our previous labors and hardships to see the devotion of the pilgrims at the Holy Sepulcher. How they rejoiced and exulted and sang the ninth chant to the Lord. It was the ninth day, the ninth joy and exaltation, and of perpetual happiness. The ninth sermon, the ninth chant was demanded by all. This day, I say, will be famous in all future ages, for it turned our labors and sorrows into joy and exultation; this day, I say, marks the justification of all Christianity and the humiliation of paganism; our faith was renewed. "The Lord made this day, and we rejoiced and exulted in it," for on this day the Lord revealed Himself to His people and blessed them.[25]

This mood was all very different from the attitude of the Byzantines, who had long withstood the Turks but without religious fanaticism. The emperors sometimes even gave their daughters to the harems of the sultans. There was more hate for the Latins than for the Turks. Hence the saying "Better to come under the turban than under the tiara."

As for the Byzantine attitude to clerical fighting, we have a very illuminating account from the pen of Anna Comnena, the daughter of the Eastern emperor of Constantinople at the time of the first crusade. Although the Franks had come to the aid of the Greeks, misunderstandings and frictions occurred and a Frankish vessel had a skirmish with the admiral of the Byzantine fleet. Anna gives this description.

A certain Latin priest stood on the stern and discharged arrows. Though streaming with blood, he was quite fearless, for the rules as to priests are different among the Latins from ours. We are taught by the canonical laws and the gospel that the priest is holy . . . but the Latin barbarian will handle divine things and simultaneously wear a shield on his left arm and hold a spear in his right. At one and the same time he communicates the body and blood of God and becomes a man of blood, for this barbarian is no less devoted to sacred things than to war. This priest, or rather man of violence, wore his vestments while he handled an oar and was so bellicose as to keep on fighting after the truce.[26]

Even monastic pacifism collapsed and there came to be monastic military orders, the Templars, the Hospitalers, and the Knights of St. John. And if St. Bernard did not write the rules for the Templars, at any rate this mellifluous commentator on the Song of Songs, celebrating the love of Christ and the Church, could exhort to fearless fighting on the ground that he who killed benefited Christ and he who died benefited himself. "Therefore, ye knights," exhorted Bernard, "attack with confidence and courage the enemies of the cross of Christ, assured that neither life nor death can separate you from the love of God which is in Christ Jesus our Lord." [27]

The medieval theologians were not aware that the crusade had written a new chapter in the ethic of war. They could accommodate the crusade to the doctrine of the just war, because by common consent the crusade was not fought to convert the infidel but only to protect the passage of pilgrims to the Holy Land; this at any rate was the initial objective. There was latent a fundamental difference, however. The purpose was not to recover stolen goods nor to repel an invasion, but to vindicate a right of religion under a foreign jurisdiction. This was after all a war of faith.

The religious character of the crusade became all the more apparent when it was used to suppress heresy at home. One of the anomalies of medieval history is that the Church itself remained united from the barbarian invasions to the peak of the papal theocracy and then, when such an amazing degree of unity had been achieved, rifts appeared in her structure. Indirectly the crusades contributed. Disillusioned crusaders, returning after disasters in the east, passed through Bulgaria and there were infected with the heresy of the Bogomili, a sect in the spiritual succession of the Gnostics who looked with despite upon the flesh. The Cathari, as these sectaries were called, looked upon the sexual act as defiling, condemned marriage, and would eat nothing related to the processes of sex, such as eggs, milk, butter, and cheese. Luckily they were not aware that plants and fish have sex. The Cathari believed in transmigration of souls, and for that reason, would not take a life. A way to detect a member of the sect was to call on him to kill a chicken. Of necessity, therefore, the Cathari rejected war, though when attacked they defended themselves. Perhaps under pressure their practice failed to conform to principle, or perhaps the discrepancy is to be explained by the division of their adherents into the perfect who observed all the precepts and the believers who were allowed a less rigorous code. The Cathari vigorously rejected the authority of the Church and threatened to supplant her in southern France. Then the crusade was unleashed. Northern Frenchmen were enlisted by an offer of indulgences in return for a service of forty days. Thirsty for loot—spiritual and temporal—they flayed Provence, hanging, beheading, and burning "with unspeakable joy." When Beziers was taken and the Papal legate was asked how to distinguish between the Cathari and the Catholics, he replied: "Kill them all; God will know which are His." [28] The claim that religious war is typically more brutal than secular war is difficult to document; but certainly the belief that the enemy is already damned is not conducive to chivalry.

The Inquisition was founded shortly thereafter to deal with the surviving remnants of the movement as well as with other heretics lately arisen. Imprisonment, torture, and the stake were employed in order to save souls by intimidation. The Inquisition was a department of the cure of souls. The motive was love for the heretic and concern for his eternal salvation as well as love for those whom he might lead to damnation. Presumably, the motive for the war against the Cathari was the same. Reviewing these events, a modern may well conclude that love is not an absolute; the pitfall of love is meddlesomeness. To be tolerable, love must be combined with humility and respect.

The crusades are commonly believed to have contributed, nevertheless, to European unity. Despite political fragmentation, medieval society from the Baltic to the Mediterranean became a *corpus christianum*, a *respublica christiana*.[29] Very probably the crusades did aid by setting Christendom over against Islam. On the other hand, a greater weight is perhaps to be assigned to those peaceful processes by which the Church unified the west sufficiently to make possible a crusade. It may well be that the many instances of the avoidance of war by arbitration, in the Europe of the thirteenth and fourteenth centuries, were due to weariness and revulsion against the crusades.

Medieval Arbitration

At any rate these centuries did exhibit a surprising degree of recourse to arbitration. Novacovitch has recorded 127 cases between the years 1218 and 1441. Such instances were rare in the twelfth century, more numerous in the thirteenth, abounded in the fourteenth and the first half of the fifteenth centuries, and then suddenly dropped off. An examination of these cases reveals several points of interest, including the geographical range—from the Scandinavian countries to Spain, England, France, the Low Countries, Poland, Lithuania, Hungary, Austria, Bohemia, the Holy Roman Empire, the Swiss Confederacy, the Italian Cities, and even the Balkans.

The disputants were less commonly the greater powers, though occasionally England, France, Denmark, Sweden, Bohemia, Hungary, Poland, and the Empire were among the litigants. For the most part, however, the list runs after this fashion: the Countess of Troy against the Duke of Lorraine; the city of Riga versus the Knights of

Christ; the Count of Ragus and the King of Serbia; the Bishop of Speyer against the city of Speyer; Aragon, Sicily, and Naples against each other as to the distribution of tribute from the sultan of Tunisia; Uri, Schwiz, and Unterwalden, later Zurich and Berne in agreement for perpetual arbitration; Holland versus Brabant; the Duke of Bar against the Duke of Lorraine; Württemberg versus Esslingen; the Count Palatine of the Rhine, the Duke of Saxony, and the Marquis of Brandenberg as to the allocation of expenses for the imperial election; the Rhine cities, Strassburg, Mainz, Worms, and Cologne in dispute with each other; and the Italian cities in like case.

The complexion of the arbitrators is striking because the Church played so small a part. Only one dispute was mediated directly by the pope, though several were handled by papal legates—a cardinal or a bishop. On the whole there was a disposition to avoid appeals to the Church, because she would inject claims of her own. On one occasion, the pope was himself a litigant and frequently bishops, convents, and orders—such as the Teutonic Knights—were among the parties. Laymen most frequently were arbiters, often the King of France or some other monarch or nobleman and not infrequently a board of arbitration set up by the contestants. Among the Italian cities churchmen were more often the judges.[30]

This comparative neglect of the Church in direct mediation must not obscure the role of the Church in the creation of an atmosphere in which arbitration flourished. On the other hand, the contribution of the Church is not to be exaggerated. The fourteenth century, when cases of arbitration were so numerous, was also the period of the Hundred Years War between England and France. The popes, then resident at Avignon, sought to avert the conflict, but during its course injected a religious issue which precluded papal mediation. For example, the emperor Louis of Bavaria was under excommunication. When, then, England made an alliance with Louis, the pope threw his support to France, and thus became a party to the quarrel. A deeper difficulty may well have been that the popes sought to eliminate only those wars which they desired to eliminate. During this very period, 64 per cent of the papal income was spent on wars

THE BATTLE OF POITIERS IN 1346 BETWEEN THE FRENCH (ON THE LEFT)
AND THE ENGLISH (ON THE RIGHT). FROM A MINIATURE OF THE FOURTEENTH
CENTURY

to recover the estates in Italy which had been overrun when the
papacy was transferred to Avignon.[31]

Medieval Pacifism

One can easily understand the revulsion which ensued against
crusades in general, and in particular against crusades to recover
papal property. Already in the twelfth century, a certain Niger protested on the ground that the cost and the risks were enough to dis-
credit the enterprise. He struck at the very root of a war under
churchly auspices, claiming that the making of war is the affair of
the secular ruler. He stoutly objected to the shedding of blood at
the hands of the clergy.[32] In the thirteenth century complaints became more general and more diverse. Some decried the financial
racketeering of crusading indulgences; some objected to shipping the
scum of Europe to the Holy Land. Military reverses and notably the
debacle of St. Louis suggested that *Deus non vult*. A Templar said

that neither cross nor faith gave protection against the Turks but that God seemed rather to favor them. Or could it be that Allah was stronger than God? There were stay-at-home farmers whom crusaders called "Flemish cows staked out to graze" and debonair troubadours who preferred to court Nicolette than to campaign for the Holy Sepulchre. One of them reproached God for sitting secure and comfortable in heaven while leaving to his harassed followers not so much as a castle, a fortress, or a battlement. Some who had no objection to shedding Saracen blood yet deplored adventures which cost so much Christian blood.

The only criticism of the crusades which verged on pacifism was that of the Franciscans. St. Francis himself had been a great preacher of reconciliation, and his followers were renowned for their ability to pacify the feuds of the Italian cities. St. Francis went in person to interview the sultan, and among the Franciscans were those who felt the entire crusading enterprise should be replaced by missionary activity. The testimony was not unequivocal, however; St. Francis did not condemn the fifth crusade which he accompanied. Some Franciscans preached crusades, as did John of Capistrano—another case of reconciling feuds at home and inciting war abroad.[33]

The purveyors of pacifism were rather the late medieval sects. We learn that a group of the Waldensians in the early thirteenth century were induced by Innocent III to return to the Church on condition that certain of their demands be granted, one of which was exemption from military service.[34] The Franciscan Tertiaries made a similar demand, and when feudal lords bitterly complained, several papal briefs supported the penitents. Any who impressed them into service would incur the indignation of the omnipotent God and of the blessed apostles Peter and Paul. The pacifism of the Cathari has already been noted.[35]

Wycliffe appears not to have been an absolute pacifist. He held war to be contrary to the teaching of Christ and considered the highest Christian ideal to require complete abstention, but allowed that on a lower level war might be waged for the love of God or to correct a people. His follower, Hereford, was less concessive, declaring

119

"Jesus Christ, duke of oure batel, taught us lawe of pacience, and not to fight bodily." [36]

The Hussite movement developed two wings, one pacifist and one crusading. This bifurcation is not as anomalous as it may at first appear. The religious sect is almost bound to be either pacifist or crusading, because the sect demands a higher level of Christian deportment than is ever attained by an entire community. If then the Church has coalesced with society so that every citizen is deemed a Christian, and Christians are not distinguishable by their behavior, then the sect must either dissociate itself from the Church and the community—and this course will commonly entail pacifism—or else must seek to impose its code upon the Church and the community—and this course will issue in a crusade.

The pacifist branch of the Hussites had its first outstanding leader in Peter Chelciky, who scathed those who scrupled to eat swine flesh on a Friday but not to shed human blood. He adumbrated many of the ideas later to be prevalent among Reformation sects—that the first age of the Church was the golden age and this age was pacifist; that Christ's law was the law of love which forbids killing; and that his weapon was spiritual only and his mission to redeem souls, not to destroy bodies. The fall of the Church began with Constantine with the union of Church and state. To be sure, the state was ordained of God, as Paul said, but only to restrain sin and should be administered by sinners. Christians should obey all commands not contrary to the Word of God, but political office they should decline and military service they should refuse. When religious war devastated the land, Chelciky was more confirmed in his view that a Christian should suffer, not inflict suffering. "Everywhere," said he, "murder, rapine and want have flourished, and multitudes have perished . . . the laboring people is stripped of everything, downtrodden, oppressed, beaten, robbed so that many are driven by want and hunger to leave their land."

Chelciky never wavered in his stand, but his branch of the Hussites made gradual accommodations, particularly when the social complexion of the group was changed, and unlettered peasants were replaced by prosperous burghers and educated intellectuals. Nevertheless a group survived; it is called from now on the Minor Party. Many secular lords had the sagacity to welcome to their estates these God-fearing, dutiful, industrious, frugal peasants. This was not to be the first time in history that pacifists proved able to survive by an unwitting vocationalism. Nonpacifist landowners and rulers argued that these men might as well be left to do the farming, since others could be enlisted to do the fighting. The Bohemian Brethren thus survived to give to the world in the Seventeenth Century the great educator and internationalist Comenius.[37]

The other wing of the Hussites, led by the blind general Ziska, flung crusading armies of peasants, as contemptible as the handful of Gideon, against the forces of the empire and put them to rout. The land was ravaged, as Chelciky reported, and the crusade was carried beyond the confines of Bohemia into Saxony. This was again warfare in the name of the Lord of Hosts.

Although pacifism was the affair of the sects, one is not to conclude that the concern for peace in the late Middle Ages was restricted to them. We have already observed the efforts of the Church to establish peace through concord or enforcement. Whereas the inadequate success of these measures turned some to pacifism others turned to the state as the appropriate organ in a Christian society to preserve the peace. The outstanding exponents of this view were Dante, Marsilius, and Pierre Dubois. They thought in terms of a universal empire like that of ancient Rome, only more extensive. Dante would include Asia and Africa. The structure of his world state was that of the Holy Roman Empire, which should, however, take up its seat in Italy rather than Germany. Marsilius perceived that a universal empire would not be free from wars of succession in a dynastic system and therefore proposed an elective constitution. Neither plan was realistic because the Holy Roman Empire was not in a position to control the rising national states and Pierre Dubois saw better the actualities when he proposed France as the Lord's chosen people to unite mankind under a single sway. But this too could not have been done without a war to end wars.[38]

Chapter 8

The Renaissance Utopia and the Revival of the Just War

THE period of the Renaissance in the late fifteenth and early sixteenth centuries was marked by three significant developments. The first was a recurrence of that political situation which is most congenial to the just war, namely, a congeries of independent sovereign states united in a common culture, each recognizing the right of the other to exist. This situation came to pass in Italy in the half century prior to the invasion by Charles VIII of France, whose advent with diabolical cannon—"son of a gun" means son of the devil—made Italy the cockpit of the European powers. Italy enjoyed an interlude of fifty years between the wars of the Guelphs and the Ghibellines and the conflict of the national states. This respite of comparative peace eventuated from the mutual weakening of the two great universal powers of the Middle Ages, the Church and the empire. Each had sought to unify Europe, the one on a religious and the other on a civil basis. The encroachment of the Church on the civil domain and the frequent confiscation by the civil power of the Church's patrimony led to conflicts in which the empire was reduced to something more indeed than pageantry, but less than world dominion, and the Church to something short of a world power, though more indeed than a spiritual society. The Italian city-states had been involved in the conflict, and each had had its papal faction, the Guelph, and its imperial faction, the Ghibelline. When the empire was weakened, and the papacy reduced to the point of itself becoming one of the Italian city-states, then these small independent political units could work out their mutual relations without subjection to the imposition of peace or war by either of their former overlords. A balance was then achieved among five states—Naples, the papacy, Florence, Milan, and Venice.

Under these circumstances, the code of the just war again came into vogue, and the conduct of the war very closely corresponded to the conditions of the Peace of God and the Truce of God. The five states adjusted their differences and pretentions by armed sorties in which mercenaries on both sides sought in seasonable weather to gain an advantage for their respective employers, with the least loss to themselves or to their fellow professionals in the opposite camp. The victory went to those who took the most prisoners, and these were not killed but were speedily released. Fighting was on horseback with conventional weapons; cannons were despised as more diabolical than human; rules were observed; ambassadors were inviolate, and private reprisals were suppressed.

Machiavelli, who viewed with contempt such gentlemanly wars, recorded that in the battle of Zagomara only three men were killed; thrown from their horses, they were suffocated in the mud. In the battle of Anghiari, there was but one casualty, that of a man who again fell from his horse and was trampled to death. In the battle of Molinella, nobody was killed; only a few horses were wounded, and a few prisoners were taken on each side.[1] To be sure, Machiavelli barbed his shafts with exaggeration. There were larger casualties. The *condottieri* sought some victories for prestige, and if they had recourse to protracted wars of maneuver, it was partly because the resources of the Italian city-states were too meagre and their power too nearly balanced to permit swift and decisive large-scale encounters. The resemblance to the Peace of God and the Truce of God was accidental, due to a new configuration of power rather than to a resurgence of the old ideal. The character of this period is of historical interest because it demonstrates that an approximation to the ideals of the just-war theory is realizable, given an equality of power and a community of culture. The traditional stipulation, however, of justice on one side only was entirely unrealistic. The five states were simply sparring for advantage and were ready to seek it without regard to justice.

The Theory of the Power State

The reduction of war's asperity in the Italy of the Renaissance was certainly not due to any peculiar goodness; this was the very period of the Italian despots from whose behavior Machiavelli derived his theory of the ruthless power state. His book, *The Prince*, though belonging to a medieval literary genre, broke with the medieval tradition of Christian morality. The ancients, said Machiavelli, fought harder for liberty than did the men of his own day because Christianity taught humility and produced no ferocity. He wrote:

Our religion has glorified rather the humble and the contemplative than the active, the *summum bonum* has been conceived in terms of humility, abjectness and contempt of the world. For as the religion [of the ancients] saw the highest good rather in greatness of mind, prowess of body and whatever else makes men courageous, our religion counsels that if you have any strength you should suffer rather than be strong. This behavior has made the world weak and has given it as a prey to the unprincipled who are able to dominate with impunity since the majority of men think the way to get to heaven is to suffer blows rather than to avenge them. That the world is effeminate and heaven disarmed arises from the cravenness of men who have interpreted our religion as indolence rather than as virtù.[2]

Machiavelli's claim that this was an incorrect interpretation of Christianity may be suspected as a sop to his time, since he was actually contemptuous of all religion save as a device for statecraft.

His political thinking was in the tradition of one strand of the classical heritage—that of the Sophists, with their glorification of brute power, of which examples in abundance could be found in the pages of Thucydides and Tacitus. Machiavelli found its locus in *virtù*, a dynamic energy in man, impelling him alike to power and greatness. *Virtù* characterizes the prince in particular, and he should seek to instill it in his subjects who possess it ordinarily only in a lesser degree. *Virtù* animates the state, though Machiavelli did not advance the view that some states are more endowed than others and have for that reason a right to impose their will. Each prince and each state, he claimed, must gain and hold power, must indeed preserve its very existence through the exercise of *virtù*. No consideration of morality should be permitted to impede. The prince, said he,

should appear pious, faithful, humane, religious and sincere, and should indeed be all of these, but should ever be ready, if need be, to change to the contrary. . . . A prince, and especially a new prince cannot observe all those qualities for which men are esteemed good. If it be necessary to maintain the state, he must be ready to violate faith, charity, humanity and religion. However, he must have a mind ready to veer with every wind and variation of Fortune.[3]

Machiavelli here suggested that not so much *virtù* as *Fortuna* is responsible for this abdication of morality, because it is she who presents those necessities to which men must react by brutality. Sometimes, however, the blame was laid upon the nature of man; if all men kept faith, then one could keep faith, but since they do not, one is not bound to be honorable with the dishonorable. Throughout the works of Machiavelli runs the assumption that one's own existence and the existence of the state are paramount. "When it is a question of the safety of the country," he wrote, "no account should be taken of what is just or unjust, merciful or cruel, laudable or shameful, but without regard to anything else, that course is to be unswervingly pursued which will save the life and maintain the liberty of the [fatherland]." [4]

This does not mean that politics is nothing but unabashed chicanery and cruelty. No state can rest permanently on hate. The *virtù* of the ruler is dynamic but not demonic, save on occasion. Ordinarily it is restrained by prudence. The wise ruler will so choose his means that he will be both feared and loved. By the same token, a state should not behave so outrageously as to provoke a concerted coalition for its destruction. Prudence and valour are alike directed to the maintenance of the security of the state. This means, of course, that the traditional code of the just war was jettisoned. Only that war could be considered just, said Machiavelli, which was dictated by interest. And there could be no nonsense in the conduct of a war. The term war did not apply "when nobody gets killed, no cities are sacked and no lands are scorched." [5]

One element of significance in the thought of Machiavelli, because appropriated by the "realists" of later times, was his personification and at the same time depersonalizing of the state. Politics for him became a game, like chess, and the removal of a political pawn, though it comprised fifty thousand men, was no more disquieting than the removal from the board of an ivory piece.

The age of the Renaissance was significant also as a link between antiquity and the modern period at the point of deterministic theories of history which regard as inevitable the recurrence of war. One form of the theory was the cyclical view with a rationalistic explanation, as in the following citation from a work of the English Renaissance:

Warre bringeth ruine, ruine bringeth povertie, povertie procureth peace, and peace in time increaseth riches, riches causeth statelinesse, statelinesse increaseth envie, envie in the end procureth deadly mallice, mortall mallice proclaimeth open warre and battaile: and from warre againe as before is rehearsed.[6]

Another form of the deterministic view was astrological and supernatural. In this view the incidence and the outcome of war depended on the courses of the stars or the caprices of the goddess *Fortuna*. A striking example of the force of such ideas in precipitating war was the case of the Peasants' War in Germany. For twenty years previously great devastations had been predicted for the year 1524, when all of the planets would be in the constellation of the Fish. The peasants indeed held back one year because of hopes that the emperor would redress their grievances. He failed and in 1525 the great Fish unloosed the waters. The practice of judicial astrology, as it was called, with specific prediction of events, incurred ecclesiastical censure not only because astrology conflicted with theology but because predictions had an unhappy faculty of procuring their own fulfillment.

Humanist Pacifism

Contemporaneous with Machiavelli was a group of Renaissance humanists who sought to resuscitate the languishing unities of Europe. They were men of many lands—Colet and More in England; Erasmus in Holland; Vives in Spain; Clichtove in Belgium; Postel, Rabelais, and Montaigne in France; Agrippa of Nettesheim Paracelsus, and Sebastian Franck in Germany. They were compelled to come to terms with the circumstances of their time. Nationalism had become a fact in politics and in sentiment. In the political realm they could do no other than reckon with realities, and their pleas for peace, unlike those of Dante and Marsilius, did not envisage a new *Pax Romana* under the tutelage of a renovated Holy Roman Empire, nor for that matter under the leadership of one of the new national states, as proposed for France by Pierre Dubois. Their hope was rather that the many sovereign states, whether the newly consolidated monarchies of France, Spain, and England, or the small territories of the German *Reich*, should dwell together in concord. To that end these states should practice political isolationism, renouncing all expansionist ambitions. Rulers should be content to govern well what they already possessed rather than seek to be encumbered with more.

The program for peace was thus focused on an aristocracy of rulers bound to each other in a code of courtesy and humanity. Almost apocalyptic hopes were entertained for the restoration of paradise at the hands of three brilliant young princes trained in humanist studies—Henry of England, Francis of France, and Charles of the Netherlands and Spain. They should abstain from inflaming their peoples with the sentiment of nationalism. The humanists varied in the degree of their own national attachments. Erasmus had the least, for seldom did he mention his native Holland, and he had but scorn for the boast of Pope Julius II that he was a Ligurian Italian. More had a deeper feeling for England, though not for the sake of England's tranquillity would he put his king above his God. Some humanists, to be sure, were intensely nationalist—for example Ulrich von Hutten and Ulrich Zwingli, but they were warriors, and even they had a sense of belonging also to a universal European republic of letters.

The philosophy and theology animating the peace pleas were a blending of the ancient Stoic harmony of the cosmos with Christian faith in the brotherhood of the sons of God, coupled with a conviction that men endowed with reason and baptized into Christ could overcome the stupidity and depravity so generally evident.

The humanist advocates of peace differed in their emphases. The sharpest variance was between Catholics and Protestants. Paracelsus, Sebastian Franck belonged to the radical wing of Protestantism. Paracelsus took his stand on the biblical command "Thou shalt not kill," [7] and the pacifism of Franck was a corollary of his view of the Church as always oppressed, ready ever to suffer but never to inflict suffering.[8] Catholics had to accept the theory of the just war, but without forsaking its formulae they could condemn all the wars of their generation. The just-war theory requires that the object of war be peace and that every expedient for reconciliation shall have been exhausted prior to the declaration of hostilities. Could Francis or Charles or Henry pretend that these conditions had been fulfilled? War against the Turks was more of a problem to the humanist pacifists, but even in this case the espousal of the ultimate crusade was not incompatible with a program of peace. That brilliant eccentric Guillaume Postel [9] dedicated his life to the conversion of the Muslim, traveled in the Orient, learned Arabic and Syriac and worked furiously to produce translations of Christian works into the Oriental tongues. After a great missionary *putsch*, he was willing to countenance a crusade to bring the obstinate residue under a world empire led by France—shades of Pierre Dubois! The emphasis was on the peaceful campaign for the *Concordia Mundi*.

Some of the individual emphases among the humanists may be noted—Rabelais scoffed at the triviality of the causes of war by recounting how some cake bakers were driving a cart laden with their goods when accosted civilly by some shepherds who wished to buy at current prices. They were met with a volley of Rabelaisan invective. The spokesman of the shepherds, without losing his *sang froid,* remonstrated and renewed the request. The chief cake baker feigned consent, but when the trusting shepherd drew near he received a lash across the shins. All the shepherds then fell upon the cake bakers, "whence arose great wars." [10]

Montaigne complained of the stupidity of those who committed their course to the capricious issue of battle, where defeat might be occasioned by a contrary wind, by the flight of crows obscuring vision, by the misstep of a horse, by a dream, a voice or a morning mist.[11]

Clichtove, the great Catholic antagonist of Luther, centered on the impropriety of war among Christians, the sacrilege of clerical participation, and the unseemliness of taking the cross into battle where it might be desecrated by trampling in the fray.[12] Vives commenced his tract on *War with the Turk* as if he were about to revamp the speech of Pope Urban II at the council of Clermont. The Spaniard pointed out that the Turk was gaining because the Christians were fighting each other. One would expect his next point to be that the Christians should stop fighting each other and unite against the common foe. Not so; however, since God does not need the unity of men in order to repulse the foe—he went on—a mere handful will suffice, and those who enjoy Christ's favor may be assured of security, apparently if they do nothing at all. The reason for the Turkish success was not so much that Christians were divided as that they were divisive, and that not merely at the political level. There were, alas, contentions between the Thomists and the Occamists, the Monks and the Minorites, the Franciscans and the Dominicans, the Catholics and the Lutherans, and among the Lutherans themselves. Let contention cease, then peace would ensue. As to the new weapons of war employed in the sixteenth century, Vives recalled the remark of one of the ancients who when the Syracusans used darts of liquid fire, commented ruefully: "Now valor is no more." "Today," said Vives, "we might better say 'humanity is no more'." [13]

The Utopia of Thomas More had the ring of righteousness. The noblest wars, in his judgment, were those undertaken by the state not on its own behalf but to succour the injured. The rules of the just war should be strictly observed, hostilities should cease the moment the objective was achieved, and during their course humanity should be practiced. For the Utopians "doo no lesse pytye the basse and common sorte of their enemies people, than they doo theyre owne; knowynge that they be driven to warre agaynste theyre wylles by the furyous madnes of theyre prynces and heades." The Utopians "do not waste nor destroy there enemies lande with forraginges, nor they burne not up their corne. . . . They hurt no man that is unarmed, onles he be an espiall. . . . All the weak multitude they leaue untouched." [14]

John Colet, the Dean of St. Paul's, likewise confined himself to the terms of the just-war theory. Yet in so doing he stressed peace to the point of disquieting Henry VIII, for whom he preached a famous sermon. Erasmus, on whom we must rely for a report, declared that Colet pointed out how few undertake a war save for hatred or ambition, and how hardly can they who thrust their swords into their brothers' blood entertain that love without which no one can see the Lord. Henry was apprehensive lest such words destroy the morale of his newly recruited troops.[15]

Agrippa of Nettesheim was less restrained than the others by the theory of the just war. After recounting war's horrors he concluded: "The whole art [of war] studies nothing else but the subversion of Mankind, transforming men into beasts and monsters so that War is nothing but a general Homicide and Robbery by mutual Consent." The Pontifical Decretals do not

at all impugne it, though Christ and his Apostles teach quite another doctrine. So that contrary to the Doctrine of Christ, it has obtain'd no small Honour in the Church, by reason of the many Orders of Holy Soldiers, all whose religion consists in Blood, Slaughter, Rapine and Pyracy, under pretence of defending and enlarging the *Christian faith;* as if the Intention of Christ had been to spread his Gospel, not by Preaching, but by force of Arms; not by Confession and simpleness of Heart, but by Menaces and high Threats of Ruine and Destruction, strength of Arms, Slaughter and Massacres of Mankind. Nor is it enough for these Soldiers to bear their Arms against the *Turks, Saracens* and *Pagans,* unless they fight also for Christians against Christians. War and Warfare have begot many bishops, and it is not seldome that they Fight stiffly for the Popedome; which made the Holy Bishop of *Camora* Affirm, "That seldom any Pope ascends the Chair without the Blood of the Saints." [16]

The most renowned and vocal of all the humanists pacifists of the Renaissance was Erasmus of Rotterdam. In his letter to the abbot of Bergen, in the commentary on the adage of Pindar "Sweet is war to him who knows it not," in the *Institute of the Christian Prince,* especially in the *Complaint of Peace,* not to mention allusions in nearly every work and in many letters, Erasmus reiterated his perennial plea. Peace was necessary for his program of the reform of the Church and society through the processes of education. Erasmus the more despised a sword in the hand because he had a rapier in his tongue. The use of such a verbal weapon appeared to him to be not incompatible with Christian love, because there are battles of truth and they should be conducted by the instruments of the mind. There is here a deep intellectualist revulsion against the ways of the brute.

As for the traditional ethic of the just war, Erasmus subscribed to it. When after his deprecation of crusades, he was pinned down as to the legitimacy of war against the Turk, he conceded that an invasion might be repelled but added the proviso that nothing should be done contrary to the will of God. Was this another of those artifices by which Erasmus nullified a concession? At any rate, when it came to the wars of Europe, he could and did condemn them all as incompatible with the stipulations of a just war. In the matter of territory, he perceived that there could never be justice on one side only, because there was no state which had not lost territories formerly possessed. If prior possession constituted a claim, Italy might take over the whole of Northern Africa, and that of course would have meant in his day an aggressive war against Islam. Erasmus would have none of it.[17]

A brief review of his best known tract, *The Complaint of Peace,* will show how he quarried afresh in the classical and Christian sources to produce a new synthesis.[18]

Here follows an epitome:

Peace enters speaking in her own person and lamenting that she is so little received among men. She marvels at this the more because the heavenly bodies, though inanimate, preserve a happy equilibrium; the very plants cling to each other and the irrational animals do not devour those of the same species. The boar does not bury his tusk in the boar, the lion shows no fierceness to the lion, nor does the serpent expend his venom on the serpent. The wolf is kind to the wolf. And if animals do fight it is only to assuage their hunger. Why then should not man of all creatures be at peace with man? The more so because he is endowed with reason and gifted with speech, the instrument of social intercourse and reconciliation, and with tears which in a shower dissolve the clouds and suffer the sun again to shine. Man depends for his very existence upon cooperation. He could not be born without the union of partners or survive without a helping hand. The human being, unlike the animals, arrives physically defenseless. Why then should man prey upon man?

Peace, not yet disillusioned, assumes that when she hears the name of man and Christian, there she will find a reception. She approaches hopefully a city begirt by walls and living in accord with laws, only to discover factions. She turns from the common rout to kings and finds them embracing with obsequious flattery while conniving at mutual destruction. The learned men, the philosophers, are little better with their wrangling schools. Nor even are the religious orders superior, though they bear the name of brother, dress in white, and carry the cross, for they are continually contentious. The home is indeed better, yet not without discord, and even in the breast of a single individual the passions are at war with reason.

All this is the more amazing when one examines the precepts of the Christian religion. In the Old Testament Isaiah foretold the coming of the Prince of Peace and in the New Testament Christ bequeathed peace as his legacy. The mark by which his disciples should be known is love one for the other. The Lord's Prayer addresses *Our Father,* but how can they call upon a common Father who drive steel into the bowels of their brethren? Christ compared himself to a hen, Christians behave like hawks. Christ was a shepherd of sheep, Christians tear each other like wolves. Christians have the same Supper of the Lord, the same heavenly Jerusalem, but they are less peaceful than the Jews who fight only with foreigners and the Turks who keep the peace among themselves.

And who is responsible for all this? Not the common people, but kings, who on the strength of some musty parchment lay claim to neighboring territory or because of the infringement of one point in a treaty of a hundred articles, embark on war. Not the young, but the graybeards. Not the laity, but the bishops. The very cross is painted on their banners and cannons are christened and engraved with the names of the apostles, so that Paul, the preacher of peace, is made to hurl a cannon ball at the heads of Christians.

Consider the wickedness of it all, the breakdown of laws which are ever silent amid the clangor of arms. Debauchery, rape, incest, and the foulest crimes are let loose in war. Men who would go to the gallows in peace are of prime use in war, the burglar to rob, the assassin to disembowel, the incendiary to fire an enemy city, the pirate to sink his vessels.

Consider the cost of it all. In order to prevent the enemy from leaving his town one must sleep for months outside of one's own. New walls could be built for less than is required to batter down old ones. When all the damage is taken into account, the most brilliant success is not worth the trouble.

How then is peace to be secured? Not by royal marriages, but by cleansing the human heart. Why should one born in the bogs of Ireland seek by some alliance to rule over the East Indies? Let a king recall that to improve his realm is better than to increase his territory. Let him buy peace. The cheapest war would be more expensive. Let him invite the arbitration of learned men, abbots, and bishops. Let the clergy absent themselves from silly parades and refuse Christian burial to those who die in battle. If we must fight, why not go against the common enemy, the Turk? But wait. Is not the Turk also a man and a brother?

Above all else let peace be sincerely desired. The populace is now incited to war by insinuations and propaganda, by claims that the Englishman is the natural enemy of the Frenchman and the like. Why should an Englishman as an Englishman bear ill will to a Frenchman and not rather good will as a man to a man and a Christian to a Christian? How can anything so frivolous as a name outweigh the ties of nature and the bonds of Christianity? The Rhine separates the French from the German but it cannot divide the Christian from the Christian. The Pyrenees lie between the French and the Spaniards but cannot break the indissoluble bond of the communion of the church. A little strip of sea cuts off the English from the French, but though the Atlantic rolls between it could not sever those joined by nature and still more indissolubly cemented by grace. In private life one will bear with something in a brother-in-law only because he is a brother-in-law, and cannot one then bear anything in another because he is a brother in Christ?

Let us then repent and be wise, declare an amnesty to all past errors and misfortunes, and bind up discord in adamantine chains which can never be sundered till time shall be no more.

This tract is a fine blending of the classical and the Christian themes. From the classical side are derived the personification of peace, the appeal to the harmony of the cosmos, the recital of the horror, cost, and folly of war. From the Christian side, the appeal to the Old Testament and the New Testament, the stress on the fatherhood of God and the brotherhood of believers and the passionate concern that swords be beaten into plowshares. Christian solidarity must not be disrupted by the new nationalism. P r i n c e s should eschew all territorial ambitions and refrain from all inflammatory propaganda.

THE WARRIOR MONK
HOLBEIN'S CARICATURE TO ILLUSTRATE
ERASMUS' *Praise of Folly*

In the colloquy, *The Fish-Eaters*, Erasmus caused the fishmonger to declare what he would do if he were emperor. He would admit that his victory over the king of France had been due only to a freak of Fortune, and would release his valiant foe with the plea that animosity be forgotten and that henceforth the two kings should vie with each other as to who should govern his own land with the greatest justice and goodness. "In the former conflict I have borne away the Prize of Fortune, but in this he that gets the better shall gain far more glory. As for me, the fame of this Clemency will get more true glory than if I have added all *France* to my dominion."

How sorely was Erasmus grieved when in the very year of the Diet of Worms, which did so much to disrupt the spiritual unity of Europe, the Holy Roman Emperor and the most Christian king of France embarked upon war.

Chapter 9

Wars of Religion

THE year 1521, in which war broke out between Francis and Charles, was also the year in which Martin Luther was placed under the ban of the Church and the empire. Thereby the *Corpus Christianum* was riven. The religious cleavage was to prove even more divisive than nationalism, and the spirit of the crusades was to be revived on a larger scale than in the war against the Cathari. Religious intolerance flared up after being largely in abeyance in the opening years of the sixteenth century, when even in Spain Erasmianism flourished for the decade of the 1520's. By the 1530's, however, the Inquisition was being revived throughout Europe, and wars of religion ensued, fanned by confessional fanaticism.

The Protestant reformers could not escape rendering judgment with regard to the morality of all the wars of their time, whether dynastic, national, religious, or what not. Luther reworked the theory of the just war of Augustine and the early Middle Ages and stoutly rejected the crusading idea. All of the Protestant state churches appropriated the just-war theory, but within its terms the Reformed churches reinstated the crusade, partly because of their theocratic pretensions and partly because of their circumstances. Pacifism, as in the late Middle Ages, was the affair of the sects—of the Anabaptists in the sixteenth century, the Quakers in the seventeenth, and the Brethren in the eighteenth.

Luther[1] almost of necessity rejected the crusade because it was a war instigated by the pope against the Turk, whereas in Luther's eyes the pope was worse than the Turk. "The mighty in the Church," said he, "fight the Turks, that is, not their vices but the rod with which God scourges their vices." [2] Because of this statement Luther,

PLUNDERING IN THE TURKISH WAR, SIXTEENTH CENTURY

like Erasmus, was understood to mean that the Turk was not to be resisted at all, a view which both men undertook later to correct. There were, however, deeper theological reasons why Luther rejected a crusade under the auspices of the Church. His objection was rooted in his view of the two kingdoms, the one the Kingdom of God or Christ, the other the kingdom of the world—the kingdom of civil affairs. The Church belongs to the former; the state controls the latter. The state includes all people, be they Christian or unchristian. The state goes back to the order of creation and arose in paradise because of man's urge to association. The coercive power of the state was introduced after the Fall by reason of Cain's murder in order to prevent a general anarchy of revenge. The state is the affair of all peoples, including the Jews and the Turks. The administration of the state is in accord with natural law implanted in the hearts of all men. In civil affairs Luther trusted so much to reason or common sense that were he faced with the choice between a ruler who was prudent and bad and another who was good but imprudent, Luther would choose the prudent and bad because the good by his imprudence would throw everything into disorder, whereas the prudent, however bad,[3] would have the sense to restrain the bad. In the kingdom of Christ reason does not apply, however, for this is the area of faith. The state rules over things outward—the body, houses, lands, and the like—the Church only over things spiritual. The state deals with crime, the Church with sin. Civil rulers are ordained of God and wield the sword, whether to maintain justice within the state or to repel invasions from without. The minister of the Church is armed only with the Word. From this it follows obviously that the minister cannot be a judge, an executioner, or a soldier—and of course not a crusader.

The sharp demarcation of these spheres has led some interpreters of Luther to say that he posited also two moralities, one for the state and one for the Church. The suggestion has even been made that his political thought resembled that of Machiavelli, but this is a perverse misreading of Luther. Because he said that the magistrate cannot rule with a foxtail and that there cannot be war without bloodshed, he is not to be understood to have jettisoned political morality. He had in mind not two ethics, but two and more than two codes of behavior. At this point his position was a simplification of the view of Augustine, who as to war had posited four codes: for the magistrate, the minister, the monk, and the citizen. Luther omitted the monk and thus was left with the other three. There is a certain correspondence here to the two aspects of God's character. For God operates in history with a left hand which is the coercive state and a right hand which is the persuasive Church.[4] He is consuming in his anger and gracious in his compassion. The magistrate is the instrument of his wrath. The positive function of the magistrate is to protect the good, for without his help they would become extinct. True Christians do not protect themselves. They are like sheep; if sheep are placed in the midst of wolves the sheep do not resist nor do they last long. That is why the civil ruler bears not the sword in vain.[5]

In the exercise of severity the magistrate is not going counter to Christian love. Though his work appears cruel, it is as merciful as an amputation performed by a doctor. The magistrate is as much subject to the Christian ethic as the minister, though in a much more difficult position because the magistrate in executing a malefactor must be completely devoid of any personal rancor, resentment, or revenge. He is solely God's instrument.[6] He must indeed perform his task with a sorrow which the minister has no need to feel. "We see then that the godly judge will be pained to condemn the guilty and he will be grieved by the death which the law imposes. This work has every appearance of wrath and unmercifulness but gentleness is so utterly good that it remains in such a wrathful work and wells up all the more in the heart when it is required to be angry and hard." [7] Here we have again the mournful magistrate of Augustine. This reference of course is to the judge, but is equally relevant for the soldier, because Luther, like Augustine, thought of war as an aspect of the police function of the state.

The role of the minister is strictly spiritual. He may curse and damn the malefactor, but he may employ no weapons other than the Word. The common citizen should never defend himself. He may serve at the behest of his prince; otherwise he should suffer. The monk is out of the picture. This meant that the soldier was given a higher status—not that Luther directly and consciously substituted the one for the other. The point was rather that the notion of a religious calling was taken away from the monk and bestowed upon all worthy occupations. Luther recognized three general categories, *Nährstand,* *Lehrstand,* and *Wehrstand.* The first included agriculture and whatever sustains the body; the second the ministry, education, and all that concerns the mind and spirit; the third applied to government, whether in peace or in war. The soldier then had a legitimate calling ordained of God.

Luther accepted the traditional view that the object of the just war is peace, and like the ancient Greeks and Hebrews extolled all her blessings.

139

Through peace we enjoy our body and life, wife, children, house and castle, yes, all of our members, hands, feet, eyes, health, and freedom. And we sit secure in these walls of peace. Where there is peace there is half of the Kingdom of Heaven. Peace can make a crust of dry bread taste like sugar and a drink of water like malmosier wine. I could more easily number the sands or count all the blades of grass than narrate all of the blessings of peace.[8]

Therefore, of course, war was to be only a last resort. The cost should be carefully reckoned, and Luther quoted with approval the remark of the Emperor Augustus that war is like fishing with a golden net.[9] The function of war for Luther was primarily the defense of territory in the medieval sense. On this ground he came at length to condone resistance to the Turk, not as an infidel but as an invader. All of the traditional limitations of the code also applied.

The conservative character of the just-war theory became most evident when Luther sharply condemned the uprising of the peasants. In so doing he was not traitor to his class, for he had always said that the common man should suffer rather than resist; only the magistrate is ordained of God to bear the sword. Luther at the outset upbraided both the lords for the injustice which had occasioned rebellion and the peasants for going beyond petition and prayer. When armed bands broke loose and ravaged the country, Luther was infuriated—doubly so because the prince, John Frederick, was disposed to follow the Counsel of Gamaliel and wait to judge by the outcome whether or no the rebellion were of God. Luther informed him that as a magistrate he was obligated to use the sword: "smite, stab, slay, and kill," because no justice can result from rebellion. It creates disorder and out of disorder only new injustice can arise. Luther appeared here to be using pragmatic arguments.

He was further outraged by the particular circumstances of the peasants' war in Saxony. In this area it was incited by that evangelical preacher Thomas Muentzer, who sired the idea of the Protestant theocracy, with the concomitant crusading idea. Muentzer believed that God's elect could be identified through the experience of the new birth. They could recognize each other and form a covenant, a

Bund, and though the Lord Jesus would soon come to reap the harvest, yet the angels, identified with the peasants, must begin the work. Muentzer rallied them to the cause by unfolding the banner of rebellion in the very church. Luther fumed. To engage in revolution against God's ordained magistrate is rebellion, but for a minister to instigate revolt in the name of the gospel is sacrilege. What then should be done if the minister thus forsook his proper role? Smite him down! Thus Luther's hardness was a corollary of his doctrine of nonresistance in the case of the minister.

Later in his life Luther was asked for a judgment with regard to another variety of war, namely, against the emperor, should he undertake to eradicate the evangelical faith. Resistance to the emperor would be rebellion and one would expect Luther to have discountenanced it. At first he did so unequivocally. He had said in good medieval fashion that only equals can make war upon equals. Peasants cannot make war upon lords and by the same token lords cannot make war upon the emperor. When in the early 1520's the question was whether Frederick the Wise could resist the emperor by arms in case he were to extradite Luther, the answer was absolutely no. After the Diet of Speyer in 1529 the question came to be, What should be the response if the emperor were to try to eradicate the Protestant faith and compel Lutherans to go to mass? Here, too, Luther was at first disposed to advise passive resistance only. He had always counseled disobedience in case the emperor were to issue a command contrary to the will of God, and argued that a private citizen might refuse to serve in war if he knew the cause to be unjust and opposed to the gospel. Luther thus highly approved of the desertion of the troops engaged by Joachim of Brandenburg ostensibly to fight the Turks, but actually to fight the Lutherans.

Could there be armed resistance? The jurists pointed out to Luther that the emperor was not a hereditary prince but an elected monarch. On the occasion of his coronation he had taken an oath that no German state should be placed under the ban of the empire without a hearing. At Speyer the Protestant princes had appealed to the emperor to call a council of the Church whose decision he should implement, but the emperor had not called the council and had given the Protestant princes no hearing. If then he should invade their territories to reinstate Catholicism, he would be violating his coronation oath. Luther's initial response to this argument was that from the legal point of view it was valid, but not in accord with the New Testament. Yet on occasion he would say that in matters political the judgment of the lawyers might be followed—and then once more he would voice his extreme reluctance.

Where Luther held back, his followers were to go forward. After his death the Lutherans of Magdeburg in 1550 developed a theory of armed resistance destined to have a long history with varied applications. It consisted in substituting constitutionalism for the graded scheme of feudalism. The prototype was found rather in classical antiquity in the example of the ephors in Sparta and the tribunes of Rome. They were all magistrates, lower magistrates, assigned the function of restraining and even resisting higher magistrates. The biblical doctrine then would not be violated if the sword were borne only by the magistrate, albeit an inferior magistrate. *Die niedrige Obrigkeit* should resist the higher. In Germany this meant that the electors might resist the emperor if he violated the terms of his oath. Observe that this was no doctrine of popular sovereignty; it was more nearly a sytem of checks, with the lower a control upon the higher. In 1555, when Lutheranism received legal recognition, this doctrine of resistance was dropped, and the conservative elements in Luther's theory were emphasized to a degree far beyond his intent. The stress was placed upon the duty of the subject to obey. Although Luther had said that the minister should be the mentor of the magistrate and the pulpit should "wash the fur of the ruler and clean out his mouth whether he laughs or rages," [10] in a state church the minister came to be so dependent for his position upon the government that any free exercise of the prophetic role was excluded. The way lay open for political absolutism and the militarization of the state.

The churches of the Reformation, with the exception of the Anabaptist, all endorsed the theory of the just war as basic. The

Thirty-nine Articles of the Church of England affirmed that "it is lawfull for Christian men, at the commandement of the Magistrate, to weare weapons and serve in the warres."

The Reformed Churches and the Crusade

Nevertheless, the Reformed Churches moved in the direction of the crusade, partly because they became involved in wars of religion and partly because of their theocratic concept of the Church. They were in a sense in the succession of Thomas Muentzer, although his name was anathema to them all. Like him they believed that the Church consisted approximately of the elect, an identifiable company, in some sense a kingdom of God on earth, with a commission to establish holy commonwealths, whether by persuasion or constraint of the ungodly. Zwingli saw in the Church the new Israel of God, the successor to the chosen people of the old covenant and realized in the church at Zurich. On behalf of this company the one-time near pacifist was to become a crusader.[11]

In his earlier years Zwingli had been revolted by the mercenary service of the Swiss and in his *Fable of the Ox*, the dog, who was Zwingli himself, counseled the Swiss Ox not to forsake his Alpine meadow in order to aid the French leopard, the imperial lion, or Venetian fox. Yet Zwingli was at that time willing to serve as a chaplain to the Swiss troops in the service of the pope and shared with them the perils of the field of Marignano where six thousand of his countrymen were left upon the field. Deeply shaken and profoundly affected by Erasmian pacifism, Zwingli renounced the papal service and wrote a poem containing the lines:

> Our honor stands on blood and war
> Nature's rights are drowned in gore,
> With all the furies loose from hell.
> How could anybody tell
> That we are Christian save by name,
> Without patience, love and shame?
> If God grant not that wars have ceased
> We shall have turned from man to beast.[12]

143

More pointed was the question which he addressed to his fellow Swiss, "Suppose a foreign mercenary should break into your land, ravage your farms and vineyards, drive off your cattle, cut down your sons where they try to protect you, violate your daughters, kick your wives as they supplicate for themselves and you, drag you out, an old man cowering in your house and stab you before the eyes of your wife and then burn home and house? If fire did not burst from heaven to consume such villains, would you not say that there is no God? And if you do this to another, will you call it the right of war?" [13]

Yet if the security of the fatherland were threatened Zwingli was not ready to renounce a war of defense, and when the gospel was imperiled war was not to be regarded as the wrangling of men but as a veritable crusade of the new Israel to vindicate the honor of God. That the Catholic cantons should not suppress the gospel in the evangelical lands, Zwingli drew up a plan of campaign, and solicited a military alliance with the German Protestants. He counseled a show of the sword at a time when the Protestants had such an overwhelming preponderance that they could win without using it. They sallied forth, Zwingli with them and armed. On the field of battle an old Swiss besought both sides to negotiate, and since the Catholics lacked bread and the Zürichers milk, each supplied the lack of the other and peace was concluded over a huge bowl of bread and milk. Zwingli was disheartened, because he believed the issue would have to be decided eventually in blood and not in milk. When the Catholics gained a military ascendancy, they marched. The Zürichers, surprised and outnumbered, rallied. Zwingli stood with them in helmet and sword and went down fighting. Luther looked upon his death as a judgment of God because as a preacher he had taken the sword.

Calvinism and the Wars of Religion

Yet Calvinism,[14] even more than Zwinglianism, is associated with the crusade. The reason is partly one of circumstance—because Calvinism rather than Zwinglianism became a militant minority fighting for a foothold in France, The Netherlands, Scotland, and

England—and partly one of ideas. Calvin spoke of "the Church restored" as the kingdom of God, and Calvinists were active in erecting holy commonwealths. The kernel of the theocratic ideal was the doctrine of election, with more and more tangible tests of the elect, who could be identified in reasonable charity by faith, upright deportment, and participation in the sacraments. The role of the state in the religious commonwealth was indeed restricted, in that church discipline and excommunication were to be in the hands of the Church alone. The state was ordained of God, not only to protect the good and punish the bad, but also to support the true religion —even to the point that the town council at Geneva conducted the heresy trial of Michael Servetus. Whereas Luther looked upon the coercive function of the ruler as a sad necessity, Calvin had none of the mood of the mournful magistrate. With such presuppositions war would have to be the battle of a religious society fought with fervor in the name of the Lord God of Hosts, and the more holy the cause the less restrained would be the means. Calvin repeatedly said that no consideration could be paid to humanity when the honor of God was at stake.[15] One recalls that Machiavelli eliminated humanity when the security of the state was in jeopardy. Calvin took loftier ground since the honor of God transcends the security of the state, but one may well inquire whether either can be conserved if humanity be flouted.

The question of war was acute during Calvin's lifetime because Geneva was constantly in danger of attack from the Catholic powers. The duke and the bishop, having been expelled, desired restoration; after Calvin's death an attack was in fact made. The atmosphere at Geneva throughout his life was surcharged, though actual war over religion broke out only in France. In that land Calvinism was from the outset a revolutionary movement, prohibited by law, spreading rapidly in the utmost secrecy. Converts were sworn, if discovered and tortured, to disclose nothing about their coreligionists. The presence of a congregation in Paris became known and there followed the massacre of the Rue Saint Jacques. A rash young nobleman thought then to avert a repetition of this tragedy by an armed uprising which should seize the person of King Francis II, assassinate the regents of the Catholic house of Guise, and seat in their stead the princes of the Protestant house of Bourbon. The conspiracy was nipped. Calvin highly disapproved of it on the ground that rebellion is never legitimate. "Better," said he, "that we should all perish one hundred times than that the cause of the Gospel and Christianity should be exposed to such opprobrium." [16] Yet Calvin had informed the conspirators that he would not object if the revolt were led by the Bourbon prince, Anthony of Navarre. Behind this concession lay the theory already set forth in the confession of Magdeburg (1550) that an inferior magistrate might resist a superior. Calvin appealed to the example of the ephors in Sparta and the tribunes at Rome and suggested that the Estates in France might fulfill the same role. In the above instance, however, he looked to the princes of the blood, and when war broke out led by Condé of the house of Bourbon, Calvin had only encouragement to offer.

His associate, Theodore Beza, had even less reservation. Earlier than Calvin he had adopted the theory of the inferior magistrate, and after the massacre of St. Bartholomew, along with Hotman and the *Vindiciae Contra Tyrannos*, even went so far as to justify a rebellion on the part of the community—because a covenant exists between God, the king, and the people[17] which, if it be violated by the king, may be vindicated by the people. In England coincidentally a more acute problem had arisen under "Bloody" Mary, because no Parliament and no nobles were willing or able to offer resistance to her. For that reason Ponet and Goodman hesitantly endorsed private resistance as a final recourse; so also did John Knox in Scotland, though less on the ground that tyranny may be resisted than that idolatry must be extirpated. At the same period Catholic authors naturally espoused similar views.

Such ideas were not without bearing on the course of the wars of religion, which were punctuated by assassinations. Huguenot sympathizers disposed of Duke Henry of Guise and his son Duke Francis, and Catholic sympathizers made away with Henry III and Henry IV, not to forget William of Orange in the Low Countries. The unsuccessful attempt on the life of Coligny set off the massacre of St. Bartholomew.

The conduct of the wars was marked by barbarities. A commander guilty of atrocities justified himself by saying, "The first acts are cruelties, the second mere justice." A Catholic commander, having captured a town on the Rhone, put the people to the sword and threw their bodies into the river with a note to the bridge keeper at Avignon to let them pass since they had paid the toll already. Huguenots wore strings of priest's ears, buried Catholics up to their necks, and played nine pins with their heads.[18] Said a contemporary, "Only Christians are permitted to rage against each other with every variety of inhumanity provided it be for the advancement of one party and the detriment of another. Those who are moderate are held suspect." [19]

Cromwell and the Puritan Revolution

The transition in the Puritan upheaval from the theory of the just war to that of the crusade is a striking illustration of the conservative character of the revolution. One may wonder why so much concern should have been felt to keep facts in accord with theory. If the Puritans meant to have a revolution, why did they not simply have a revolution? The reason was that they were of no mind to disrupt the British constitution and to introduce a general chaos. They were desirous of proving to the public and to themselves that, granted certain rights, they would leave the political structure intact. For the same basic reason they were loath to exceed the traditional ethic of the just war. As we have seen, however, a revolution against the prince cannot be squared with a war under the prince. The Puritan preachers struggled manfully to find a formula of accommodation.[20] The first was that they were not fighting the king but only his evil counselors, the Malignants. Charles I dispelled this evasion by lining up with the Malignants. The next approach was by way of the theory of checks and balances. England was held to be a mixed monarchy consisting of king, lords, and Commons, and the Commons might correct the king—to which he replied that the three were coordinate and the Commons was no more empowered to correct him than he the Commons. Next came the familiar argument of the right of the inferior magistrate to curb the superior. The difficulty here was that Parliament was acting as the superior, and the claim naturally shifted to the assertion that Parliament was a supreme court of judicature competent to pass even upon the life of the king. Then the entire argument was confused when the army asserted as great a right to resist the parliament as had the parliament to resist the crown. The army pretended to be the custodian of the welfare of the people of England even against their will, just as, when the pilot is drunk, inferior mariners must take over. Finally, some argued that if the king were a tyrant he was no longer a king, and in that case even a private citizen might bring him to book.

Oliver Cromwell grew impatient with the quest for the authority of the prince as a guarantee for the justice of the cause. How can the prince determine the justice of a holy war? If it is holy, it is holy no matter what prince, parliament, or people may say to the contrary. All of these quibbles about the seat of authority may be but "fleshly reasonings." The Lord himself has given the answer. "Let us look unto providences; surely they mean somewhat. They hang so together; they being so constant, so clear and unclouded." [21] The crusading theory in these words is complete.

If the formulation had waited thus long, the mood had been present for some time in the sermons of the parliamentary divines and the dispatches of the parliamentary leaders. The crusading idea requires that the cause shall be holy (and no cause is more holy than religion), that the war shall be fought under God and with his help, that the crusaders shall be godly and their enemies ungodly, and that the war shall be prosecuted unsparingly. Examples of all of these points are abundant.

The cause was deemed holy because religious. Whether or no the preachers were realistic at this point is irrelevant. The schools of modern thought divide over this, as over every war. Some look to social and economic causes, some to the force of ideas including the religious. The contemporary preachers recognized both and not uncommonly declared that they were fighting for religion, liberty, and laws. Take, for example, the title of the tract, *The Declaration of the Kingdomes of England and Scotland Ioyned in Armes for the vindication and defense of their Religion, Liberties and Lawes, against the Popish, Prelaticall, and Malignant party.*[22] Some of the preachers went further and insisted that religion was a primary factor in the struggle. Heyricke, for example, exclaimed, "Religion is the very Nerves and sinews of the Common-wealth, the very heart and prime fountain of life and livelihood, the Crown, the glory of a Nation, the beauty, the strength, the perfection, the Spirit, the soul of a Kingdome; in Religion is Embarqued the publicke safety; when that is aimed at, the danger is dreadfull, the losse beyond recovery." [23] Edmund Calamy, urging upon the Commons the summoning of the Scots in October, 1643, defended himself that as a minister he pleaded for war. Did not the priests in the Old Testament blow the silver trumpets? "And certainly, if this were the way of God in the Old Testament, certainly much more in such a Cause as this, in which Cause Religion is entwin'd and indeed so interlac'd, that Religion and this Cause, they are like Hippocrates his twins, they must live and die together." [24] Obadiah Sedgewick on the same occasion maintained the cause to be the cause of God, the cause of Christendom, "for if this Cause be carryed against us, certainly the Protestant Cause throughout all of Europe, will fare the worse for it." [25]

The war was fought, under God.

The Saints receive their commission from the great King, King of Kings, to have a two edged sword in their hands, to execute judgment upon the Heathen, and punishment upon the people; *To binde their Kings with chaines, and their Nobles with fetters of iron;* to execute upon them the judgment written, *This honour have all the Saints.* Hence then we see what a type of Holy Writ lies upon our Parliament and Army, to execute judgment upon the King and his wicked Adherents.[26]

God might be trusted to scatter his enemies. So George Walker preached before the Commons in 1644,[27] and did not Oliver Cromwell pause with his army at St. Abb's Head to sing the sixty-eighth psalm, "Let God arise, Let His enemies be scattered"? [28] Victory was regarded as the Lord's doing and the manifest proof of his approval of the cause. Cromwell referred to his success as "an unspeakable mercy," [29] and emphasized the disparity of the forces in order that divine assistance might be the more apparent. "Sir, this is nothing but the hand of God. Praise onely belongs to him." [30] Addressing the Speaker of the House the general exclaimed, "Sir, what can be said to these things? Is it an arm of flesh that does these things, Is it the wisdom, the counsel, or strength of men? It is the Lord only. God will curse that man and his house that dares to think otherwise." [31]

When the Presbyterians held back from touching the Lord's anointed and Cromwell pressed on with the aid of the Congregationalists and the Baptists to the execution of the King, the crusading note was struck in the sermons of the period. Joseph Caryl inquired: *"How can we be quiet seeing the Lord hath given us a charge* against Askelon? . . . May this Sword and Bow of all the upright in heart be like the *bow* of Jonathon, *and the sword of* Saul, *not turning backe nor returning empty, from the blood of sinne slaine, and from the fat of our mightiest corruptions both in Church and Commonwealth."* [32] The old favorite crusading text was revived: "Cursed he that keepeth backe his hand from sheding of blood." [33] *The Souldiers Pocket Bible* compiled by Edmund Calamy in 1643 manfully disposed of the Sermon on the Mount by placing together the following verses: "Matthew 5:44. But I say unto you, Love your enemies. 2 Chronicles 19:2. Wouldst thou help the wicked and love them that hate the Lord? Psalm 139:21-22. Do not I hate them, O Lord, that hate Thee? . . . I hate them with an unfeigned hatred as they were mine utter enemies." The summary is that the soldier must "love his enemies as they are his enemies, and hate them as they are God's enemies."

The conduct of the war was affected by the religious alignment. Catholics received no quarter from the Puritans. The garrison at

Drogheda was massacred. Hugh Peters is reported to have sent this dispatch. "Sir, the truth is Drogheda is taken, 3,352 of the enemy slain, and 64 of ours . . . Ashton the governor killed, none spared. . . . I came now from giving thanks in the great church . . . Dublin, September 15, 1649." [34] Cromwell justified this exercise of severity in the following words: "I am persuaded that this is a righteous judgment of God upon these barbarous wretches, who have imbrued their hands in so much innocent blood; and that it will tend to prevent the effusion of blood for the future, which are the satisfactory grounds to such actions, which otherwise cannot but work remorse and regret." One who had talked with Cromwell said that he adduced also the consideration that "there are great occasions in which some men are called to great services in the doing of which they are excused from the common rule of morality," as were the worthies of the Old Testament. [35]

The Presbyterians in Scotland, however, were treated with leniency which made possible the resumption of the union of the two lands. In England the differences between the Dissenters and the Anglicans did not dispel the amenities which obtain among gentlemen.

In the meantime the Thirty Years' War raged on the continent. The beginning was over a point of religion, though the course of the war became increasingly a struggle for power. The sack of Magdeburg was considered one of the great atrocities of the age. A modern author is inclined, however, to believe that it was not the result of deliberate fanaticism and brutality on the part of Tilly and Pappenheim, but was due rather to the license of uncontrollable troops. It is an illustration not of the point that a religious war is less humane than a secular war, but rather that all war unleashes hell. [36]

Chapter 10

The Historic Peace Churches
and War with the Aborigines

THE sixteenth and seventeenth centuries, which witnessed the wars of religion, saw also a rise of pacifist sects, remarkable because they have largely preserved their testimony against war until our own day. The Anabaptists (now the Mennonites and the Hutterites), the Quakers, and the Brethren are popularly called the "historic peace churches," not because other churches are not concerned for peace but because these groups have refused to take part in war. They have differed somewhat among themselves in their emphases. The Anabaptists have been the most aloof from society and averse to participation in government. The Quakers have been the least segregated and have been willing even to assume political office up to the point of war. The Brethren have taken a median position. In the colonial period in Pennsylvania the Mennonites would not vote; the Quakers sat in the legislature; the Brethren would vote only for Quakers. The differences are due to divergent estimates as to the redeemability of human nature here on earth. Pessimism and optimism on this score in the case of these three may not be unrelated to the circumstances of their origins. The Anabaptists began subject to the penalty of death, the Brethren to that of banishment, the Quakers only to that of imprisonment. The Anabaptists, being burned by Catholics and drowned by Protestants, saw no hope in man. The Quakers, able to use trials and imprisonments as instruments of propaganda, were more hopeful that their witness would affect the mind of all England, and not without reason—witness the way in which William Penn in the course of his trial won the battle for the nonintimidation of juries.

The Anabaptists

The Anabaptists[1] made a sharp distinction between the two kingdoms, the kingdom of the world and the kingdom of Christ. The kingdom of the world comprised the unredeemed who live according to the lusts of the flesh and prey upon whom they can. To restrain their villainy God instituted the state and endowed it with coercive power.[2] The sword was ordained because of sin; in Paradise there was no sword until after the Fall—some said until after the Flood, when the descendants of Noah proved to be as vile as his contemporaries.

Then Christ instituted a new order, an order of love and meekness in which there is no constraint. This is possible because the Christian is a new creature and will not avenge himself. As a sheep before the shearers is dumb, so he opens not his mouth. The Good Shepherd called his flock sheep. "By sheep Christians alone were meant. A sheep is a suffering defenseless, patient beast, which has no other defense save to run so long as it can and may. A sheep is no more comparable to the governance of the sword than to a wolf or a lion." [3] The deportment of Christians is wholly different from that of the children of the world. Said Menno, "Our fortress is Christ, our defense is patience, our sword is the Word of God, and our victory is the sincere, firm, unfeigned faith in Jesus Christ. Spears and swords of iron we leave to those who, alas, consider human blood and swine's blood well-nigh of equal value." [4]

The Christians who endorsed the just war or the crusade confronted the Anabaptists with many examples of warriors approved of God in the Old Testament. The reply was that the New Testament represents the radical new order of Christ. This suggests that the Old Testament belongs to the kingdom of the world under the administration of God and the New Testament to the kingdom of

Christ. The danger is here implicit, and had to be refuted, that the Anabaptists were setting the kingdom of God the Son over against that of God the Father. How to handle the Old Testament was of course a problem for all Christians. None rejected it completely but all to a degree. Paul himself had said that the law of Moses was binding only until Christ. How much more, then, would one expect the new dispensation to reject the immoralities of the patriarchs,[5] such as the suicide of Samson, the theft of the Israelites from the Egyptians, the tyrannicide of Judith, the lie of Abraham, the polygamy of the patriarchs, and the conquest of Canaan in contravention of the requirements of the just war? Some answered that all of these were allowed by reason of a special revelation from God which had not been subsequently repeated. Some, however, affirmed that certain of the above acts, such as tyrannicide, were in accord with natural law and might recur. Luther considered polygamy permissible under natural law, though not to be practiced because contrary to statute law. There was general agreement that a war of invasion without provocation, such as the conquest of Canaan, was no longer permissible. The Anabaptists were of all parties the most radical because, though steeped in the imagery of the Old Testament, they yet rejected its ethic as having been superseded by that of Christ.

His kingdom they held to be based upon the Sermon of the Mount and his injunctions to be literally obeyed, not only with regard to war but also with regard to the oath. Here, then is a New Testament legalism. Obedience, discipleship, and the imitation of Christ are the recurrent words in the Anabaptist confessions. They suggest something more than individual behavior and stand in the context of a program for the Church which must itself first be restored to the purity of the apostolic time, when Christianity was persecuted rather than supported by the state. The great fall in the history of the Church came with Constantine when the two kingdoms were fused and the sword of the empire intimidated the heretics. The restitution of the Christianity of the golden age was the object of the Anabaptists' endeavor, and to this end adherents were expected to embark upon missionary tours for the conversion of the heathen Christians, whether Catholic or Protestant. The gathering of the pure Church would be the prelude to the coming of the Lord to establish his kingdom upon earth. Thus they held hope for society, but only through the conversion of individuals and the intervention of Christ.

Critics faced the Anabaptists with the problem with which Luther had wrestled. He too had defined Christ's kingdom in these terms, but he had pointed out that the lion and lamb cannot lie down together unless the lamb is frequently renewed. He argued that if, as the Anabaptists admitted, the sword of the magistrate had been ordained by God, Christians who would renounce it for themselves should employ it for others. Out of love they should collaborate with God's left hand. The Anabaptists almost said that God's right hand should not know what his left hand was doing. They recognized the need of government for sinners.

But our will and mind are not to do away with civil government, nor to refuse it obedience in matters good and right, because there must be government among men in the world, just as there must be daily bread and a schoolmaster with a rod over the children. Since the great mass of this world will not allow God's Word to hold and rule, therefore they must be held and ruled by the sword, that the scamps and rascals, the children of this world, who will not walk uprightly through Christ, may do so through fear of the gallows. . . . Therefore the magistracy is ordained of God.[6]

The Christian may not be a magistrate, however.

Wherefore? Because the governance of the world is according to the flesh; the governance of Christians is according to the spirit. The houses and dwelling of the worldly are in this world, whereas the dwelling of the Christians is in heaven. The citizenship of the world is in the world; the citizenship of the Christians is in heaven. The warfare and weapons of the one are of the flesh and fight only with the flesh; the weapons of the other are spiritual against the rampart of the devil. The worldly are armed to fight only with the flesh; the Christians have put on the armor of God, that is "truth, righteousness, peace, faith, salvation and the Word of God." [7]

The Anabaptists were told that if they abstained from the maintenance of justice by the sword, justice would suffer. They answered that there would never be any lack of persons ready to assume the office of the magistrate. This rejoinder savors very much of vocationalism. Functionally it is just that, but not in theory, for the office of the magistrate, though ordained of God, did not belong in their view to the kingdom of Christ. If all men would enter the kingdom of Christ, the magistracy would at once cease. So long as men did not, the citizenship of the Christian could be only in heaven, and he must even now walk as if heaven were here.

Would not that mean suffering for those who were not protected? The Anabaptists were aware that it would, and offered the weak only the protection of the sword of the Spirit. Suffering in the body there would be, but it was not a suffering from which the Christian was exempt while others endured. He would be subject to the sword because of his rejection of the sword. This must be expected because the world would always be the world and the Church would always be rejected, poor, and persecuted. Every Abel must have have his Cain and every Christ his Caiaphas. So would it be until the Lord came.

Appeals to princes therefore were deemed fatuous, and plans for world peace were considered futile. The Anabaptist could not, like Erasmus, write an *Institute of the Christian Prince,* because there could not be a Christian prince. The true Christian could do no other than withdraw from all political life—and in the sixteenth century the Anabaptists were compelled to withdraw from all social life. Survival was possible only by accommodation or withdrawal. Those who preserved the witness were those who withdrew. To find a place where they could go and behave fully in accord with their conviction was not simple. A group of the Hutterites, for example, was granted an asylum on the estates of Count Leonard of Lichtenstein. When the Austrian authorities threatened to extradite the Anabaptists the Count replied that if the Austrians came they would be met with cannon balls. The Hutterites thereupon informed him that they could not in conscience remain. With wives, bairns, and goods they took to their wagons until they found a nobleman who would grant toleration without protection.[8]

An unusual situation developed in Poland, where a number of noblemen were themselves converted to the faith of the Brethren and discarded the sword in favor of the staff. Faustus of Socinus was for a time of this persuasion. Their position was again that of the Anabaptist's radical distinction of the two kingdoms. Faustus began to make concessions, however—for example, that a Christian might serve in the army provided he did not take a life. This position had not been unrealistic in the days of the early Church, when the Roman soldiers were engaged primarily in police work. It was not realistic in the wars of Poland, and this accommodation speedily proved to be the undoing of the pacifism of the Polish Brethren.

The Quakers

The Quakers occupied a median position between Erasmus and the Anabaptists. The Quakers were ready to address pleas to rulers and even to offer counsel as to the use of the sword, while themselves refraining from its employment. To a degree they have sought peace through politics. While separating the kingdom of Christ from the kingdom of the world, they have not utterly despaired of the world. As already noted, their attitude may have been related to the comparative mildness of their punishment, but perhaps also to the fact that many of them had come out of the army and knew that the ranks still held godly men. Several Quakers had been converted while in the army and had not at first been impelled to leave. Rather they were expelled, not because they were pacifists, but because the unpredictable promptings of the light within were incompatible with army discipline. General Monk said that they were fitted neither to command nor to obey and that their social equalitarianism liquidated the distinction between officers and privates. Some after and some before expulsion were persuaded of the word of George Fox, who when asked why he would not fight for Cromwell against the king replied, "I live in the virtue of that life and power that takes away the occasion of all wars." [9] When William Dewsbury joined the army in the spirit of a crusade,

The word of the Lord came unto me and said, "Put up thy sword into thy scabbard; if my kingdom were of this world then would my children fight. Knowest thou not that, if I need, I could have twelve legions of angels from my Father?" Which word enlightened my heart, and discovered the mystery of iniquity, and that the kingdom of Christ was within; and the enemies was [sic] within, and was spiritual, and my weapons against them must be spiritual, the power of God. Then I could no longer fight with a carnal weapon, against a carnal man, for the letter, which man in his carnal wisdom had called the Gospel, and had deceived me; but the Lord . . . caused me to yield in obedience, to put up my carnal sword into the scabbard and to leave the Army.[10]

Quakers thus recognized that those in the army had a conscience and a code to which they were bound until they should receive further light. Edward Burrough set forth the point, which, however incongruent it may appear, goes far to explain Quaker behavior. He exhorted soldiers to observe their duty. "What do you know but the Lord may have some good work for you to do if you be faithful to Him? . . . The Lord hath owned and honoured our English Army, and done good things for them in these nations in our age, and the Lord once armed them with the spirit of courage and zeal against many abominations, and gave them victory and dominion over much injustice and oppression and cruel laws." They should avenge innocent blood and break down the thorns and briers which impede the work of the Lord. "And yet though such a victory would be honourable unto you, yet there is a victory more honourable, to wit, the victory over sin and death and the devil in yourselves. . . . Your work hath been, and may be, honourable in its day and season, but he hath a work more honourable to work after you; that is, to destroy the kingdom of the devil and the ground of wars." [11]

In this spirit, Barclay set the case very clearly when he said:

As to what relates to the present magistrates of the Christian world, albeit we deny them not altogether the name of Christians, because of the public profession they make of Christ's name, yet we may boldly affirm, that they are far from the perfection of the Christian religion; because in the state in which they are they have not come to the pure dispensation of the Gospel. And therefore, while they are in that condition, we shall not say, that war, undertaken upon a just occasion, is altogether unlawful to them. For even as circumcision and the other ceremonies were for a season permitted to the Jews, not because they were either necessary of themselves, or lawful at that time, after the resurrection of Christ, but because that Spirit was not yet raised up in them, whereby they could be delivered from such rudiments; so the present confessors of the Christian name, who are yet in the mixture, and not in the patient suffering spirit, are not yet fitted for this form of Christianity, and therefore cannot be undefending themselves until they attain that perfection. But for such whom Christ has brought hither, it is not lawful to defend themselves by arms, but they ought over all to trust to the Lord.[12]

The distinction between a Christian and a sub-Christian ethic makes possible appeals to those who operate on other presuppositions that they be faithful to their own. On such grounds Quakers have often been able to address themselves to an entire nation in the name of justice and humanity, if not in the name of nonresistance and pacifism.

The question would not down: if Quakers held that those who believed in just wars should fight just wars, why should not Quakers join them that justice might prevail? The answer given was that war as a method is not appropriate for the achievement of peace. This is a pragmatic consideration, but the ground was deeper. Said Isaac Pennington, "Fighting is not suitable to a gospel spirit, but to the spirit of the world and the children thereof. The fighting in the gospel is turned inward against the lusts, and not outward against the creatures." [13] This sounds very much like the word of Erasmus, who was constantly pitting the inward against the outward. The Quakers applied to the sword the word "carnal," and carnal meant not only the fleshly but also the irrational, the entire lower nature of man. George Fox proclaimed his mission "to stand a witness against all violence and against all the works of darkness, and to turn people from the darkness to the light and from the occasion of the magistrate's sword. . . . With the carnal weapon I do not fight, but am from those things dead." [14] John Lilburne, who had served long in the army, testified after becoming a Quaker: "I am already dead, or crucified, to the very occasions and real ground of outward wars and carnal sword-fightings and fleshly bustlings and contests; and that therefore confidently I now believe, I shall never hereafter be a user of a temporal sword more, nor a joiner with them that do so." [15]

Another Quaker objection to war arose out of respect for the conscience of the enemy. This was a particularly telling point in the English Civil War, when men equally conscientious were fighting both for and against the king and the bishops. Again the point was made in colonial Pennsylvania, and a petition was addressed by the Quakers to the government in 1740 pointing out the great difference between "killing a soldier fighting (perhaps) in obedience to the commands of his sovereign, and who may possibly think himself in the discharge of his duty, and executing a burglar, who plundered our goods and perhaps would have murdered too and who must know that by his acts he justly rendered himself obnoxious to the punishment which ensued." [16] Killing appeared here to be allowed in the case of a burglar but not against a soldier acting in accord with his conscience.

Still another Quaker objection to war was predicated upon ignorance. Incipient English democracy—let alone scrupulously conscientious Quakerism—could not rest with the injunction of Augustine to leave the decision to the magistrate in case of doubts as to the justice of the war. Barclay advanced ignorance as one of the grounds for declining to engage in war.

If to revenge ourselves, or to render injury, evil for evil, wound for wound, to take eye for eye, tooth for tooth; if to fight for outward and perishing things, to go a warring one against another, whom we never saw, or with whom we never had any contest, or anything to do; being moreover altogether ignorant of the case of the war, but only that the magistrates of the nations foment quarrels one against another, the causes whereof are for the most part unknown to the soldiers that fight, as well as upon whose side the right or wrong is; and yet to be so furious, and rage one against another, to destroy and spoil all, that this or the other worship may be received or abolished; if to do this, and much more of this kind, be to fulfill the law of Christ, then are our adversaries indeed true Christians, and we miserable Heretics, that suffer ourselves to be spoiled, taken, imprisoned, banished, beaten, and evilly entreated, without any resistance, placing our trust only in GOD, that he may defend us, and lead us by the way of the cross unto his kingdom.[17]

The Quakers by their allegiance to conscience convinced the government of the rights of conscience, and for the first time were accorded exemption from military service on this ground in 1802.[18] The claims made by them, and indeed by all Puritans, on behalf of conscience were now much more sweeping than those allowed by Aquinas and the Protestant reformers, who had attached conscience to knowledge in such fashion that conscientious objection to participation in war was admitted only on the basis of positive information as to the injustice of the conflict. The struggle for religious liberty had done much in the meantime to relativize conscience as inward conviction, no matter to what it applied and regardless of objective correctness.[19] Such a conscience is binding upon the individual so long as he remains convinced. This Aquinas would have said, but he would have insisted that unless he were right he had no claim to recognition by the state. The English state, however, agreed at last to accord a civil status to an internal conviction deemed wrong by the state.

The Problem of Conscience

A severe ethical and political dilemma is posed here. The Quaker recognized that the soldier might be conscientious and the magistrate conscientious. Might not then the magistrate be conscientious in imprisoning the Quaker, and might there not then be a clash between those equally conscientious, a clash capable of reconciliation only by a struggle of body for body? Early in the eighteenth century, Pierre Bayle raised the problem in the case of a conscientious tyrannicide such as the assassins of Henry III and Henry IV. If an individual conscientiously believes himself called upon to kill the monarch, he must follow his conscience, but at the same time the magistrate must punish him.[20] Samuel Johnson wrestled with the difficulty. When asked whether the Roman magistrates were justified in persecuting the early Christians, the doctor replied, "Sir, the only method by which religious truth can be established is by martyrdom. The magistrate has a right to enforce what he thinks; and he who is conscious of the truth has a right to suffer. I am afraid there is no other way of ascertaining the truth, but by persecution on the one hand and enduring it on the other." [21]

The position of Johnson has become a commonplace in modern political thought; L. T. Hobhouse said, for example, "that we have to admit as correlative to the ultimate right of conscience an ultimate right of coercion." [22] At the same time, although the state may in conscience place restrictions upon the conscientious objector, yet there are considerations of prudence and humanity which dictate restraint. On the mere score of expediency the state needs to recognize that unwilling soldiers do not make good soldiers. Further, since so many services are requisite in wartime, the state is most unwise to try to turn an industrious farmer or a good dentist into a dragheel private. A more serious and loftier consideration is that the conscientious objector to military service is not antisocial nor ordinarily antipolitical. His very integrity makes of him the finest citizen and the most effective civil servant in a post which he can in conscience accept. The man who may have to be imprisoned in war may become a prime minister in time of peace. In England, men who opposed particular wars, like Lloyd George and Ramsay MacDonald, did become prime ministers, and Bertrand Russell now sits in the House of Lords. The state therefore should employ only that minimum of constraint required to neutralize the objector during a period of crisis that he may be utilized when the emergency is past. Of all considerations the deepest is that conscience is worthy of honor and is not lightly to be constrained.

Undeniably the entire Quaker program of abstention from war and participation in politics was predicated upon a greater hopefulness for the world than that held by the Anabaptists. When Isaac

Pennington was told that his program was fit only for "a world in the moon," he retorted:

After a long night of apostasy, the spirit of Christ is awakening again and gathering men together to the true Church, making them pure and peaceable. "As the Lord does this so will it go on, and the nations, kings, princes, great ones, as this principle is raised in them, and the contrary wisdom, the earthly policy (which undoes all) brought down, so will they feel the blessings of God in themselves, and become a blessing to others." [23]

Not merely individuals, then, but magistrates also belong to the kingdom of Christ. William Smith contemplated the spiritual army marching under the banner of love which would reach such strength that "wars would cease, cruelty end, and love abound." [24] This was to be the work of the Lord, but his instruments were men "who have given up their bodies and spirits unto God."

In the case of the Brethren, who arose in the eighteenth century, there is little to be said, because the information is scant in regard to their early peace stand. One of the utterances from the time of their origin has the ring of Mennonite statements. "The higher powers bear the sword of justice, punishing the evil and protecting the good. In this we acknowledge them from the Word as the ministers of God, but the sword belongeth to the kingdom of the world." [25]

A Quaker Example

A concrete example of the dilemmas, predicaments, problems, and behavior of the early peace churches is afforded by the case of a Quaker, Thomas Lurting by name,[26] who lived in the time of the Commonwealth and the Restoration. He was first a fighting sailor who had no scruple against firing a shot into the powder hold of a Spanish galleon and blowing up ship and crew. On his own vessel were some Quakers whom he maltreated until convincement came upon him and he joined himself to the Friends. Thus far, none of them had any compunction as to war. First to Lurting in the midst of an engagement came the word of the Lord that he should not kill a man. He brought the other Friends to be of the same mind. Then a vessel, presumed to be Spanish, bore down upon them, and the captain summoned all to their posts. The Friends headed by Lurting appeared in a body on deck and told him they would not fight. He drew his sword promising to "put it into the guts of any who denied to fight." Lurting was distant from him five paces and six steps. Eyeing him steadily, he stepped the five paces. At the third step, "the captain's countenance changed pale," and leaving his sword he turned away. The vessel proved to be friendly and thereafter the captain became "respective." At the end of the voyage Lurting was released.

Subsequently, he was impressed on another man of war. For five days he refused to eat, saying that if he took of the king's victuals he would be the king's man. The commander then offered him noncombatant service. He should haul the ropes. No! He should hand out the beer. No! Then, he should engage in a piece of charity and assist the doctor. No! Because this, too, was assistance. He was willing to load grain onto a warship. Was not this also assistance? To which he replied, "I am commanded to love my enemies." In this reply there may be a touch of legalism, but basically Lurting was trying to find a line between a direct contribution to war with humanitarianism and a direct humanitarianism with an incidental assistance to war. His opponents were employing the familiar tactic of driving one who seeks a middle ground of nonconformity into either a complete withdrawal from society or a complete conformity.

Lurting's great testing was yet to come. He took service on a merchant ship in the Mediterranean under a Quaker captain, with a non-Quaker crew. The defense of this vessel was not guns but sails. When a Turkish pirateer swooped down, the English ship let out all sail to a point beyond her capacity. Something gave way and she was taken. The Turks boarded. They were ten; the English were nine. But the Turks were armed. A storm separated the English and the Turkish vessels. Lurting proposed to lull the Turks by compliance; then to disarm them. The men were ready to cut throats, the Quaker captain said no. Lurting reassured him, though doubtful whether he could hold his men. The Turks were persuaded to bed in different cabins. While asleep, their arms were collected and the pirates were locked in the hatch with the English all on the deck. The Turks wept, but were promised that they would not be sold into slavery. Lurting feared to put into a Spanish port lest he should not be able to keep his word and made instead for the Barbary Coast. As they neared the shore, the English saw the difficulty of landing the Turks. The rowboat would not hold more than fourteen. If an equal number of English and Turks got in, two trips would be necessary and the Turks first put ashore might give the alarm. But if there were ten Turks to four Englishmen, the Turks might make them captive. Lurting resolved to risk it. He took charge himself, with three of his own men and no arms save blunt instruments. The Turks were quiet until one of the English called out, "There are Turks in the bushes." Lurting was smitten with fear. The Turks saw it and rose. He confronted them in silence until his composure returned. Then with a boathook he struck the master of the Turks, who sank into his seat, and the rest followed. As the Turks landed, they invited the English to come and enjoy much wine in a town three miles distant. They declined. The Turks were given supplies of food and their arms, "and so we departed in great love, and stayed until they had all gone up the hill, and they shook their caps at us and we, at them." When the English vessel sailed up the Thames, King Charles and the Duke of York came aboard and plied the Friends with many questions. "Said the King, 'I should have brought the Turks to him.' I answered, 'that I thought it better for them to be in their own country.' At which they all smiled and went away."

War with the Aborigines

A frightful strain was placed upon every form of the Christian ethic by the struggle with the natives for possession of the world discovered by Columbus. The Spaniards in the Caribbean, the government at any rate, tried to conserve the code of the just war.[27] The Puritans in New England revived the crusade. The Quakers in Pennsylvania adhered resolutely to the Sermon on the Mount.

The conquistadores were themselves a mixed breed, some concerned for souls, some only for loot. Pizarro frankly averred that he had come for no other reason than "to take from the Indians their gold." De Soto and his men raped the Vestal Virgins of the Incas and by treachery assembled and butchered the princes and took over the empire. Cortez responded to the proposal that the Spaniards, instead of enslaving the Indians, should themselves work the land, by saying, "I came to get gold, not to till the soil like a peasant." Others strove for the conversion of the Indians, but how much good conversion did them, in some instances, is evidenced by the case of a chief in Chile who requested baptism. With solemn rites he was baptized and then riddled with arrows. A combination of motives was expressed by one who said, "We came here to serve God and also to get rich." The conditions for the just war with the Indians were set forth by Francesco Vittoria.[28] The natives were not to be converted by force nor killed because of a rejection of the gospel, but they might be constrained if they denied the natural right of travel through their territories and also if they refused to permit the preaching of the gospel. The just war required an announcement of the conditions on fulfillment of which war could be avoided. These were set forth in a document called The Requirement in 1513. The natives must acknowledge the Church as the ruler of the world and the king of Spain as its representative, and they must permit the preaching of the faith. A modern historian reports that "Captains muttered its theological phrases into their beards on the edge of sleeping Indian settlements, or even a league away before starting the formal attack, and at times some leather-lunged Spanish notary hurled its sonorous phrases after the Indians as they fled into the mountains."

Later the great theologian Sepulveda adapted the theory of the just war to the new situation by having recourse to its most ancient formulation declared by Aristotle, who had said that a just war is one waged to enslave those who by nature are destined to be slaves and who resist their destiny.

Protests against the rapacity of the conquistadores and the subterfuges of theologians were persistently voiced by not a few, among whom the most celebrated was Bartolomeo de las Casas, himself a conqueror revolted by what he had seen and done. First as a layman and then as a friar, he dedicated himself to the Indians, to the abolition of forced labor in the encomienda system of slavery, to peaceful conversion, and to free labor for the Indian with agricultural work for the Spaniards. Free Indians would not work the mines, however, and Spaniards would not till the lands. Attempts at peaceful conversion were subverted by the invaders who did not want peace. Las Casas took his case to Spain and so impressed the Emperor Charles V that even after the conquest of Mexico he ordered a halt to all further expansion until the theologians should have pronounced on the justice of the cause. There followed a long and inconclusive debate between Las Casas and Sepulveda. In the meantime the conquistadores thumbed their noses alike at the friars and the government. The historian cited above says of all the experiments and peaceful conquests, that today they appear "as tragic comedies enacted on doomed little islands around which the ocean of the conquest boiled and thundered until it overwhelmed them."

The Spanish Christians so behaved that an aged chief in Nicaragua inquired, "What is a Christian, what are Christians? They ask for maize, for honey, for cotton, for women, for gold, for silver; Christians will not work, they are liars, gamblers, perverse, and they swear." In Peru Benzoni wrote that Spaniards committed such cruelties that the Indians "not only would never believe us to be Christians and children of God, as boasted, but not even that we were born on this earth or generated by a man and born of a woman; so fierce an animal, they concluded, must be the offspring of the sea." [29]

If the Spaniards appealed to Aristotle, the New Englanders appealed to Moses. In so doing they reversed all previous Christian exegesis. For by common consent the conquest of Canaan had been the only instance of a just aggressive war, and it was just only because commanded by God. But God was commonly held no longer to issue such commands. They were reinstated by the theocratic holy commonwealth in the wilderness, which regarded itself as the New Israel of God commissioned to subdue the Indians as the Amalekites. In his *Soldier's Counselled* written in 1689, Cotton Mather affirmed that the New Englanders had acquired all of their land by just and fair purchase and not by encroachment like the Spaniards, but the Indians, said he, were "a treacherous and barbarous enemy." [30] He was of course ignorant of their political institutions and expected them to conduct their foreign relations after the manner of European sovereigns. Since they did not, he pronounced them to be "the veriest tigers" and summoned the colonists to go forth against "Amalek annoying this Israel in the wilderness." One would have thought that he might have been as generous as Vittoria, who saw justice on both sides in Indian wars, on the side of the Spaniards who were vindicating the right of free travel in accord with natural law and on the side of the Indians because of their invincible ignorance. Cotton Mather did not make even this less than tender concession, however. For him, the eradication of the aborigines was a crusade.

The behavior of the Puritans was little better than that of the Spaniards, although the Puritans came to colonize and to till the soil themselves. They, too, made slaves and they, too, made holocasts. Miles Standish rounded up the Indians into their villages and set fire to the whole. Piety was no impediment. Pyncheon, the author of "The Meritorious Price of our Redemption" carried the scalps of the murdered sachems from Hartford to Boston.[31] The early crusading mood continued well into the eighteenth century. Herbert Gibbs in 1704 thankfully commemorated "the mercies of God in extirpating the enemies of Israel in Canaan," and ended his sermon with the text, "Curse ye Meroz." [32] In 1742 Samuel Phillips declared that with regard "to the Aboriginal natives . . . there is no method so likely to subdue, or to humble them, as to march forth in quest of them." In this we should try to "engage the Lord of hosts on our side." [33] The point, of course, was, as in the Old Testament, that if Israel were recreant the Lord would withdraw from the field.

In the eighteenth century the feeling against the Indians was intensified because these "Amalekites" came to be allied with the minions of Antichrist, the French Papists. The sermons of the period spew the wrath of God upon them both: "Our Indian neighbors, under the influence of Popish priests treacherously and barbarously" fall upon us. France is a "proud, haughty, blasphemer, persecutor and disturber of the Common peace." "By flattery she seduced her Huguenot subjects and then polluted their temples." [34] "The Israelites of old by the immediate command of God Almighty made war on the nations of Canaan . . . and God was exceedingly displeased with Saul . . . for not entirely destroying Amalek." This took care of the Indians. As for the French: "Endeavor to stand the guardians of the religion and liberties of America; to oppose Antichrist and prevent the barbarous butchering of your fellow countrymen." [35]

When Cape Breton was captured in 1745, Thomas Prince of the South Church in Boston said that he had long regretted the transfer by treaty in 1713 from the British to the French of this island abounding in the finest coal in America. In the intervening thirty years the French had so developed the island as well-nigh to capture the trade of Spain, Italy, and Portugal. He had considered that a war for its recovery would be expedient, and now the Lord had been pleased to instigate the French to "precipitate the war upon us," with the result that all of their prodigious labor "has accrued to us. It is the Lord's doing and it is marvelous in our eyes." [36]

When Montreal fell in 1760, when in consequence the "treacherous Aboriginals" and the "perfidious papistical French" were defeated, when the holy Protestant religion was thus vindicated, when the door was thereby opened for the propagation of the Gospel, then the new Israel sang with Moses, "The Lord is our strength." [37] One of the preachers exulted that God had proceeded with "awful and righteous solemnity to pour the vials of His wrath upon the Romish beast." [38]

In New England as in the Spanish possessions there were protests against the maltreatment of the Indians. John Elliott, Roger Williams, David Brainerd, and Jonathan Edwards sought by peaceful means to save the souls of the Indians. Unhappily, success in this endeavor imperiled the Indians' temporal existence, since converts were esteemed neither white nor red. And, conversions or no conversions, "Westward the course of empire took its way."

Be it observed however that in dealing with fellow Protestants such as the Dutch the Puritans adhered to the code of the just war.[39]

The Quakers and the Indians

A very serious attempt to keep peace with the Indians was made in Quaker Pennsylvania. William Penn was the son of the admiral of the British fleet. The old sea dog disowned him for joining the Friends. Though young William Penn renounced "the treasures of Egypt," he did not escape from the treasures of the Admiral, and Charles II, in order to discharge a debt of the crown to the father, gave to the son the colony of Pennsylvania. He who "refused to be called the son of Pharoah's daughter" and kept his hat on in the presence of the king did not on that account forfeit the friendship of princes, though no doubt they thought it more pleasant to have him on the other side of the ocean.

William Penn was ready to abandon England's thrust for a maritime empire, but he saw no reason to renounce the colonial enterprise, since he assumed that it could be pursued peaceably through the exercise of justice and friendliness toward the natives.

The Quakers tried resolutely for nearly a century to implement his experiment but never had a completely free hand.[40] The colony was a grant from the crown, and the crown was not pacifist. The governors were appointed by the crown and, after William Penn, they too were not pacifist. Residence in the colony was open, and those who flocked in were sometimes in accord with the Quaker dream, but sometimes they were not. The Mennonites and the Schwenckfelders could be counted as allies, but not the Anglicans, and by no means the Scotch-Irish Presbyterians, whose slogan was: "And when the Lord thy God shall deliver them before thee; thou shalt smite them, and utterly destroy them; thou shalt make no covenant with them, nor shew mercy unto them." [41] The Quakers controlled the legislature. They did not control the king. They did not represent all of the constituency and they were opposed to coercing the consciences of others.

At first there was no great problem, because the Indians were few. They were of the tribe of the Delawares, subject to the Iroquois, and by them forbidden to engage in war. Their enforced situation well accorded with Penn's holy experiment. He treated them justly and generously. No finer example of the treatment of the aborigines is to be found in history.

By and by came the French. The struggle for the American continent was not simply with the red man, but with other Europeans for the opportunity to exploit and exterminate the red man. The French found a way to the Ohio Valley through the territory of Pennsylvania. There they sought to enlist the Iroquois as allies, and the English countered in kind. Both supplied rum and rifles. The Iroquois desired to be neutral, to let the French and the English fight it out and the more killed the better. An Indian complained of the encroachments from both sides, saying that if an Indian found a bear in a tree an owner of the land would pop up and forbid him to kill it. The Indians veered to the French, partly because the French intermarried with the Indians, partly because the French were fur traders and clashed less with the Indians' way of life, and partly because the English were divided into several colonies striving with one another. The Delawares had even less desire than the Iroquois to be drawn into war, but the pressures were increasing, and they were infuriated by the treacherous "walking purchase" which by trickery alienated their land.

Wars were under way. Braddock was defeated. Benjamin Franklin was pushing Pennsylvania toward energetic participation. The Quakers still controlled the legislature. They had long since refused to vote military appropriations as such, but they voted money "for the King's use" and left the use to his conscience. In 1756, a bill authorizing a military force was before the house. The Quakers in conscience could not vote for it; they hesitated to vote against it, thereby impeding the exercise of the conscientious persuasion of the non-Quakers. The bill exempted Quakers. Franklin justified this clause on the ground that he would not refuse to pump the ship because in saving himself, he would also save the rats. Let the

Quakers pay for the war, said he, and others could do the fighting. The Quakers at last voted for it, because of their own exemption. On April 14, 1756, the government declared war on the Delawares.

This was too much for the conscience of John Woolman and others like him, who sensitized the Friends again to the repudiation of such equivocation. At the next election the Friends declined candidacy for the legislature, and the few who were elected without their consent tendered their resignations. Thus faded the Quaker dream.

In general one may say with reference to the treatment by Europeans of the Indians of South and North America that one people imposed itself upon another, sparing the conquered when they could be used or if they could not be reached, and exterminating them if they were in the way. To be sure disease accounted for more casualties than war since the natives had no immunity to smallpox, measles, typhus, and tuberculosis. Complete dislocation of the social fabric was likewise a factor. Yet, though war alone was not responsible and despite all protests and efforts at amelioration, the word to be written over the dealings of the white man with the red man is ruthlessness.

Chapter 11

The Enlightenment

Peace Plans and Limited War

THE age of the Enlightenment, roughly the eighteenth century, was marked by a revulsion against the wars of religion. These wars were now over. The military struggle was terminated in France by the Edict of Nantes in 1598, though the struggle was in a measure renewed by the revocation in 1685 and the banishment of the Huguenots. In England, the end of the convulsion was marked by the Glorious Revolution at the end of the century. In Germany the Thirty Years' War was terminated in 1648. These wars, of course, had never been exclusively religious. They became increasingly secular and ended in simple power struggles such as those between Louis XIV, the English, and the Dutch. But whatever the causes of the

HORRORS OF THE THIRTY YEARS' WAR

173

carnage, men were sick of it. Already in the seventeenth century and more particularly in the eighteenth, there emerged protests and pleas, plans for peace and the actual amelioration of war.

One of the greatest changes was in mood. The age of the Enlightenment saw the return of pity. Not that pity had been extinct, no great human motif ever fully succumbs. Yet, the absence of the theme of pity for the victims of war, in the great literature from the Renaissance to the Enlightenment is worthy of remark. Racine and Corneille made use of Euripides' *Trojan Women* not to appropriate compassion for the women of the enemy, but only to borrow certain dramatic techniques.[1] Shakespeare, otherwise so universal, lacks this theme.[2] The poor conscripted devils, Ralph Mouldy and Peter Bullcalf, impressed by Falstaff, are introduced only for burlesque. To be sure, Aufidius, the Volscian, can shed a tear over Coriolanus, his fallen Roman foe: "My rage is gone, and I am struck with sorrow." This is only the theme of the medieval duel, in which he who fell could still in dying declare that he who felled him was his greatest friend. The golden warless age of the Stoics is relegated in *The Tempest* to the realm of diverting fantasy, and the "quality of mercy" is invoked for the victim of extortion, not for the multitudes whom war despoils. In Henry V the king expressed qualms as to the invasion of France, but his scruples were speedily allayed by the Archbishop of Canterbury.

Pity in war returns with Voltaire. His novel *Candide* may serve as an example. Candide is a gentle youth who is well received by a baron and baroness in an elegant chateau. Candide learns from the tutor, Pangloss, that this is the best of all possible worlds, but because of too intimate attentions to the charming Cunigunde, the daughter of the house, Candide is booted out of this best of all possible chateaux. In penury, he is picked up by the impressment officers of the King of the Bulgars, engaged in fighting the Abars. Nothing could be more beautiful, more fascinating, more brilliant than two well-ordered armies: the trumpets, the fife, the hautboys, the drums, and the cannons form a harmony such as there never was in hell (a crack at the portrayal of war as music). The artillery disposes of some six thousand on each side. The musketry removes from this best of all possible worlds about nine thousand miserables who infest its surface. The bayonets take care of several thousand more; in all there might be some thirty thousand casualties. Candide escapes to a village of the Abars, fired by the Bulgars, and thence to a village of the Bulgars, fired by the Abars. At length he encounters a pitiable beggar who turns out to be the tutor, Pangloss, the proclaimer of the best of all possible worlds. Candide asks about Cunigunde, only to learn that she is dead. "Cunigunde dead! Oh, best of all possible worlds, of what disease?" "She was disembowelled," Pangloss tells him, "by the Bulgars, after having been raped as many times as possible. The baron who tried to protect her had his head bashed in, and the baroness was dismembered. As for the chateau, there is nothing left—not a stone, not a barn, sheep, duck, or tree. They were well avenged, however, because the Abars did the same thing to a nearby estate of the Bulgars."

The themes of peace characteristic of the Renaissance and classical antiquity were revived in this period. Erasmus was to have a great vogue in the age of enlightenment. Actually the number of editions of his peace tract was greater in the seventeenth century than in the eighteenth,[3] but by way of compensation, the eighteenth brought out a complete edition of the entire Erasmian corpus.

Jonathan Swift, in *Gulliver's Travels*, pillories the trivialities of war when he describes the conflict between the great empires of Lilliput and Blefuscu.

It began upon the following occasion: It is allowed on all hands that the primitive way of breaking eggs before we eat them was upon the larger end; but his present Majesty's grandfather, while he was a boy, going to eat an egg, and breaking it according to the ancient practice, happened to cut one of his fingers. Whereupon the Emperor, his father, published an edict, commanding all his subjects, upon great penalties, to break the smaller end of their eggs. The people so highly resented this law, that our histories tell us, there have been six rebellions raised on that account; wherein one Emperor lost his life, and another his crown. These civil commotions were constantly fomented by the monarchs of Blefuscu;

and when they were quelled, the exiles always fled for refuge to that empire. It is computed that eleven thousand persons have at several times suffered death rather than submit to break their eggs at the smaller end. Many hundred large volumes have been published upon this controversy; but the books of the Bigendians have been long forbidden, and the whole party rendered incapable by law of holding employments. During the course of these troubles the emperors of Blefuscu did frequently expostulate by their ambassadors, accusing us of making a schism in religion, by offending against a fundamental doctrine of our great Prophet Lustrog, in the fifty-fourth chapter of the Brundecral (which is their Alcoran). This, however, is thought to be a mere strain upon the text; for the words are these: That all true believers break their eggs at the convenient end. And which is the convenient end seems, in my humble opinion, to be left to every man's conscience, or at least in the power of the chief magistrate to determine. Now, the Bigendian exiles have found so much credit in the Emperor of Blefuscu's court and so much private assistance and encouragement from their party here at home, that a bloody war hath been carried on between the two empires for thirty-six moons, with various success; during which time we have lost forty capital ships, and a much greater number of small vessels, together with thirty thousand of our best seamen and soldiers; and the damage received by the enemy is reckoned to be somewhat greater than ours. However, they have now equipped a numerous fleet, and are just preparing to make a descent upon us; and his Imperial Majesty, placing great confidence in your valour and strength, hath commanded me to lay this account of his affairs before you.

On a subsequent voyage, Gulliver found himself among the most repulsive creatures he had ever encountered, the Houyhnhnms. In their language he was called a Yahoo. He described to the chief of the Houyhnhnms how wars arose among the Yahoos over such questions as to whether flesh be bread or bread be flesh and whether the juice of a certain berry would be blood or wine. The chief was not greatly disturbed at this recital because nature had constructed the Yahoos incapable of doing much damage to each other. They could not bite very effectively, nor had they claws upon their feet.

I could not forbear shaking my head, and smiling a little at his ignorance. And, being no stranger to the art of war, I gave him a description of cannons. culverins, muskets, carbines, pistols, bullets, powder, swords, bayonets, battles, sieges, retreats, attacks, undermines, countermines, bombardments, sea-fights; ships sunk with a thousand men; twenty thousand killed on each side, dying groans, limbs flying in the air; smoke, noise, confusion, trampling to death under horses' feet; flight, pursuit, victory; fields strewed with carcasses, left for food to dogs and wolves, and birds of prey; plundering, stripping, ravishing, burning, and destroying. And to set forth the valour of my own dear countrymen, I assured him that I had seen them blow up a hundred enemies at once in a siege, and as many in a ship; and beheld the dead bodies come down in pieces from the clouds to the great diversion of the spectators.

The monster at this recital reflected that "when a creature, pretending to reason, could be capable of such enormities, he dreaded lest the corruption of that faculty might be worse than brutality itself."

Eymeric Crucé in his *Le Nouveau Cynée* revives the theme of the fickleness of fortune and the risk of war. Princes should recall that only a little wind is necessary to push them into the abyss. At this point Crucé betrays the classical origin of his idea, for with the passing of sailing vessels a little wind could no longer determine the fortunes of battle. His observation was sound enough, however— that the sovereign of today might be the slave of tomorrow.

Above all he revives the great theme of humanity. Nationalism, as in the Renaissance, was accepted as a political fact but derided as a sentiment. Hostilities between people, he avers, are

only political and cannot take away the connection that is and must be between men. The distance of places, the separation of domicile does not lessen the relationship of blood. It cannot either take away the similarity of nature, true base of amity and human society. Why should I, a Frenchman, wish harm to an Englishman, a Spaniard, or a Hindu? I cannot wish it when I consider that they are men like me, that I am subject like them to error and sin and that all nations are bound together by a natural and consequently indestructible tie which insures that a man cannot consider another a stranger.[4]

Religious intolerance as a source of war was especially decried in this period, and the struggle for peace coincided with the struggle for freedom in religion. Voltaire composed an "Ode on Fanatacism" in which this verse occurs.

> Jansenists and Molinists
> Who battle in our day
> With reasons of the Sophists
> To teach mankind the way,
> Must you lose humanity,
> Brandish the flare of hate
> To show us what is verity? [5]

The pacific mood of the Enlightenment brought forth a great many plans for peace.[6] One striking characteristic among them is that, although written by Christians, they are so little Christian in the ground of their ethic. The ground of motivation, to be sure, is Christian but the appeal is sub-Christian. The explanation may be twofold. One reason was that these schemes generally went beyond the confines of Europe and envisaged a universal peace embracing the Turk and the Hindu. Plainly if non-Christians were to be included, the basis of the peace could not be exclusively Christian. The other reason was that the confessional cleavages had so far divided Christians that they themselves could not find a common Christian denominator. Therefore recourse to the ancient classical tradition of natural law was necessary. Grotius, in his famous tract on the *Law of Peace and War*, already in the seventeenth century delineated the program for the eighteenth. The basis, said he, must be a morality self-validating and true, "even if there were no God, which God forbid." [7] A Christian himself and a confessional Christian who suffered for his adherence to a particular creed, Grotius must in international relations revert to the classical heritage. Incidentally, though he aimed at peace, his position did not preclude war. Rather it sought to repristinate the just war theory—to make war again the servant of law, the instrument of justice, and the tool of peace.[8]

Nowhere is the secular tone more amazing than in William Penn's *An Essay Toward the Present and Future Peace of Europe*. To be sure there is a conclusion in which the Christian note is struck. Christians are upbraided for

invoking the merciful God to prosper their brethren's destruction: yet their Saviour has told them that He came to save, and not to destroy the lives of men: to give and plant peace among men: and if in any sense He may be said to send war, it is the holy war indeed; for it is to send against the devil, and not the persons of men. Of all His titles this seems the most glorious as well as comfortable for us, that He is the prince of peace. It is His nature, His office, His work, and the end and excellent blessings of His coming, Who is both the maker and preserver of our peace with God. And it is very remarkable, that in all the New Testament He is but once called lion, but frequently the Lamb of God; to denote to us His gentle, meek, harmless nature, and that those who desire to be the disciples of His cross and kingdom . . . must be like him.[9]

Apart from this peroration, the tract is pitched in accord with what was to be a common Quaker tactic, on the level of sub-Christian presuppositions. The essay is not replete with biblical texts, and the arguments in favor of peace are to a large degree prudential and even mercantile. Penn speaks of "the mighty prey" which in war "winds and waves have made upon ships and men." Not for nothing was he the son of an admiral, though he had an eye also to the losses which he had witnessed in the Palatinate on land. Penn speaks, after the manner of the Greeks and Erasmus of the uncertainty and the expense of war. What were better than that "our trade should be free and safe and we should rise and lie down without anxiety"? His plan would insure freedom of travel and traffic, "a happiness never understood since the Roman Empire has been broken into so many sovereignties." "The devouring expenses of war" might be diverted into "public acts for learning, charity and manufacturers." This is well-nigh the voice of Jeremy Bentham. There was no insincerity in this appeal, however, because the assumption was that idealism and practicality would in the long run coincide, nor did the Quaker who eschewed none of the economic virtues foresee that business might be as inimical to the Christian ethic as war.

Penn's scheme was one of those which transcended the boundaries of Europe and would include the Turks and the Muscovites. The notion of a crusade was utterly gone, and this is significant because in his day it was not extinct. James I tried to marry his son Charles to the Spanish Infanta in order to cement a political alliance which would drive the Turks from the Mediterranean, where they were still preying upon European commerce and selling Europeans into slavery. Recall the case of Thomas Lurting.

Within Europe, Penn betrayed no trace of English nationalism. He planned a parliament of nations which should surrender national sovereignty in international affairs and retain home rule in matters domestic. When it came to voting he would give to the German Empire twelve votes—the aura of the Holy Roman Empire had not yet vanished—while France should have ten, Italy eight, and England only six.

He advocated in this writing no absolute pacifism, perhaps because it was not addressed to Quakers. There should be an international police force to coerce the recalcitrant. If all other armed forces were abandoned, such a force need actually never be invoked. Above all he sought to eliminate war by the exercise of justice. The just war was supposed to vindicate justice but in practice, said Penn, "the remedy is almost ever worse than the disease. The aggressors seldom getting what they seek, or performing, if they prevail, what they promise." If justice is first of all practiced, however, there will be no occasion for war. "Thus peace is maintained by justice, which is a fruit of government, as government is from society, and society from consent."

Eymeric Crucé was a Catholic, but his scheme was not conspicuously Catholic.[10] He thought the greatest step toward universal peace would be an agreement between the two great powers of his day—namely Christendom and Islam—by which he certainly did not mean that the Turks must submit to the Pope. Therefore, his pleas already cited were those of antiquity and the Renaissance. He, too, desired a world assembly. When it came to the order of rank in seating, he would, as a Catholic, give the first place to the Pope, but the second should go to the Emperor of the Turks, the third to the Emperor of the Christians, and the fourth to the King of France. Crucé, good Frenchman that he was, placed the Emperor higher than his own sovereign. The fifth was accorded to the King of Spain; the sixth should be shared by Persia, China, Tartary, and Muscovy; and the seventh by Great Britain, Poland, Denmark, Sweden, Japan, Morocco, and the great Mogul. French nationalism is evident in the place assigned to Great Britain. On the whole, however, there is here a singular world-mindedness and also a remarkable secularity of tone.

Comenius, a Moravian, in *The Angel of Peace* (1667) takes his own stand on the Sermon on the Mount, but says to his readers, "if you are not equal to the precepts of Christ, at least imitate the concessive Abraham." Let the English and the Dutch divide the spheres of their trade and let not one try to rule the waves. Conflict will impoverish both. "Is it wise to fish with a golden hook or to scuttle the ship on which thine enemy is traveling with thee?" [11] The cure for trade wars is to renounce Asiatic gewgaws. In all essentials each nation is capable of economic self-sufficiency. Abandon avarice as Christ was poor. Here is the Christian note, but it is reinforced by an appeal to Seneca, Epicurus, and Socrates, and by the reminder that if Christians do not follow the gospel, the pagans will rise up in judgment upon them.

Emanuel Kant, a Lutheran, in his *Perpetual Peace* (1795) grounded his appeal primarily upon reason and prudence. He believed strongly in the practice of political morality and was at the same time convinced that ultimately it would prove to be the course of enlightened self-interest. The principle is sound, said he: "Let justice be done, though the earth perish." But it will not perish. "The universe would not totter if there were fewer wicked men in it." Statesmen do wrong to act on the principle "Act first, excuse afterwards; disclaim what you have done; divide and conquer. . . . True politics can never take a step without having previously rendered homage to morality." This is ultimate prudence, however, because honesty is better than all policy, even though temporarily a statesman might have to sacrifice the interests of his own country in order to bring the constitution into accord with "national right founded on reason."

Even an impassioned plea against colonial exploitation is combined with the observation that the enterprise is unprofitable. He exclaimed:

How far are the nations of Europe from exercising the natural right of universal hospitality! At what an excess of injustice do we not behold them arrive, when they discover strange countries and nations? . . . The Chinese and Japanese, whom experience has taught to know the Europeans, wisely refuse their entry into the country. . . . The worst, or to speak with the moralist, the best of the matter is, that all these outrages are to no purpose . . . the sugar islands, that den of slavery the most refined and cruel, produce no real revenue, and are profitable only indirectly . . . to form sailors for the navies, consequently to carry on war in Europe, which service they render to powers who boast the most of piety and who, whilst they drink iniquity like water, pretend to equal the elect in point of orthodoxy.[12]

His objection to the just war was chiefly pragmatic, because it would never succeed in being just. The very concept was based on the analogy of government, and that analogy he held to be false. There never has been a system in which war was the instrument of an international justice determined by an impartial tribunal. Even the papacy never functioned in this way. Rather, each party determined justice for itself. Kant observed that "the field of battle is the only tribunal before which states plead their cause; but victory . . . does not decide." This statement would seem to imply that war might be legitimate if conducted by an international army enforcing a decree of an international court; but this, too, Kant rejected. "From her highest tribunal of moral legislation, reason without exception condemns war as a means of right." There are ambiguities in his position. He condemned a peace of mere indolence and was enthusiastic over the American and French Revolutions.

The most secular and the most penetrating of all the peace plans of the century was that of Jean Jacques Rousseau in his *Extran du Projet de Paix Perpetuelle de M. L'Abbé de Saint Pierre* and his

Jugement sur la Paix Perpetuelle. Rousseau's religion sat more lightly than that of the others. He did not scruple for convenience to change from Catholicism to Calvinism. Still, he could be a Christian without being passionately addicted to either, and in any case, his treatise moves on a secular level.

First of all, he takes his departure from a résumé of the scheme of the Abbé de Saint Pierre (written in parts from 1712 to 1733), who would have frozen the victories of Louis XIV by a European federation to maintain thereafter the *status quo*. His plan, unlike those noticed above, did not include the Turks and the Tartars. It was to have been simply a confederation of Europe which formed an entity united by religion, letters, commerce, customs, and the law of nations. The sovereign states within this entity should federate and use constraint against any recalcitrant. After the union was once formed, there would be no fear of rebellion. Forts then could be demolished and troops disbanded.

"All very well," commented Rousseau, "but how is it to be brought about?" He recalled the still earlier scheme of Sully, the minister of Henry IV, who desired to establish a *Pax Gallica* by first breaking the power of all of the rivals of France. "And how else can it be done?" inquired Rousseau. The Abbé assumed that princes would be willing to form such a confederation. But princes do not distinguish between the good of their independence and the greater good of perpetual peace. The Abbé assured the princes that they need not fear rebellion but could give no such assurance unless the people were at the same time assured that there would be no tyranny, but what prince will ever endure to be forced to be just? A voluntary federation cannot be realized. The only way to federate is by force. In that case, we should not write books but raise troops.

Two inferences are possible from these assertions. One is that the federation of peoples might be achieved if the princes were first removed. This would be the way of the French Revolution. The other possibility is that one prince might impose his way upon all the rest; that was the way of Napoleon. The peace plans of the eighteenth century thus began in appeals by Christians to *humanitas,* and ended in a tocsin for war in the name of *l'humanité.*

Limited War

The eighteenth century is not to be written off as if it had done nothing but compose abortive tracts. In this period the magnitude of war was reduced and the cruelty of war restrained. This happened not because men as men became less cruel. Civil life was brutal; death was the penalty for trivial offenses; prisons stank; amusements were cruel; but war was reduced in intensity and extent. For this change there were a number of contributing factors—sociological, political, and ideological. Europe had again become more unified. Religion had ceased to divide. One might almost say that there was again one religion—this time, the religion of deism. Science was more developed, and science was not divided along national lines. French culture was universally admired and imitated, even by Frederick the Great and Katherine the Great, and commerce, though it might incite war, yet imposed restraints because it was not prudent in destroying a rival to wreck a market.

One of the most important factors in the changed practice of war was political and consisted in the centralization of power in monarchy—this was the age of the enlightened despots—and, above all, in the stabilization of finance so that armies could be maintained without pillage. The troops were composed of mercenaries; their pay was kept up, and they were restrained from plunder by an iron discipline, especially in Prussia. So strong was the control that the Prussian army retreating from Jena endured the rigors of a winter's night without fires rather than burn the wood stacked up near the encampment, because the troops lacked money with which to pay for it. Looting was held in supreme detestation, and when the Russians did it in East Prussia in 1757 there was an outcry.[13]

Bloodshed was reduced, not altogether for humanitarian reasons. Mercenary armies could not be trusted. They might desert for more pay from the other side, to escape combat, or to avoid killing their own countrymen among the "enemy." In the Anglo-Dutch War from

1665 to 1667, three thousand English and Scotch were serving in the Dutch fleet.[14] There were desertions every day. In the American Revolutionary War the claim was made, of course with exaggeration, that the British and the American forces were made up in each case of deserters from the other side.

Since actual battles were costly of men set in mass formation against artillery, the course of prudence was to wear out the enemy by maneuvers rather than to defeat him on the field. Defoe said that in his day it was customary for armies of fifty thousand men to spend the whole campaign in dodging each other. The art of war was said by another to consist less in knowing how to defend a fortress than in knowing how to surrender it honorably.

Wars interfered less in this period with the civilian population. There was no restriction on travel for noncombatants, and passports originated as safe conducts. When Laurence Sterne went to France without a passport during the Seven Years' War, he readily secured one after his arrival from a French Duke engaged in prosecuting the war, who gave it when assured that "a man who laughs is never dangerous." [15]

The conduct of war and the making of peace were restrained by chivalry. War again became a game. At the battle of Fontenoy, "When the head of the English column was twenty paces from the French line, the officers of the other side saluted, and Lord Hay, the captain of the Guards, called out: 'Tell your men to fire!' But, 'No, Sir, you have the honor,' replied the Count d'Auteroche. The first volley mowed down the French." [16]

Vattell in his great work, *Le Droit de Gens* (1758), ransacked history for examples of chivalry to hold up as examples to his age. He told how Leopold in 1318 threw a bridge across the Aar to reach Soleure. When a sudden rise in the river washed it out and threatened to drown his men the enemy rushed to their rescue and Leopold called off the siege. Again, the Duke of Cumberland, being wounded, was waiting for the attention of a physician when a French officer in worse plight was brought in. The English Duke yielded his turn.

As for his own day, Vattell testified that "the humanity with

185

which war is waged cannot be too highly praised. If occasionally a soldier refuses quarter, this is contrary to orders." Noncombatants, he added, are spared. An invading army behaves in friendly fashion, said he, "to the inhabitants of the occupied territory and the peasants come to sell their goods in camp." [17]

Montesquieu similarly lauded the moderation of his day, where the conqueror continued to govern a country in accord with its own laws. How different from the behavior of the Spaniards in the New World! "What might not the Spaniards have done for the Mexicans! They might have given them a gentle religion. Instead they gave them a furious superstition. They might have freed the slaves; instead they enslaved the free. They might have enlightened them as to human sacrifice; instead they exterminated them." [18]

There was in this period genuine reluctance to invent and to employ cruel weapons. This note did not originate in the eighteenth century. Leonardo had invented some sort of submarine but, said he, "This I do not divulge on account of the evil nature of men who would practice assassinations at the bottom of the seas by breaking the ships in their lowest part and sinking them together with the crews who are in them." Sir John Napier invented a mechanism which enabled him to clear four square miles of life, as he demonstrated on sheep, but refused to disclose his device. The eighteenth century went further and refrained from using weapons already known and available. The Swedes refused to use the bayonet except against the Poles, and the Russians and Louis XV refused to have the French armies use an improved form of gunpowder because it was too destructive of human life.[19]

Yet when all is said, one cannot deny that many features of the eighteenth century were making for new wars. One was injustice. The iron rule of the army was itself an aspect of despotism, and the treatment of the serfs in France was to produce the Revolution. Peace is not secure when based only on chivalry; there must also be justice. If this be true in Europe, how much more in the colonial world, where some of the excesses of the conquest were tempered but where the white man still exploited all those of color! At the same time, the industrial revolution provided the means for more deadly weapons. The French Revolution swept away courtesy and reintroduced plunder, and the democratic revolution ended the

AN EDITION OF THE MARSEILLAISE IN 1792

system of professional mercenaries in favor of citizen armies, with the result thereafter that war could no longer be isolated from the entire population. One of the most sinister developments was the exaltation of the state as a counterpoise to the Church and as a bulwark against disorder. The right of resistance to the state was repudiated by

187

Grotius and Bayle,[20] and Hobbes even went so far as to deny the injunction to obey God rather than man. He did say that in a Christian state such an alternative could never arise, because God requires of man for salvation only that he be minded to obey God and love his neighbor. No Christian sovereign would ever infringe upon these duties, and if a pagan sovereign should do so the Christian should be content to believe in his heart. If he felt compelled to make a public testimony, then let him be prepared to suffer and receive his reward in heaven.[21] Such sentiments obviously anticipated the totalitarian state of modern times.

The American Revolutionary War

The eighteenth century occasioned no significant changes in Christian views of war, except that the American Revolution posed a much more difficult form of the discrepancy of any revolution from the theory of the just war waged under the authority of the state. In the Puritan revolution the insurgents had claimed the authority of Parliament as an inferior magistrate resisting the king. This time the colonists professed loyalty to the crown and opposition to Parliament.[22] There was no religious difference with England, and the "perfidious French Papists" were now allies. On the score of religion the most that could be said was that if political liberty were lost religious liberty would be insecure. The colonial preachers did not quite venture to beseech the Lord to hew Agag to pieces over a tax on tea. The only remaining recourse was the secular solution that the colonists, by reason of England's violation of the compact, had lapsed into a state of nature in which they could make a new compact with each other and form a new government. Although the theory of the war was secular, the mood still had much of the crusade, at any rate for the New England Congregationalists. Among them regard vanished for the old rule of clerical abstention. Several of the Connecticut clergy served not only as chaplains but recruited and led companies of militia.[23]

Other churches followed more nearly their own traditional lines. The Anglicans were frequently Tories out of devotion to the king, the head not only of the state but also of the Church. The Methodists, only just emerging as a body separate from the Church of England, shared the same political outlook. John Wesley printed a tract on "Taxation no Tyranny," and in general the Methodists were cool to the revolutionary cause. The peace churches of Pennsylvania —the Mennonites, the Brethren, and the Quakers—maintained their witness and suffered at the hands of their compatriots, for Pennsylvania had long since ceased to be under Quaker control. The Lutherans were ready to support the war but were averse to clerical participation. There was one notable exception. John Peter Gabriel Muhlenberg in his farewell to his congregation in January, 1776, declared: "In the language of Holy Writ, there is a time for all things. There is a time to preach and a time to fight; now is the time to fight." After the benediction he removed his vestment and stood in the uniform of a Virginia colonel. He never went back to his vestment; one or the other it must be. This the Lutherans still felt.[24]

Chapter 12

From Waterloo to Armageddon:
A Century of Comparative Peace

AFTER the Napoleonic Wars, Europe was to enjoy a century of comparative peace from 1815 to 1914. The primary reason was that the Napoleonic conflict did not disrupt the balance of power which had obtained during the eighteenth century. The French failed to establish a hegemony in Europe, and the victorious Allies were wise enough, after their victory, not to eliminate the vanquished from the power conclave. Throughout the nineteenth century the powers to be taken into account were England, France, Germany, Russia, and Austria. Spain, Holland, and Sweden had lost the pre-eminence of former years. Britannia ruled the waves and intervened on land only to keep the balance, as in the Crimean War to prevent Russia from cutting through Turkey to the Dardanelles. By no means negligible as a stabilizing factor was the American frontier, which eased the strains on the European social fabric by affording an outlet for the indigent and the insurgent. During the century 66,000,000 persons emigrated.[1] Even more important was the survival of the sense of European unity. Christendom lived on, at least as a cultural entity, and for most statesmen also as a religious society.[2] Bismarck had a deep sense of his responsibility to the Great Task Master, and that old sea dog Admiral Fisher was facile with scripture. The concept of Europe as a family of sovereign states imposed restraints, and when Bismarck had rounded out the confines of Germany, he refrained from Napoleonic adventures.

Peace makes possible reform, and the nineteenth century was an age of reform in Europe and in America. The abolition of the slave trade and of slavery, the ending of child labor, the reduction of hours and the increase of wages for adults, the repeal of the Corn Laws in England, the improvement of prisons, the reduction or abolition of the death penalty, the extension of the franchise, women's suffrage, the restraint of alcoholism, and social legislation—these were the reforms agitated and in large measure achieved. The technique developed for fostering these reforms was the founding of societies, each directed to a specific objective and recruiting all who agreed on the one goal, however diverse their religious or other affiliations. In consequence, Christian influence in this period cannot be traced by observing the actions of churches. One must rather examine the religious allegiance of the individual members of societies. When this is done, the primary motivation is seen to have stemmed from Christian idealism.

The Peace Movement

Among the reforms which peace fostered, none is more important than the abolition of war. This was the period in which the peace movement first organized itself on an international scale and took measures to impress its views upon governments.[8] Peace societies were formed in England, Germany, France, Scandinavia, Italy, Austria, Switzerland, The Netherlands, and the United States. Congresses were held in Brussels, Paris, Boston, and elsewhere. The movements were inspired in part by revulsion against the Napoleonic wars, and in the United States the War of 1812. The general mentality was still that of the eighteenth century, and the effort now was not so much to advance new ideas as to implement politically the peace plans of the previous century. The societies were Christian in their outlook, save in France, where the *fraternité* and *humanité* of the revolution were still the slogan. The forces for peace were divided in this period, as they commonly are, between those who sought peace through world

191

government, or even through an international police force, and those who renounced all war and violence.

In the United States one ingredient in the philosophy of peace came from the mellowing of the rigors of Calvinism. Even Samuel Hopkins, accounted a high Calvinist, stressed the utter benevolence of God, while his onetime parishioner William Ellery Channing, a Unitarian, inveighed alike against the inhumanity of God in the Calvinist picture and the inhumanity of man in war. The Calvinist dream of a holy commonwealth to be won and maintained by the might of the Ironsides was transformed by extending the terrain to embrace not merely the original Puritan colonies but the whole of the United States. The goal was to be a world at peace, with America taking the lead through her emancipation from the dynastic quarrels of a decadent Europe. Ralph Waldo Emerson in his "Address on War" voiced alike the faith and the hope. In 1838 he said:

Not in an obscure corner, not in a feudal Europe, not in an antiquated appangage where no onward step can be taken without rebellion, is this seed of benevolence laid in the furrow, with tears of hope; but in this broad America of God and man, where the forest is only now falling, or yet to fall, and the green earth opened to the inundation of emigrant men from all quarters of oppression and guilt; here, where not a family, not a few men, but mankind, shall say what shall be free; here, we ask, Shall it be War, or shall it be Peace? [4]

One of the most novel turns of the peace movement was the re-examination of historical wars. A Unitarian minister in Maine, Sylvester Judd, published a tract entitled *The Moral Evils of Our Revolutionary War*, as a result of which he was dismissed as the chaplain of the state legislature.[5] John Humphrey Noyes was so incensed by the treatment accorded in the past and present to the Indians and the Negroes that he resigned from the United States.[6]

The peace movement developed two wings. The moderates who organized the American Peace Society in 1838 would allow defensive war and trusted for the abolition of war to the establishment of world government with an international court and an international congress of the nations, after the manner of the peace plans of the previous century.

The pacifists organized the New England Non-Resistance Society in 1838. Their leader, Adin Ballou, went further than anyone hitherto in advancing a prudential pacifism which, he claimed, would afford actually greater security than would reliance upon arms. Not invariably, to be sure, but ordinarily one could assume that if one turned the other cheek, one would not be hit. His examples were taken almost entirely from private life, though in one instance groups were involved. An army was commanded to capture a town in the Tyrol. Finding there only women and children, the soldiers withdrew, not knowing what else to do because their instructions covered only fighting with soldiers.[7] They had been born too soon!

The American societies were recruited from the membership of the churches, among whom the more prominent were the Quakers, the Unitarians, the Methodists, the Baptists, the Congregationalists, and the Presbyterians. The Episcopalians, the Catholics, and the Dutch Reformed held aloof. Sometimes the churches as churches made pronouncements on the subject of war, as when the Congregationalists in Massachusetts and Vermont in 1816 and 1817 denounced war and lauded peace.[8] At the same time in particular wars, as we shall see, the clergy were often highly belligerent; so much so, that Mark Twain was prompted to compose this satire on a wartime prayer:

O Lord our Father, our young patriots . . . go forth to battle—Be Thou near them. With them—in spirit—we also go forth from the sweet peace of our beloved firesides to smite the foe. O Lord our God, help us to tear their soldiers to bloody shreds with our shells. . . . Help us to wring the hearts of their unoffending widows with unavailing grief; help us to turn them out roofless with their little children to wander unfriended the wastes of their desolated land in rags and hunger and thirst . . . imploring Thee for the refuge of the grave and denied it. . . . Blast their hopes, blight their lives, protract their bitter pilgrimage, make heavy their steps, water their way with tears, stain the white snow with the blood of their wounded feet. We ask it in the spirit of love, of him who is the source of Love, and who is the ever-faithful refuge and friend of all that are sore beset and seek His aid with humble and contrite hearts. Amen.[9]

In England the great drive came from the Quakers; their attitude will be delineated below in connection with Bright's critique of England's wars. In Germany the *Uncle Tom's Cabin* of the peace movement was the novel *Lay Down Your Arms* by the Baroness Bertha Von Suttner. She dealt in the story with Bismarck's three wars against Denmark, Austria, and France. Two themes in the book are recurrent. The first is the frightfulness of war:

Fighting in the open country is terrible enough but fighting amongst human beings is ten times more cruel. Crashing timber, bursting flames, stifling smoke; cattle run mad with fear; every wall a fortress or a barricade, every window a shot-hole. I saw a breastwork there which was formed of corpses. The defenders had heaped up all the slain that were lying near, in order, from that rampart, to fire over onto their assailants. I shall never forget that wall in all my life. A man, who formed one of its bricks, penned in among the other corpse-bricks, was still alive, and was moving his arm. . . . If there were any angel of mercy hovering over the battlefields he would have enough to do in giving the poor creatures—men and beasts—who are "still alive" their *coup de grâce*.

The other theme is the circuitous and fallacious reasoning of those who regard war as inevitable. Her father in the story quotes to her the old saying

Si vis pacem para bellum: we are only preparing out of precaution. And the other side?
With a view to attacking us.
And they also say that their action is only a precaution against our attack.
That is malice.
And they say that we are malicious.
Oh, they say that only as a pretext, to be better able to make their preparations.[10]

The baroness animated the German peace movement until her death just before the outbreak of the First World War.

Russian pacifism in this period, represented by the sects, was without impact not only in Europe but even in Russia. The Dukhobors were few and were persecuted and segregated. Their aversion to miltary service appears, as a matter of fact, not to have arisen from pacifism at all, if the charge be true that they were guilty of murdering any deserters from their cult. The reason would seem rather to have been hatred for the czars' government, which had inflicted upon them such frightful persecution.[11]

The Molokans were different.[12] In them came again to expression an early and persistent strain in Russian piety, the imitation of the kenotic Christ. The word "kenotic" comes from the Greek and means emptying, "for Christ counted not the being on an equality with God a thing to be grasped, but *emptied* himself." Long before St. Francis this ideal of complete abnegation animated Russian monasticism. It was to reappear in the nineteenth century among the atheist aristocracy, who renounced wealth and position to share the life of the peasants.[13] Specifically the Molokans justified their pacifism as obedience to the commands "Thou shalt not kill" and "Put up thy sword." A broader consideration was that the right of life and death belonged only to the Creator of heaven and earth.

The obscurity of these sects was not shared by Tolstoy, whose name became a symbol of pacifism throughout the literate world. He, too, stood in the tradition of the kenotic Christ. Man, as a son of God, must renounce himself; he alone is above others who humbles himself. Christ did not command us to suffer, but to resist not evil, and this will entail suffering. Violence is to be used neither to defend oneself or others, though force may be employed to rescue a child from imminent danger. The Christian must renounce all recourse to law as well as to war. He who does so will of necessity be at variance with the state and society, which rest upon violence. The renunciation of violence was made to rest by Tolstoy partly on obedience to the divine commands and partly on the hope of a better future. He believed that the day would surely come when the scientific activity dedicated to destruction would be the derision and pity of future generations.[14]

Arbitration and Disarmament

When we review the peace efforts of the nineteenth century they appear at first glance to have been utterly unavailing; nothing is more depressing than to walk through the library stacks of shelves and shelves of pamphlets, periodicals, and books of that era advocating peace. Yet there were concrete gains, valid at least for their own time. International arbitration received an enormous impetus. The number of cases successfully arbitrated in Europe in approximately the nineteenth century is as follows:

1794-1800	4	1841-60	25
1801-20	12	1881-1900	111
1821-40	10	1901-10	25 [15]

The establishment of the Hague Tribunal in 1899 provided a convenient machinery for adjudication, but it has been hampered by the failure of the nations to surrender their sovereignty to the degree of submitting all disputes to juridical decision. High hopes were entertained for this goal when in 1910 President Taft declared that even questions involving national honor should be resolved in this way. There was even greater enthusiasm when, under Woodrow Wilson, the Secretary of State William Jennings Bryan negotiated thirty treaties requiring that prior to hostilities a "cooling off" period should intervene, in which all disputes should be submitted to an investigating commission. Bryan presented to each of the diplomats of the signatory powers a plowshare paperweight beaten from a sword supplied by the War Department. Bryan never received the Nobel peace prize, which earlier had been conferred upon the swashbuckling Theodore Roosevelt for negotiating on request the peace between Japan and Russia.[16]

Efforts at disarmament during this period achieved some tangible results, to which one may well believe the agitation of the peace societies had contributed. The most spectacular accomplishment was the Rush-Bagot Agreement of 1816 which demilitarized the entire frontier between the United States and Canada. Naval vessels on the Great Lakes were dismantled. The agreement has been continuously in force ever since and has never resulted in any untoward incident from either side.

Agitation for similar but much more extensive peace action among the great powers was persistent on the continent and in England, where the dissenting churches threw their whole weight into the endeavor. Statesmen and parliamentary bodies discussed the idea. Yet all were amazed when in August of 1898, a call for a disarmament conference was issued by the Czar Nicholas II of Russia, in which he lamented that the desire of the great powers for a general pacification had yielded no results during the preceding twenty years. Hundreds of millions were being spent on engines of destruction, regarded today as the latest inventions of science but discarded tomorrow as obsolute. "It is the supreme duty, therefore, at the present moment of all States to put some limit to these unceasing armaments." Accordingly, a conference was summoned. "Such a Conference, with God's help, would be a very happy augury for the opening century. It would concentrate in one powerful effort the strivings of all States which sincerely wish to bring about the triumph of the grand idea of universal peace."

"Could it be that the Czar really meant it?" gasped an astounded Europe. Was this perchance a ruse? He did in fact mean it, for he had been influenced by the work of Von Bloch, who predicted that future war would bring "not fighting but famine," the bankruptcy of nations, and the disruption of the social order. The Czar's ministers —did they agree? Did they also mean it? There was reason to believe that they did because Russia wished peace with the West in order to expand toward the East. The conference met, and it did accomplish the establishment of the Hague Tribunal, a very relevant achievement since the corollary to disarmament is the settlement of disputes under law.[17]

Actual disarmament made no strides, however. President Roosevelt thought it would mean abdication by civilized nations in favor of the barbarians. When it came to summoning another conference, he graciously yielded the initiative to the Czar. The assembly met in 1906, but Russia, after her defeat at the hands of Japan, desired now to increase her armaments. The dictum of Theodore Roosevelt prevailed, that the highest civilizations must be masters of the world.

The Churches and the Wars of the Nineteenth Century

The statement that the nineteenth century was one of comparative peace is entirely valid, but this is only to say that there were no conflicts of equal magnitude to the Napoleonic wars earlier or to the First and Second World Wars afterward. There were wars during the nineteenth century. England had the Crimean War with Russia and the Boer War. Bismarck, as we have observed, fought with Denmark, Austria, and France. The United States was involved in the War of 1812, the Mexican War, the Civil War, and the Spanish-American War. The attitudes of the churches in the respective countries to these wars call for review. In the United States, peopled mainly by the dissenting religious bodies of Europe, the traditional varieties of the Christian ethic were less displaced by the attitude of the enlightenment than had been true in Europe. One observes that during the Civil War there was a recrudescence of the old alignments, notably on the part of the Northern churches. Those who had come from the established churches of Europe—the Catholics, the Anglicans, and the Lutherans—looked upon the war less as a crusade for the emancipation of the slaves than as the suppression of a rebellion. They talked in terms of "inevitable necessity" (Lutheran), "support of the constituted authority" (Catholic), and "unfaltering allegiance to the Government" (Episcopalian). The churches of the Calvinist tradition—the Congregationalists, the Unitarians, the Presbyterians, and the Baptists, as well as the Methodists—looked upon the war as a crusade for the abolition of slavery. For them the soldier in such a cause was an imitator of Christ. "As he died to make men holy, let us die to make men free." [18] The peace churches, for the most part, adhered to their historic stand and in this witness they were joined by the Disciples. The Quakers suffered agonized searching of heart. They had been in the van in disowning any of their members who did not emancipate their slaves. Here now was a war for the emancipation of all slaves. Could Quakers continue at the same time to oppose both slavery and this war to end slavery? Some Quakers became colonels, but the Society as a whole continued to combine the campaign for the emancipation of slaves with the condemnation of all war.

Cutting across the old lines was sectionalism. This was at no time so evident as in the Civil War. The churches in the South supported the Confederacy, and three of the great denominations were split: the Methodists, the Presbyterians, and the Baptists. The two former have since been reunited. The Mexican War to a lesser degree disclosed a sectional rift. Support for the war came from the churches close to the Mexican border, and opposition came from New England. The Christians nearest to the Rio Grande shrieked their *Deus vult*. The Southern Baptists, being closest, were the most vociferous. The Congregationalists and the Unitarians, in the area converging on Boston, were emphatic that *Deus non vult*.[19]

The War of 1812 may have exhibited sectionalism, but the matter has not been sufficiently investigated to admit of final analysis. The pressure of the war came from what was then the frontier, running in a crescent from New Hampshire to Buffalo, on through Kentucky and Tennessee to Savannah. There was no division along the lines of North and South, because the North desired to annex Canada and the South, Florida. Since England and Spain were, at the moment, allied in fighting Napoleon, war with England was also war with Spain and thus provided an opportunity for annexation in two directions. But if the North and South were united, the East and the West were split. The war was not popular on the Atlantic seaboard and especially in New England. The Federalist party, which opposed the war, consisted of the commercial interests in the coast towns, as well as the college-bred and the professional men, who looked upon Napoleon as anti-Christ and upon England as "the world's last hope." [20] The clergy in this area denounced the war, but whether the clergy on the frontier supported the war is a question which remains to be investigated.

A growing tendency on the part of the churches to coalesce in their attitudes, not only with one another but also with the prevailing mood of the country, became evident in the Spanish-American War. It was an expansionist war, pushed by men like "Teddy" Roosevelt, the Rough Rider, who was convinced that the civilized nations must keep the barbarians in tow. Popular passion was fanned by the propaganda of the Hearst Press, which disseminated fabricated atrocity stories illustrated by Remington. Though Spain had conceded our demands, President McKinley declared war and took over not only Cuba, where Spain's misrule was claimed to be intolerable, but also the Philippines. The full facts were not available to the public at the time. The Church press at the outset exhibited an admirable moderation, refusing to become hysterical over the blowing up of the Maine. When Senator Proctor visited Cuba and came home with reports of Spanish misrule, however, the churches sounded the tocsin of a holy war for the vindication of the oppressed. This was true in general of the Congregationalists, the Presbyterians, the Baptists, the Methodists, the Disciples, and the Unitarians. The Episcopalians, the Lutherans, and the Roman Catholics were more temperate.[21]

In England the dissenters were the core of the Liberal party, even though it was headed by an Anglican, William Ewart Gladstone. The dissenters were not pacifists, but political liberals and opponents of imperialism. Thoroughgoing and consistent opposition to England's wars came, as one would expect, from the Quakers. The full implications of their position were well exemplified in the career of their great statesman John Bright. He was a Quaker; he believed in Quaker principles. He opposed all of England's wars during his lifetime, but not on Quaker principles; rather on the principles of those whom he addressed.

I shall not read the Sermon on the Mount to men who don't acknowledge its authority, nor shall I insist on my reading of the New Testament to men who take a different view of it; nor shall I ask the members of a church whose articles especially justify the bearing of arms to join in any movement which shall be founded upon what are called abstract Christian peace doctrines. But I will argue this question on the ground which our opponents admit, which not professing Christians only, but Mohammedans and heathen and humanity will admit. I will argue it upon this ground, that war is probably the greatest of all human calamities.[22]

After the Indian mutiny he responded to the question whether the English should do nothing but allow every Englishman in India to be murdered.

I don't think so. They must act on their principles, seeing they admit no others. . . . I have not pleaded . . . that this country should remain without adequate and scientific means of defense. I acknowledge it to be the duty of your statesmen, acting upon the known opinions and principles of ninety-nine out of every hundred persons in the country, at all times, with all reasonable moderation, but with all possible efficiency to take steps which shall preserve order within and on the confines of your kingdom. But I shall repudiate and denounce the expenditure of every shilling, the engagement of every man, the employment of every ship, which has no object but intermeddling in the affairs of other countries, and endeavoring to extend the boundaries of an Empire which is already large enough to satisfy the greatest ambition, and I fear is much too large for the highest statesmanship to which any man has yet attained.[23]

On the grounds, not of Quaker nonresistance, but of public policy, he would point out that England's intervention in Europe's wars had been not only unnecessary but calamitous. Had she refrained, "We should indeed have had less of military glory. We might have had neither Trafalgar nor Waterloo; but we should have set the high example of a Christian nation."

With regard to the Crimean War, Bright urged that England was not called upon to defend Turkey against Russia. If she should do so on behalf of every down-trodden people, why had she not intervened on behalf of Hungary against Russia? After the war with Russia was actually in progress and members of the Cabinet were treating the subject with flippancy, Bright rose to rebuke the buffoonery of the noble Lord Palmerston, the Prime Minister. Bright went on to say that he was ready enough to debate the justice of this war on the principles of the noble lord himself, and on such principles it could not be justified. He continued:

I am not, nor did I ever pretend to be, a statesman; and that character is so tainted and so equivocal in our day, that I am not sure that a pure and honourable ambition would aspire to it. I have not enjoyed, for thirty years, like these noble lords, the honours and emoluments of office. I have not set my sails to every passing breeze. I am a plain and simple citizen, sent here by one of the foremost constituencies of the empire, representing feebly, perhaps, but honestly, I dare aver, the opinions of very many, and the true interests of all those who have sent me here. Let it not be said that I am alone in my condemnation of this war, and of this incapable and guilty administration. And even if I were alone, if mine were a solitary voice, raised amid the din of arms and the clamours of a venal press, I should have the consolation I have tonight—and which I trust will be mine to the last moment of my existence—the priceless consolation that no word of mine had tended to promote the squandering of my country's treasure or the spilling of one single drop of my country's blood.

Bright sat down in the midst of a complete silence in which the tittering ministers had become grave.

On another occasion he addressed a plea to Lord Palmerston:

The Angel of Death has been abroad throughout the land; you may almost hear the beating of his wings. There is no one, as when the first born were slain of old, to sprinkle with blood the lintel and the two sideposts of our doors, that he may spare and pass on; he takes his victims from the castle of the noble, the mansion of the wealthy, and the cottage of the poor and the lowly, and it is on behalf of all these classes that I make this solemn appeal.

I tell the noble lord, that if he be ready honestly and frankly to endeavour by the negotiations about to be opened at Vienna to put an end to this war, no word of mine, no vote of mine, will be given to shake his power for one single moment, or to change his position in this House. [Hear, hear]

The noble lord has become "the foremost subject of the Crown." Let him achieve "a still higher and nobler ambition: that he had returned the sword to the scabbard." [24]

In these speeches of Bright a number of principles come to light: that a pacifist may legitimately appeal to the nonpacifist to live up to

202

his own ethic, by refraining from military adventures, wars of aggression, wars of expansion; and that the pacifist may sound the note of pity and compassion. As the member of a legislative assembly the pacifist should not, however, stand in the way of those measures which are necessary for the implementation of the policies adopted by the majority in accord with their principles. He could not of course share in the framing or the execution of policies not in accord with his principles. Therefore he could not hold executive office. He could do no more than retain his seat in the House.

The Boer War divided even the dissenting churches in Britain. Some held it to be an example of unabashed imperialism. W. T. Stead, a Congregationalist, and Lloyd George, a Baptist, together with many others, were of this mind. Their position was well stated by the Liberal Lord Morley, not himself a churchman. When he went to speak in his native Manchester to an audience of between eight and ten thousand persons, he was hooted down until in a pause he managed to call out "I am a Lancashire man." Then they gave him a chance.

After an hour of a judicious mixture of moderation, breadth, good-temper, with a slight guarded Lancastrian undertone of defiance, which they rather liked than resented, I sat down amid universal enthusiasm. The grand potent monosyllable with which I wound up was not to be resisted. "You may carry fire and sword into the midst of peace and industry: it will be wrong. A war of the strongest government in the world with untold wealth and inexhaustible reserves against this little republic will bring you no glory: it will be wrong. You may make thousands of women widows, and thousands of children fatherless: it will be wrong. It may add a new province to your empire: it will still be wrong." [25]

There were others among the British dissenting churches who held that the war was being fought on behalf of the South African natives, who would not be accorded equality in status by the Boers, as they would be the British. The English won the war at the cost of instituting concentration camps for Boer civilians. The war was followed by a generous peace which granted to the Boers home rule, but the outcome of this idealistic war for the native has come to be *apartheid*.

As for the attitude of the churches on the continent to the wars of the nineteenth century, we know in general that all supported their governments, but no detailed studies are available save one. This chronicles the sequel to the Franco-Prussian War, when the German Protestants extended a hand of reconciliation to the French Protestants in a document which began by stating that the Germans were not disposed to be vainglorious because God had given their fatherland the victory in a war forced upon them by the French. This preamble nullified the gesture.[26]

In Russia the Orthodox Church throughout supported the czar. The sects protested and were unheard. Only Tolstoy reached the world. During the Russo-Japanese War he lamented:

All over Russia, from the palace to the remotest village, the pastors of churches, calling themselves Christians, appeal to that God who has enjoined love to one's enemies—to the God of Love Himself—to help the work of the devil to further the slaughter of men. . . . The same thing is going on in Japan. . . . Japanese theologians and religious teachers no less than the military . . . do not remain behind the Europeans in the techniques of religious deceit and sacrilege, but distort the great Buddhistic teaching by not only permitting but justifying that murder which Buddha forbade.

Specifically Tolstoy pilloried the statement of the Czar and his general that not more than fifty thousand men would be needed to dislodge the Japanese from Manchuria.

That ceaseless stream of unfortunate deluded Russian peasants now being transported by thousands to the Far East—these are those same— not more than 50,000 live Russian men whom Nicholas Romanoff and Alexis Kuropatkin have decided they may get killed and who will be killed in support of those stupidities, robberies, and every kind of abomination which were accomplished in China and Korea by immoral, ambitious men now sitting peacefully in their palaces and expecting new glory and new advantage and profit from the slaughter of those 50,000 unfortunate defrauded Russian workingmen guilty of nothing and gaining nothing by their sufferings and death.

On the publication of this indictment in England, the *London Times* commented, "The enormity of bloodshed is the gist of his [Tolstoy's] doctrine; yet he holds the governing classes of his own country up to the execration of ignorant peasants with a recklessness which might lead in certain circumstances to the cruelest of all bloodshed—the bloodshed of social war." [27]

The First World War, the Crusading War

The shot at Sarajevo ended Europe's century of comparative peace. In August, 1914, the First World War began. The causes have been much debated. Among the more remote were the closing of the American frontier and of the frontier of colonial possessions, leaving Germany with inferior holdings. The Allies at the time ascribed to Germany sole guilt for the disruption of the peace. Subsequently, the revisionist historians have taxed Russia with even greater responsibility. In this land one of the world's great revolutionary upheavals was already astir and one could hear the bellowing of the milling herd. The Czar's government may well have supposed that the proletariat insurgence could be deflected by a foreign war and that in the melée Russia might achieve her ancient goal of an ice-free port on the Mediterranean. Whatever Russia's guilt, Germany is not to be exonerated. She had been engaged in a feverish race of naval armaments in order to challenge Britannia's "dominion over palm and pine." Germany had become highly industrialized. She needed to be sure of raw materials and markets abroad. Had she been able to conclude a partnership with England, the one to control the land, the other the sea, with both dividing the spoils, the balance might have been preserved. But Germany could not trust a commercial rival in control of the seas to be solicitous for her interests.

In conjunction with this rivalry of goods and power, a subtle change of outlook had been taking place, which divided Germany from the world of the West. With singular acumen, Ernest Troeltsch took cognizance of this change.[28] It consisted in this: that the West, meaning especially England, the United States, and France, retained the tradition of natural law, whereas in Germany it was supplanted by the Romantic movement. The ancient theory of natural law, as we have observed, rested upon the assumption that a principle of rationality pervaded the cosmos, immanent in the world and man, implanting in his heart the principles of a morality intelligible to and binding upon all. The Romantic movement denied the possibility of a universal morality, claiming instead that men are not equally endowed with reason and with energy. On the contrary, in particular periods particular peoples are the recipients and custodians of a dynamic vitality which lifts them above their fellows. By virtue of this special endowment, they make their own rules which others cannot understand but should be compelled to obey. Here we have a secularization of the concept of the chosen people. God's elect have here become the *Herrenvolk*.

Hegel in the realm of ideas and Bismarck in the realm of politics are often regarded as the prime architects of this attitude, though as a matter of fact, neither was as extreme as were his followers. Hegel held that private morality does not apply between nations; for them the only morality is fidelity to agreements of their own making. The sovereign nation is subject to nothing save the *Weltgeist*.[29] Precisely what this means depends upon the definition of the *Weltgeist*. If it can be the cosmic rationality of the Stoics, then natural law is not excluded, but if it be the *élan vital* which appears erratically in this nation or that, then the universal morality of natural law is at an end. Politically, as we have noted, Bismarck set out to achieve Germany's destiny by blood and iron, but having attained his goal, he then stopped. Alike, Hegel and Bismarck would have been aghast at Hitler—and probably at Bethmann-Hollweg when he referred to the treaty over Belgium as a "scrap of paper." Yet the lines do run from the restrained precursors to their less inhibited successors. A distinct difference has appeared between German and notably English and American attitudes. Bethmann-Hollweg's remark was defended in Germany, but when Admiral Fisher, head of the British Navy, proposed to "Copenhagen" the German fleet, after the manner of Nelson who, at Copenhagen, fell without warning upon the fleet of Denmark, British leaders were horrified and promptly disavowed his proposal. Troeltsch summarized by saying that to the Germans the Anglo-Saxon attitude appeared to be compounded of moralism and pharisaism. To the English and Americans the German attitude seemed to be a blend of mysticism and barbarism.

Whatever may be the proper assessment of responsibility, whatever the relative roles of sensate and ideological factors, the war did come and the churches in every land gave support to their governments. In Germany the Catholic Mausbach [30] and the Protestant Holl [31] looked upon Germany as begirt by foes bent on her strangulation. For Germany to defend herself against their encirclement was nothing other than a just war.

In England, the mood fluctuated between that of the just war and the crusade. The latter outlook became the more prevalent as fabricated atrocity stories were disseminated and believed, to the effect that the Germans had cut off the hands of babies in Belgium and had crucified a Canadian.

The Bishop of London regretfully but candidly called on young Englishmen to do that which in war has to be done: "Kill Germans—to kill them, not for the sake of killing, but to save the world, to kill the good as well as the bad, to kill the young men as well as the old, to kill those who have shewn kindness to our wounded as well as those fiends who crucified the Canadian Sergeant. . . . As I have said a thousand times, I look upon it as a war for purity, I look upon everyone who dies in it as a martyr." [32]

The Archbishop of Canterbury was more temperate and more troubled. He recognized the legitimacy of a righteous wrath, but feared that it might degenerate into a "poisonous hatred" which would coarsen, corrupt, and defile England's high aims, "transforming what was a righteous—yes, a wholesome—wrath against wrong into a sour and envenomed hatred of whole sections of our fellowmen." [33]

In December, 1914, Richard Roberts, a Presbyterian minister, and

Henry Hodgkin, a Quaker, founded the Fellowship of Reconciliation.

In the United States the mood was a blend of hysterical nationalism and crusading idealism. The rancor was the greater because of the fervent desire of the nation to be neutral. Hence virulent resentment against those who, contrary to our will, dragged us into the conflict. Wilson was re-elected on the slogan "He kept us out of war." At the beginning of hostilities in Europe his intervention was confined to

WHEN WILLIAM COMES TO LONDON

YOU'LL HEAR THE TIN-GOD OF POTSDAM SAY:
"ACCEPT THIS IRON CROSS, MY RAMSAY."

OPPONENTS OF WAR RIDICULED IN ENGLAND AND AMERICA
DURING THE FIRST WORLD WAR

protests against interference with the rights of neutrals on the high seas. England had thrown a tight blockade around Germany and was preventing all trade from going in, while Germany was seeking to break through by means of the newly invented submarine. Passenger ships bearing arms were sunk. Of such was the Lusitania—though only later did it become generally known that she carried munitions. Both England and Germany interfered with American travel and trade. Complete and consistent defense of neutral rights would have involved the United States in hostilities with both countries, but

Wilson's sympathies were with England, because he shared her blood, her ideas, and her ideals. England was a democracy, Germany a monarchy, and though the ostensible occasion for entering the war was still the defense of neutral rights, once America became involved the goal was declared, "to make the world safe for democracy."

A surprised and outraged nation rallied to the support of the president. American churchmen of all faiths were never so united

OPPONENTS OF WAR RIDICULED IN ENGLAND AND AMERICA
DURING THE FIRST WORLD WAR

with each other and with the mind of the country. This was a holy war. Jesus was dressed in khaki and portrayed sighting down a gun barrel. The Germans were Huns. To kill them was to purge the earth of monsters. Nor was such action incompatible with love, because their deaths would restrain them from crime and transplant them to a better land. The Lord God of battles was rolling up the hosts of Armageddon to destroy the great beast of the abyss that the new Jerusalem might descend from the sky. To be sure, not all ministers were so immoderate. There were eighty pacifist clergymen.[34] Nor were churchmen so savage as the general populace. The press engaged in vilification of isolationists, IWW's, and pacifists. All of them were branded as agents of the Kaiser. Violence sprang up against those suspected as pro-German. The language of Germany became taboo and sauerkraut had to be called "liberty cabbage." For refusal to put on a uniform, a Dukhobor was sent to Alcatraz, and there was subjected to hosing under cold water so that he died of pneumonia. When his widow came to claim the remains, the corpse was dressed in a uniform.[35]

Strategically the war bogged down into trench warfare. Mirred in mud and gore, the choicest of Europe's youth went over the top and fell in no man's land. The war ended, as winter was about to set in, on November 11, 1918. When spring returned, the poet sang:

> So when the Spring of the World shall shrive our stain
> After the winter of war,
> When the poor world wakes to peace once more,
> After such night of ravage and rain,
> You shall not come again.
> You shall not come to taste of old Spring weather,
> And gallop through the soft untrampled heather,
> And bathe and bake your body on the grass.
> We shall be there. Alas!
> But not with you. When Spring shall wake the earth
> And quicken the scarred fields to a new birth,
> Our grief shall grow. For what can Spring renew
> More fiercely for us than the need of you? [36]

Chapter 13

From the Outlawry of War
To the Atom Bomb

AFTER the war to end war came the crusade for an enduring peace. This mood of the 1920's has come to be incomprehensible to the 1950's. The young today inquire how people could have been so unrealistic as to suppose that there could ever be an enduring peace. Were they impelled by an incredible naïveté as to the goodness of human nature? On the contrary, not the goodness of man but the hideousness of war fired the resolve that it should never happen again.

If one would understand the mood of that hour, listen to these words of Herbert Hoover:

I was one of but few civilians who saw something of the battle of the Somme. In the distant view were the unending trenches filled with a million and a half men. Here and there, like ants, they advanced under the thunder and belching volcanoes from 10,000 guns. Their lives were thrown away until half a million had died. Passing close by were unending lines of men plodding along the right side of the road to the front, not with drums and bands, but with saddened resignation. Down the left side came the unending lines of wounded men, staggering among unending stretchers and ambulances. Do you think one can forget that? And it was but one battle of a hundred. . . .

In another even more dreadful sense I saw inhuman policies of war. That was the determination on both sides to bring subjection by starvation. The food blockade by the Allied Governments on the one side, and the ruthless submarine warfare by the Central Powers on the other, had this as its major purpose. Both sides professed that it was not their purpose to starve women and children. But it is an idiot who thinks soldiers ever starve. It was women and children who died of starvation. It was they who died of the disease which came from short food supplies, not in hundreds of thousands, but in millions.

And after the Armistice came famine and pestilence, in which millions perished and other millions grew up stunted in mind and body. That is war. Let us not forget.[1]

Because men had not yet forgotten, Woodrow Wilson was hailed as a messiah by delirious throngs who saw in him the leader through whom a new world order should come into being.

The revulsion against the misery of war was intensified by the disclosures and failures which followed in its wake. The sole guilt of Germany was called into question by the Revisionists. The atrocities in the conduct of the war were demonstrated to have been the fabrications of propagandists. Evidence was presented pointing to the conclusion that an international ring of munitions makers, selling to both sides, had had a hand in fomenting and prolonging the war. Disillusionment as to the cause and conduct of the struggle was augmented by despondency over the failure to realize in the peace the ideal objectives for which the war had been waged.

The war to end war had been followed by the invasion of Manchuria and Abyssinia. The campaign to make the world safe for democracy had as its sequel in some lands the rise of totalitarianism. The slogan of "No annexations and no idemnities" was evaded by mandates and reparations. The attempt to recover "normalcy" was thwarted by economic upheaval, depression, inflation, widespread unemployment, and more or less violent social unheavals.

For all of these failures war itself was widely blamed, on the ground that peoples frenzied with fury cannot immediately on the cessation of hostilities display the magnanimity, rationality, and co-operativeness needful for the establishment of world order, democratic institutions, social and economic stability.

Many of the leading literary and ecclesiastical figures in England became pacifist—Bertrand Russell, Vera Brittain, A. A. Milne, Aldous Huxley, Canon Raven, and Dick Shepherd. They were joined

WHAT DID YOU DIE FOR?

in the United States by Archibald MacLeish and Harry Emerson Fosdick, who put himself on record as resolved never to bless another war.[2] The churches resolved to make every effort to see that there should never be another war to bless. With characteristic ardor the churches of the United States embarked on a crusade for peace. Three ways were tried: the first looked to the State to eliminate war, the second looked to the Church to excommunicate war, the third looked to the community to find an alternative to war.

War No More

The first strove progressively to eliminate war by reduction in armaments. To this end a four-power treaty was signed in 1921 by the United States, Great Britain, Japan, and France. It was really not disarmament but only proportional limitation in accord with the actual *status quo*. It applied only to naval construction and set ratios at five for the United States, five for Great Britain, three for Japan, and 1.7 for France. The United States gained heavily because, by agreement, she now equaled Britannia in the ruling of the waves. The new treaty abrogated the alliance between Great Britain and Japan, and thus relieved the United States of concern as to the Pacific, where, however, Japan was to have a free hand. The greatest renunciation was made by Britain, depleted by the war and in no mood to combat the pretensions of the United States. Already the shift in the center of power was becoming apparent. The point here is that this and subsequent attempts at disarmament were motivated by revulsion against war. Yet they never really amounted to disarmament and exhibited no genuine sacrifices or even risks on behalf of peace.[3]

A few years later, in 1929, an attempt was made to outlaw war by treaties between sovereign states. The Kellogg-Briand treaties, called the Paris Pact, bore the signatures of fifty-nine nations. A peal of jubilation arose from the American Protestants, and the historic peace churches were pleased to see governments actually ready to beat swords into plowshares. In a few years the resolutions of church bodies made it apparent that they did not wish to see all swords converted to agriculture. The phrase used in the treaties was "renunciation of war as an instrument of national policy." Precisely what did this mean? That a nation should not defend itself, or merely that it should not use war to enforce its will by aggression? Baptists, Methodists, and Presbyterians, among others, made plain that they did not propose to outlaw a war of defense or a war of ideals. In other words, the just war and the crusade were still intact.[4]

A second line of attack was religious and moral rather than political, relying on the actions of churches and not of governments. A number of Protestant churches recorded their unwillingness *as churches* to bless any war whatever, but leaving to individual members the decision as to conscientious objection, with full support of the church either way. Yet traces of the old alignments were still visible. In 1934 more than twenty thousand of the Protestant clergy were asked this question: "Do you believe that the churches of America should now go on record as refusing to sanction or support any future war?" The affirmative list was headed by one of the historic peace churches, that of the Brethren. The Methodists and the Disciples were near the top; the Congregationalists and the Unitarians in the middle; the Baptists, the Presbyterians, the Episcopalians, and the Lutherans in descending order at the bottom. As for the Catholics some were doubtful whether in modern times the conditions of the just war could be realized.

A third approach to the elimination of war was an effort to discover alternate techniques which could be employed by the world community for the settlement of disputes between nations. One technique was the erection of an international machinery of justice comparable to that already existing within the framework of well-ordered states. The World Court and the League of Nations received warm support from many churches, in the hope that they would achieve this end.

Another alternative to war, which commended itself especially to Christian pacifists, was the attempt to resolve conflicts by the exercise of nonviolent pressure. The example and the comparative success of Gandhi in the interval between the two world wars gave strong stimulus to the exploration of the power of nonviolence.

The Assault on Liberal Optimism

A drastic shift in attitude was underway. It was rooted in the doctrine of man. All of the programs for the elimination of war rested on the assumption that man is good enough and wise enough to abolish war. Such confidence received a succession of shattering blows. Karl Barth in Europe revived the Calvinist picture of human depravity, and Hitler arose to illustrate it. The year before the Nazi accession to power in 1933, Reinhold Niebuhr in the United States struck at naïve optimism by reviving in *Moral Man and Immoral Society* (1932) the essential features of Luther's tract *On Civil Government*. Luther had drawn a distinction between the little flock of real Christians and the mass of nominal Christians. The one could dispense with control, the other must be ruled by the sword. The masses would never be genuinely Christian, hence the sword could never be eliminated. Niebuhr's distinction was not quite the same. He did not segregate believers into true and nominal Christians. His point was rather that the very best of Christians act differently as private individuals and as members of large groups. The moral in both cases was that in public relations conflict would never be overcome. Consequently restraint would always be necessary. The only questions were how much restraint and how it should be exercised. Here Niebuhr was scornful of the outlawry of war and much more respectful of Gandhi's nonco-operation, but insistent that nonco-operation was not nonresistance. It may have definite moral advantages because it can be more readily controlled, does not so easily alienate the one against whom it is directed, and leaves the door open for a rational agreement. It may succeed under some circumstances, though not under others, and it does not preclude recourse to violent action if the nonviolent should fail. The conclusion was that war should not be ruled out as an ultimate recourse.

On the Brink

Hitler came into power in 1933 and initiated the sequence which ran directly to the Second World War. Whether his advent could have been prevented, and whether after his accession the war could have been averted are still questions for rueful speculation. The Treaty of Versailles was certainly not as magnanimous and wise as the Treaty of Vienna. Germany was saddled with immense reparations on the ground that she was solely responsible for the outbreak of the conflict. When the historians in the Allied countries later came to the frank avowal that this was not the case, the treaty was not in consequence revised. Actually, of course, the reparations were never paid in full, but if only there could have been an open remission with a disavowal of the accusation of sole guilt, how gratifying would have been the effect upon the German public mind, instead of the course actually taken of continuing the demands for reparations and financing the payments by American aid! [5]

Another step which might have forestalled Gehenna would have been sincerity in the matter of disarmaments. The Treaty of Versailles exacted disarmament of Germany and promised disarmament on the part of the Allies. The exaction was executed, the promise not fulfilled. Repeated disarmament conferences were abortive. In 1931 Bruning pleaded that if he could return to Germany with a real pledge of disarmament on the part of the Allies, he could overcome the Nazis. He was sent back empty-handed, to be removed by Von Hindenburg and replaced by Von Papen—who said that Germany had "struck out the word pacifism from her vocabulary. . . . Pacifism cannot understand the old German aversion to death on a mattress." Hitler understood it. When he followed swiftly, he still claimed that what Germany demanded of the powers was equality in the matter of armaments. It could be achieved by universal disarmament—and this he would accept—or by the rearmament of Germany. If the Allies would not agree to the one, he would grasp the other. This he did. [6]

Even so, perhaps he might have been contained had not England and France each hobbled the technique of the other. England wished to let Germany up, France to hold her down. Had Germany been permitted to rise by voluntary grant rather than in response to pressures, Hitler would have been deprived of his most persuasive talking point. On the other hand, had there been prompt intervention before Germany was rearmed, Hitler might have been held in leash. But England impeded France, and France, England. They were all playing the game of the balance of power, and it did not balance.[7]

Hitler sought the unification of Europe by the revival, with even greater brutality, of the way of Napoleon; unification by the hegemony of one power. This England was bound to resist, because it would destroy the balance. Hitler claimed that Germany needed room to live. He set out to get it by robbing Russia and by expelling and in the end exterminating the Jews. Never has there been a more unmitigated exemplification of the slogan of Lord Fisher, "Ruthless, Relentless, Remorseless." [8]

The outbreak of the Second World War in 1939 demanded quick decision by governments, peoples, and churches as to what should be done and what could be justified. In England, endorsement of the war was compounded of the resolve to defend the nation and the empire and a determination to protect the minorities of Europe and the decencies of life. British pacifists were driven to a re-examination of their position, and not a few changed their minds. Maude Royden summarized the new mood by citing the word of a man who said, "I used to be a pacifist. I know now that I would rather go to hell for fighting than have my son brought up to think that it was funny to kick a Jew in the stomach." [9]

Canada joined with Britain in the struggle. The United States, spared by her geographic location and political independence from immediate decision, watched and waited, trying to decide where her interest and her duty lay. The government of the United States moved stage by stage toward intervention in Europe and in the East. Neutrality legislation was repealed so that the opponents of the Axis could buy munitions on a cash and carry basis. Supplementary lend-lease was subsequently introduced. Economic pressure on Japan commenced with the freezing of Japanese assets in the United States as early as July 25, 1941. Trade restrictions were progressively applied until December 2, 1941, five days before Pearl Harbor, the *New York Times* cited the report of the National Industrial Conference Board that "Japan has been cut off from about 75 per cent of her normal imports as a result of the Allied blockade." Before hostilities were declared we were already so nearly embarked on an undeclared war that the *Saturday Evening Post* on May 24, 1941, revised its noninterventionist editorial policy without retracting a single argument in its favor, on the sole ground that the country was by this time too involved for retreat. "For the truth is that the only way now to avoid the shooting, if it has not already begun, is to repudiate the government."

The Drift Toward War

Public opinion in the United States was torn between sympathy for Great Britain and the desire to stay out of the war. A Gallup poll in February, 1941, registered 85 per cent in favor of abstention, yet 68 per cent would aid Britain even though war might be the outcome. The opinion in the churches was not far different from that in the country at large. The prevailing sentiment was for staying out of the war but there was no absolute unanimity. The Episcopalians were ready to support Britain; the Presbyterians were of divided counsels; the Disciples were noninterventionist; while the Methodists and the Congregationalists still reflected the strong pacifist sentiment of the previous decade. Curiously, while the other Protestant churches were veering toward war the Lutherans were detaching themselves from their traditional adherence to the doctrine of the just war. As for the Catholics, a poll of 54,000 students disclosed 97 per cent opposed to our entry into the conflict.

Some of those who opposed participation contended like John Haynes Holmes that the issues were not sufficiently clear because the Allies bore a heavy burden of guilt for the outbreak of hostilities. Others held the cause to be just but the means inappropriate. One is not to suppose, said they, that "after a long-drawn-out orgy of indiscriminate killing . . . people may be expected to think rationally and act justly." [10]

This entire analysis was most stoutly opposed by a group who urged at first all aid to Britain short of war and in time came to favor even military intervention. They rejected the characterization of the war as merely a struggle between rival imperialisms. To speak in such terms was to strain out the British gnat and swallow the German camel. Granted that all were tainted with sin, that all stood in need of repentance, nevertheless there were still relative rights and relative wrongs, to distinguish between which was of extreme importance. To be sure, the war might not establish democracy, liberty, and a just and enduring peace. The only thing war can ever do is to restrain outrageous villainy and give a chance to build again. A victory of the Allies would ensure none of the ideal ends which Christians entertained, but a victory for the Axis would preclude them. And an Axis victory could be prevented only by military strength. To suppose that the patient endurance of evil would soften the heart of the wolf was sheer nonsense. To talk of influencing history by bearing the cross was to forget that the crucified is blotted out of the historical process. If a pacifist wished to take his stand upon an absolute, regardless of consequences, he was on logically impregnable ground, but let him not pretend by his stand to determine the course of events, and above all let him not prate of the cross when by his very abstention from the struggle he was not so much bearing the cross as fastening it upon the shoulders of others.[11]

All such discussion was cut short in the United States by Pearl Harbor. As usual in war, pacifism receded, though the recession was far from complete. Three thousand ministers in the United States enrolled in the Fellowship of Reconciliation to continue their pacifist witness, and the membership of the society increased both in Britain and in the United States after the outbreak of hostilities. By and large, however, concerted opposition to the war had folded up. The main reason was that the Japanese attack had solidified the country. Many Americans who had opposed intervention in Europe saw no recourse after Pearl Harbor but to defeat Japan and Hitler too, since he had followed suit. The Axis Powers certainly did their best to provide for the United Nations all the normal conditions of the just war. Many former pacifists argued that under the circumstances the best way to further the peace was to finish the war.

No Crusade

If pacifism largely collapsed, its place was not taken by a crusade in which the knight could fight without qualm, assured that the cause was holy, that God was with him and Christ beside him, and that victory would be a triumph of the cross. Such a mood recurred but slightly this time and chiefly in secular quarters. Practically every church pronouncement was replete with the note of contrition.

A lone crusader like Stanley High was somewhat irritated that "prayers for use in wartime fairly reek with penitence, and the sons of God are being sent forth to war clad only in sackcloth." Paul Ramsay reminded the mournful warrior that he had better not "blubber over his gun-powder" but "get on with the shooting." [12] Such exhortations only reinforced the observation of Willard Sperry that "we cannot recover either for better or for worse the feelings of World War I for the needs of World War II"; we are no longer wielding "the sword of the Lord and Gideon." The English, he said, at the outbreak of the war thought of themselves sometimes as a patient about to undergo a dangerous operation and sometimes as the doctor who, by a slip of the scalpel "might infect himself with the poison in the bloodstream of the patient." [13] Either way the attitude was sober, matter-of-fact, and entirely unsentimental. No more poignant exhibition of the prevailing mood could be found than in the words of a Canadian minister who said, "this is the saddest war in history. We are not jubilant, but infinitely dejected. There is not a jot or atom of hatred in our hearts. . . . We expect nothing from this war except that everything sweet and precious will be crushed out of life for most of us. Nevertheless, we could do no other." [14]

The Just War Through a Glass Darkly

If pacifism and the crusade are excluded, the only position remaining in historic Christian thought is the ethic of the just war. The traditional concept of the just war had been subject to so much criticism, and the incompatibility of its conditions with modern war so cogently displayed that some Christians who rejected the other two positions could not find a refuge here, however. Hence, the quest for a fourth position was undertaken by the *Christian Century*. With extraordinary sensitivity to the pressure of the contemporary, this journal responded to the impact of the times. All the confusion inherent in the situation itself was vividly sensed: the all-engulfing quality of modern war which draws to itself every constructive effort despite the unwillingness of the contributor; the irrational character of a struggle which embraces the globe though no people desire it; the futility of the effort which vitiates the use of power for ideal ends; the undisciplined quality of a force which brooks no restrictions impeding victory; the impersonal character of a fight in which combatants strike invisible foes; the undiscriminating nature of weapons which smash alike arsenals and cathedrals and shatter equally troop trains and air-raid shelters filled with children; the blindness of a strife, the precise reasons for which may not become clear until ten years after its termination; the complexity of a war where rival imperialisms, nationalistic interests, and clashing ideologies crisscross inextricably on a loom shaken by shifting alliances, so that the solemn pronouncements of one day appear ironic to the next. In such a struggle, the *Christian Century* could discover no meaning and no morality. This was not a just war; it was just war. We were in the war, and none of us could get out. We should have to see it through in a spirit of inexpressible grief.

This abdication of morality was due to concussion. When full consciousness returned, the just-war theory was revived in terms of the edge of justice. The case was well stated by Reinhold Niebuhr, who protested against allowing contrition to obliterate moral distinctions. "We do not find it particularly impressive," he wrote, "to celebrate one's sensitive conscience by enlarging upon all the well-known evils of our western world and equating them with the evils of the totalitarian systems. It is just as important for Christians to be discriminating in their judgments, as for them to recognize the element of sin in all human endeavors." [15] John Bennett protested very strongly against making the soldiers regard themselves merely as "victims of a common tragedy or of God's judgment. It would make a vast difference to many of them if they could know that on what they do depends the possibility of justice and freedom of men everywhere." [16]

The Ultimate Degradation of Warfare

In the meantime the moral problem was being accentuated by the culmination of a process which had been underway for a century and a half, namely the progressive degradation of warfare since the eighteenth century. There was nothing essentially new in this development, but rather a reversion to the methods of warfare which had prevailed in the centuries preceding the eighteenth. Nor was the subsequent decline due to any deterioration in Western man. On the contrary, the nineteenth and twentieth centuries have seen a great increase in humanitarian feeling manifest in civilian life. The eighteenth century was brutal in its treatment of criminals, underlings, and unfortunates; in its amusements; and in its sports. The modern age spends incredible sums to reclaim the reclaimable and to keep alive the irreclaimable. There has emerged an ever widening discrepancy between sensitivity in civilian relations and callousness in military behavior.

Coleridge already observed it in the very last years of the eighteenth century. Upbraiding his fellow Englishmen, he wrote that they were unmindful of their mercies,

> Thankless too for peace . . .
> Secure from actual warfare, we have loved
> To swell the war-whoop, passionate for war!
>
> . . . .
>   Boys and girls
> And women, that would groan to see a child
> Pull off an insect's leg, all read of war,
> The best amusement for our morning meal.[17]

In the early twentieth century the Baroness Von Suttner observed it. As she was crossing the Atlantic a vessel was sighted in flames. The ship on which she was a passenger at once raced to the rescue. The burning vessel proved to be a derelict with none aboard. Had there been so much as one passenger, what pains, what risk would have been taken to save him! But when the next morning the Marconi (the wireless) brought word of a blood bath at Port Arthur or Mukden, it was only an interesting piece of news.[18]

The war of etiquette prevalent in the eighteenth century is thought by some to have been broken down by the struggle in the New World with the Indians, whose code the white man adopted. One may doubt, as a matter of historical fact, whether the Indians could teach the white man anything on the score of cruelty and treachery. The point is rather that when the French, the English, and the Spaniards fought each other on the terrain of the new world, and with Indian allies, they no longer lined up and said, "You shoot first, dear colleague." The methods of the savages were taken over by the civilized and turned against each other.

Another stage in the brutalization was marked by the American Civil War, which differed from the European conflicts of the eighteenth century in two respects. In the first place, it was not organized under strong monarchs able to pay and control their troops. In the second place, to the eyes of the North it was a crusade. These two factors may have contributed to Sherman's use of the scorched earth technique in his march through Georgia. Said he, "War is hell," and the way for the enemy to avoid it is to surrender. In Europe the makers of modern Prussia were through with politeness. Clausewitz said, "To introduce into the philosophy of war a principle of moderation would be absurd. War is an act of violence pursued to the uttermost." [19]

The great change came through technology. New weapons precluded humanitarian restraint. The submarine could and did send out a wireless as to the location of a stricken vessel, but it lacked accommodation for the removal of the crew and passengers. Poisoned gas cannot be palliated. The blockade in the Middle Ages had been applied usually to cities from which non-combatants were sometimes permitted to withdraw before the commencement of the siege. Such permissions could not be granted when the whole of Germany was ringed around and the object was to break the war potential of the populace.

In an earlier age sea powers like England had never refrained from throwing cannon balls from ships into enemy ports, even though civilians were killed. How much more deadly was this procedure when the missile was released not from the sea but from the air! The First World War had seen the advent of the airplane. It was then used only to strike at troops and military installations. In the Second World War it came to be used to break the morale and the resistance of civilian populations. Strategic bombing was followed by obliteration bombing. The first step was taken by England as an extension of the principle of naval bombardment. This is not to forget that Hitler first bombed Warsaw and Rotterdam, where civilian populations were destroyed. His object was still strategic—to pave the way for the entry of invading troops rather than to shatter civilian morale.[20] Churchill, in January, 1940, stigmatized obliteration bombing as "a new and odious form of attack." President Roosevelt, in 1939, before the United States became involved in the war, addressed an appeal to the German and Polish governments in which he affirmed that "the ruthless bombing from the air of civilians in unfortified centers of population . . . has profoundly shocked the conscience of humanity. . . . I am therefore addressing this urgent appeal to every government to affirm its determination that its armed forces shall in no event and under no circumstances undertake bombardment from the air of civilian populations or unfortified cities." [21]

In May, 1940; only five months after Churchill's excoriation of "the new and odious form of attack," Britain, by an extension of her old naval policy, gave to an aerial warfare a new turn in the bombing of cities—no longer to facilitate the movement of troops, but to wreck the will to resist in the enemy population. Germany, in September, retaliated with attacks on Coventry and Birmingham. Churchill informed the House, in 1942, that Germany was to be subjected to "an ordeal, the like of which has never been experienced by any country." A year later he declared, "There are no sacrifices we will not make, no lengths of violence to which we will not go." [22]

Vera Brittain in her book *Seeds of Chaos* documented the havoc: "According to a member of the German Government Statistics Office

NEPTUNE'S ALLY

(THE FIRST LORD OF THE ADMIRALTY CALLS IN A NEW ELEMENT
TO REDRESS THE BALANCE OF THE OLD.)

Punch IN 1914 (MARCH 25) PICTURED WINSTON CHURCHILL AS
AEOLUS SUMMONING THE AIRPLANES TO THE AID OF NEPTUNE

THE DISHONOURS OF WAR

MARS: "I USED TO BE THE GOD OF BATTLE—NOT BUTCHERY."

Punch IN 1938 (JUNE 15) PORTRAYED MARS REFLECTING RUEFULLY
ON THE BARBARITIES OF AERIAL WARFARE

in Berlin, 1,200,086 German civilians were killed or reported missing, [most of them] believed killed in air raids from the beginning of the war up to October 1, says a Zurich message. The number of people bombed out and evacuated owing to air-raid danger was 6,953,000."

Concretely what this meant in human terms was described by a witness of the bombing of Berlin who reported: "It was nerve-shattering to see women, demented after the raids, crying continuously for their lost children, or wandering speechless through the streets with dead babies in their arms."

In Hamburg the heat was so intense that even in cellar shelters bodies were incinerated more completely than in the process of cremation. The hurricane of flame sucked to itself the oxygen from surrounding regions so that many who escaped the fire died of suffocation. Men, having greater power of resistance, suffered less than women and children. The loss of life at Hamburg was sixty times greater than at Coventry. To such wanton destruction—for even Churchill described the attacks only as an experiment not certain to achieve a military objective—some Britons were cynically indifferent. In one district a children's competition was organized for the best essay or poem on the target to be preferred for the bombs. Those more remote from the devastation in England were even more unfeeling with regard to the bombings in Germany. In distant Ontario a blockbuster was inscribed as "a Christmas card to the Reich." [23]

Nuclear Warfare

Then came the atom bomb. The eyewitness descriptions of the destruction, compounded at Hiroshima and Nagasaki by aftereffects, dwarfed even the accounts of the mass incinerations of Hamburg and Dresden. Ten years later Mrs. Hizume of Hiroshima reported:

"All of the houses were demolished. The crumbled walls and heaps of tiles stretched for many miles. Many people rushed from the centre. Their bodies were burnt. Their skin was hanging down like rags. Their faces were swollen to twice normal size. They were holding their hands to their breasts. They were walking, embracing one another and crying out with pain. Someone was walking, dragging something along. To my great surprise it was his intestines. His stomach was ripped open and it came out and he was dragging it along without knowing what he was doing. . . . My eldest daughter had only two slight wounds. . . . A month after the bombing she died. My second daughter had no wounds at all, but one day in July, *six years* after the explosion, she told me about pains in the throat and shoulder and she said she could not walk very well.

She died six days after having been taken ill. "It is more than ten years since the war was over, but the sufferings from the bomb have not yet been cured." [24]

The world was shocked. Herman Hagedorn wrote:

In a splendor beyond any that man has known, the new age we have claimed came to birth.
The brightness of its drawing was the fierce shining of three suns together at noonday, shedding, for golden seconds, such beauty over the earth as poets, painters, philosophers and saints have imagined and striven in vain to reveal to man in symbols and parables.
And we used it to destroy a hundred thousand men, women and children.
.   .   .   .
What have we done, my country, what have we done?
Our fathers knew greatness.
What shall the shrunken soul do to fill out and be itself again?
Our fathers knew mercy.
What shall the wet stick do to burn once more? [25]

The A bomb has been followed by the H bomb. The test at Bikini affected twenty-three Japanese fishermen far beyond the range of estimated radioactivity. They returned to land and were hospitalized; a month after, radiation still appeared in their urine. One died after six months. The United States apologized, indemnified, and prepared to test again.

In the meantime public feeling in this country has become so narcotized that the sale of a soft drink can be advanced by calling it a Hydrogen Bomb Ice Cream Soda.

Chapter 14

Past and Present

———

WHEN we come to appraise the traditional Christian positions with regard to the ethic of war we must bear in mind that the situations in confrontation with which they were originally conceived no longer exist. The development of technology and the dehumanizing of war have progressively excluded middle courses and narrowed the range of choice. Two colossi now face each other each possessed of the power to paralyze the other if not to liquidate the globe. Against nuclear destruction there is no military defense. The experts are agreed that intercontinental ballistic missiles cannot be completely intercepted and only a few H bombs would suffice to incinerate our cities. The Russians by a surprise attack could destroy, according to some estimates, as many as a hundred million persons in the United States. Other estimates regard these figures as an exaggeration and would halve the sum, but even fifty million exceeds the population of Sodom and Gomorrah.

Others again reassure us that even so we should not be disabled. They point out that obliteration bombing against civilian populations did not destroy the military potential of either Germany or Japan and now that we are forewarned, as they were not, we can take preventative measures either by the dispersal of our cities or by reverting to the rabbit stage of civilization of living in holes in the earth. We are not to forget, however, that the balance of weapons is not static. Every new instrument of attack is followed by a new device for defense, and if it is successful there is then a new instrument of attack. When the atomic submarine succeeded in cruising beneath the seven seas and emerging undetected in Boston harbor, the cry was immediately for a counter contrivance, because the assumption is that any newly invented weapon of attack will soon be in the possession of the enemy. We must then invent a defense which will also soon be in the hands of the enemy, and then we must both devise a new means of attack. In the present instance should we succeed in circumventing nuclear annihilation the enemy will shift to bacteriological warfare, which is harder to ward off, because it can be directed not only against men but also against cattle and crops. There may also be a reversion to poison gas. The public, inarticulately aware of all this, is actually not going underground, but, convinced that the only defense is massive retaliation, is content to strew the floors of the Florida seas with billions of dollars' worth of debris from experimental missiles. We are preparing ourselves likewise to retaliate with bacteriological weapons with regard to which extensive research is being conducted at Porton in England, Suffield in Canada, and Fort Detrick in the United States. In the meantime advance in technology is continually restricting our choices. Some of the military experts are now telling us that a surprise nuclear attack would incapacitate us for counterattack. Massive retaliation in that case is already obsolete, and the only recourse is preventative war, to which thus far our government has been unwilling to commit itself.[1]

Some again seek to assuage our fears by the assurance that despite nuclear weapons war can be limited. As a matter of fact there have been seventeen limited wars since the Second World War. With this in mind a study committee of the World Council of Churches advocated among the nations "the development of that discipline . . . which will enable them to stop, even if necessary on the enemy's terms, rather than embark on an all out war." [2] What this statement overlooks is that limited war is possible only within the framework of unlimited war, unless, of course, both sides abandon major weapons. If one side only renounces nuclear arms a war can be limited only if the better armed does not regard the issue as crucial. Hanson Baldwin has well observed that if war is to be kept limited the enemy must know that if he exceeds the limit we shall "clobber" him.[3] To do this we must have the full panoply of nuclear arms in reserve and we must be willing to use them. Kissinger, who has done most to popularize the idea of limited war, recognizes that it must not be "our only strategy. We must maintain at all times an adequate retaliatory force and not shrink from using it if our survival is threatened." [4] Some Christians suggest that we might achieve our end by bluff.[5] We should be prepared to retaliate, but resolved not to retaliate, but we should not let the enemy know that we would not retaliate. This sounds like the practice of a Quaker merchant of the eighteenth century who mounted on his ship wooden cannons. There was, however, this difference. His cannon could not shoot. The sum of the matter is that we have reached an impasse where the only feasible military defense is massive retaliation, or if that be obsolete, then preventative war. It we reject this possibility the alternative is unilateral disarmament.

For this our nation is not ready. Neither are our churches. All exhibit divided counsels with an increasing readiness to follow the lead of the state. Fear of the expansion of Communism, on the one hand, and on the other, recoil before the ghastliness of the only deterrent available, have prompted them to avoid unequivocal statements.

At first obliteration bombing elicited shocked protests from Protestants and Catholics. In the United States a group of twenty-eight Protestant churchmen, all pacifists, issued a summary of Vera Brittain's book with an appeal to Christian people to

examine themselves concerning their participation in this carnival of death. . . . In our time, as never before, war is showing itself in its logical colors. In the First World War, some shreds of the rules of war were observed to the end. Laws of war are intrinsically paradoxical; but so far as they went, they bore witness to the survival of some fragments of a Christian conscience among the combatants. But today these fragments are disappearing. The contesting parties pay little heed to the former decencies and chivalries, save among their own comrades.[6]

The *Christian Century* commented: "If the war goes on, with obliter-

ation bombing continuing to wipe out whole regions and populations, it is quite possible that in the hour of triumph the victors will
find that they have created so much destruction, so much hate, so
much misery, so much despair that the very well-springs of Occidental
life have been poisoned not only for the vanquished but the victors
also." [7]

For the Catholics in this country Father Ford, in 1944, came out
with an article on "The Morality of Obliteration Bombing" in which
he declared that the moral line is to be drawn between precision
bombing of specific military objectives and indiscriminate area bombing with vast killing of noncombatants. The justification for such
warfare, said he, is extremely flimsy. "Not merely the conscience of
humanity, not merely international law, but the teaching of Catholic
theologians for centuries, the voice of the Church speaking through
her Councils and through her hierarchy and through the Supreme
Pontiff down to the present day, uniformly insist on the innocence
and consequent immunity of civil populations." His conclusion was
that "Obliteration bombing, as defined, is an immoral attack on the
rights of the innocent. It includes a direct intent to do them injury.
Even if this were not true, it would still be immoral, because no proportionate cause could justify the evil done; and to make it legitimate
would soon lead the world to the immoral barbarity of total war.
The voice of the Pope and the fundamental laws of the charity of
Christ confirm this condemnation." [8]

The use of atomic weapons as instruments of obliteration bombing
caused a new shock and brought forth renewed protest. Protestant
churchmen in the United States declared that even if the attack
could have been defended on grounds of military necessity:

We have never agreed that a policy affecting the present well-being of
millions of non-combatants and the future relationships of whole peoples
should be decided finally on military grounds. . . . In the light of present
knowledge, we are prepared to affirm that the policy of obliteration
bombing as actually practiced in World War II, culminating in the use
of atomic bombs against Japan, is not defensible on Christian premises.[9]

A footnote revealed, however, that some were unwilling to renounce the restraint of aggression by the fear of reprisals.

The discussion has continued with a tendency to retrench. In 1950 a new Protestant commission rendered this judgment:

> If atomic weapons or other weapons of parallel destructiveness are used against us or our friends in Europe or Asia, we believe that it could be justifiable for our government to use them with all possible restraint to prevent the triumph of an aggressor. We come to this conclusion with troubled spirits but any other conclusion would leave our own people and the people of other nations open to continuing devastating attack and to probable defeat.

In a dissenting comment Professor Calhoun observed that the "Christian conscience in wartime seems to have chiefly the effect . . . of making Christians do reluctantly what military necessity requires." [10]

In 1947 the Catholic Association for International Peace no longer visited upon atomic bombing the condemnation which Father Ford had pronounced against obliteration bombing with conventional weapons. The author assumed a situation in which the destruction of the enemies' cities would be *"absolutely necessary."* If, for example, the enemy had invaded our shores and could be repelled only by an attack on his cities as the source of his productive capacity then "a proportionate reason" would exist for using our bombs on his cities "to preserve our country and our whole remaining people from utter enslavement." [11]

More recently Cardinal Ottaviani has declared *bellum omnino interdicendum,* war is to be entirely interdicted, by which he meant that modern war is incampatible with the just war. He stressed the principle of proportionate damage. A just war is one in which the foreseeable good exceeds the predictable evil. In modern war the damage is entirely unpredictable. The popes have neither confirmed nor repudiated this statement of the cardinal. [12]

When the pope does not speak and the World Council contents itself with no more than a statement of the dilemma, [13] the individual Christian is left to make his own decision. As one among the multitude in this extremity I will now proceed to my own analysis and conclusion.

Prior Assumptions

First, however, certain presuppositions must be declared as to man, God, and morals. If man by his nature or destiny is doomed to strife, war cannot be eliminated and modern war cannot be mitigated.

As to the nature of man and his terrestrial destiny history has something to say. The picture is mixed. When man ate of the tree of the knowledge of good and evil he became capable of rising above the angels or of sinking lower than the brutes. He has been guilty of bestiality, cruelty, and sadism. He has also exhibited nobility, self-sacrifice, heroism, and martyrdom. Man in the aggregate has been continuously engaged in wars large and small and yet has made notable achievements by way of peace in limited times and areas. There have been examples of peace by conquest—the *Pax Romana*—of peace by concord as between the principalities in the Middle Ages, the Italian city-states in the Renaissance, the modern national states in the eighteenth and nineteenth centuries, and most notably between the United States and Canada with an unfortified and unguarded frontier. There has been peace by federation as in the case of the Swiss and the United States. No one of these instances exhibits perfection. Rome had occasionally to subdue revolts. The Middle Ages, the Renaissance, and the eighteenth and nineteenth centuries could be called peaceful only in comparison with our own time. Federation did not prevent civil conflicts in Switzerland at the time of the Reformation or between the American states in the Civil War. Nevertheless these periods were less lethal than our own. If it be said that the past does not warrant hope for Utopia the reply may be that without achieving Utopia we should be vastly better off could we but recover the lost Atlantis.

If we consider Christian man operating through the Church the record is again mixed. The Church has promoted peace and fomented wars. The reason is partly the divergence of view with regard to the ethical implications of the gospel. In part, however, it is due to the abandonment of the gospel through coalescence with culture. The Christian has simply done what his neighbors were doing and has so far compartmentalized his religion as to be unaware of the discrepancy. Thus churchmen have shared in the enslavement and extermination of the aborigines. In other instances the instigation to war on the part of the Church has arisen from the perversion of the noblest in the Gospels. The concern for justice has led to cruelty toward those deemed unjust, and love, untempered by respect, has issued in meddlesomeness to the point of using the stake to save souls. Yet, when the full indictment is in, one is not to forget that the Church has never failed to pray *dona nobis pacem,* and in our own day has made and is making valiant efforts to avert the holocaust.

Some there are who take a gloomy view of man's predictable behavior not because his heart is bad but because his hands are tied. Determinism exercises a persistent lure. A contemporary historian commenting on Churchill's reference to the Second World War as "an unnecessary war" remarks: "Churchill probably would not deny, however, that there is an overriding necessity in the course of history, grounded not so much in political events as in the moral and intellectual fiber of nations and men." [14] This observation is unquestionably sound if it means that a nation frenzied by war is scarcely equal to the magnanimity requisite to prevent a recurrence. The statement is true if it means that a given decision or series of decisions may set up an ineluctable sequence from which there is no turning back. George Kennan has said it well in his comment on what led to Pearl Harbor:

I suspect that in the developments leading to World War II in the Pacific there must have been a dividing line between the phase when something hopeful could still have been accomplished by our own efforts and the phase when circumstances were beyond repair—the point at which sheer tragedy overtook human frailty as the determinant of our misfortunes. But I cannot promise you that there was such a point, and I certainly cannot tell you where it lay.[15]

The author avows his ignorance as to the location of the point of no return, but concedes that there may have been an anterior point; this concession is enough to destroy determinism.

Certainly history does not support the view of a necessary recurrence of wars in a cyclical pattern. Sorokin's graph of the frequency of wars exhibits no periodicity, no predictability. There has never

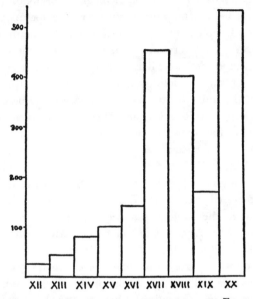

MAGNITUDE BY CASUALTIES OF THE WARS OF EUROPE
(FRANCE, GREAT BRITAIN, AUSTRIA-HUNGARY, RUSSIA)

been a period without some war somewhere, but there has been great fluctuation in the frequency and magnitude of wars.[16]

Admittedly the picture is not encouraging. The most disturbing observation is that social change is slow, and we cannot afford to be slow. Furthermore if the future is not to be vastly worse than the past it must be vastly better. To pass from the Swiss and American federations to the union of the world, the abandonment of nationalism, the surrender of sovereignty, the union of peoples of diverse faiths and cultural patterns—from the kraal to the Kremlin and the Pentagon—requires a social adjustment as great as the technological advance from the javelin to the H bomb. Man may not be equal to it. Perhaps we are so trapped by our previous mistakes and crimes that we can only play out the drama to its tragic end. We do not know. But history does not preclude hope.

When we turn from man to God theological presuppositions appear at first glance to be irrelevant. From every theological position divergent ethical applications have been deduced. Theism undergirds alike pacifism and the crusade. Atheism has been the creed of the occasional pacifist Bertrand Russell and the militant revolutionary Lenin. Humanism may solidify humanity in order to frustrate the harshness of the universe, and again humanism may become crusading against a foe devoid of humanity. Among theists the fatherhood of God entails for some the brotherhood of man, but for others brotherhood is restricted to the elect. Belief in immortality has deterred bloodshed on the ground that premature death would prejudice the lot of the soul in the hereafter, but the argument has also been reversed because the death of the body cannot hurt the soul. Appeal to the Bible is not determinative. Some look to the Moses who slew the Egyptian and some to the Moses who for the sake of his people asked to be blotted out of the book of life. Some imitate the Christ upon the cross, and some the Christ on the rainbow at the judgment day. The expectation of the speedy coming of the Lord has led some to quietism, others to revolution to hasten the coming. The appeal to Christian love does not settle the case, because if God be love, then love and killing cannot be incompatible, since God in the end terminates every life, and often prematurely. The irrelevance of theology may be inferred from the fact that when a theologian, after an elaborate exposition of his principles, comes up with a program of political action it is one which a secularist can endorse.

This is not to say that theology is irrelevant, but only that agreement on a given course of action may be possible on the basis of varying assumptions. The assumptions are not unimportant and, if circumstances alter, may lead to divergence. More to the point is this, that theological assumptions are not so ultimate as to be solely determinative for ethics. Morals have to do with men, and men have to take each other into account whether or no there be a God. Any theology which justifies the sacrifice of Isaac, the burning of Servetus, or the incineration of a hundred million persons in an act of massive retaliation has gone wrong somewhere along the line.

Among the necessary assumptions for a Christian ethic as to war and peace the most fundamental is the goodness of life. This affirmation is implied in the Christian doctrine of creation. God made man. God made man in his own image. God saw that his work was good. God saw that it is not good for man to be alone and gave to him a helpmate and told them to be fruitful and multiply. The denial of the goodness of life in Gnosticism and Manicheanism has been emphatically rejected by the Church. Life is good. But is life absolutely sacred? Certainly one is not to regard one's own life as worthy to be preserved at any cost. "He that loses his life shall save it." Neither is the indefinite continuance of man on this planet the chief end of creation, for in the apocalyptic denouement the present order is to pass away. The survival of man is neither to be despised nor to be inordinately cherished.

May man take life? In the biological realm he has to. There life lives from life, and man cannot live unless he consume either animal or vegetable life. He must destroy germs and the carriers of germs— flies, fleas, mosquitoes, and rats. Schweitzer set up the principle of reverence for life and averred that "ethical man shatters no ice crystal, tears no leaf, breaks no flower, crushes no insect." But Schweitzer at the same time recognized that man must kill to live. Yet in killing he should be remorseful. "A good conscience is an innovation of the devil." [17] Why should man feel remorse for the unavoidable? Why might he not rather blame God for such necessities? To eschew wanton killing is certainly sound, but reverence for life compels some killing, for without killing there can be no life.

This applies to the lower orders. But may man kill man? God obviously takes the life of man, but God may do so because he gives

239

life. The creature is not to usurp the office of the Creator. This is the principle on which our hospitals are conducted, and there we exhaust every resource of medical skill to keep life going even at a vegetative level, whereas in war we squander the choicest of our youth.

The distinction, we are told, lies here, that life ceases to be sacred when it menaces life. Life may be taken to protect life. The plea is not specious and was pointedly posed in recent years for a divinity student who at the outbreak of the Second World War declined professional exemption and refused to register. In consequence he served a term in the penitentiary. After his release and the completion of his ministerial training, he went out as a missionary to India and arrived at the time when the Hindus were massacring the Moslems. The latter were seeking only to escape but at the very railway stations were mowed down by the Hindu police. Corpses were piled up by the thousands and were carried away in trucks. Two occurrences contributed to the restoration of order. The first was the assassination of Gandhi, which sobered the Hindus and demonstrated the reality of "soul force." The second was the arrival of government troops ready, if need be, to fire upon the Hindus. This missionary conscientious objector said that he had reached the point where he would prefer martial law to sheer chaos.

In this situation the restoration of order might have taken some lives. To justify such action means that one does not subscribe to an absolute nonresistance. It means that the command to turn the other cheek is not an absolute when it is somebody else's cheek. It means that the command "Thou shalt not kill" is also not an absolute. It means that the police protection which Paul accepted is not ruled out. To concede all of this is not to justify war, however, because war is not an act of protection, except incidentally. Primarily it is self-vindication without due process of law. Those Christian troops who came to halt the Hindus were intrinsically policemen, acting not in their own cause and with no intent other than to restrain violence. Under such circumstances incidentally the amount of violence they would have to exercise would be minimal. Men do not wage implac-able warfare against those who are not seeking to harm them. In the quelling of riots tear gas commonly suffices. Here technology has assisted the reduction of violence. There is a further difference in that the numbers involved were fewer than in war, and therefore the Christian ideal of handling offenders as individuals with an eye to reclamation could be more nearly achieved. One of the most serious indictments of modern war is that it deals not with men but with millions.

The question may be raised as to what is to be done in a frontier situation where no police force exists. Are vigilantes then justified? Here one observes that in history the establishment of orderly gov-ernment has been achieved by the coincident operation of two forces, on the one hand by the consolidation of power and on the other by the renunciation of power. Kings have built up monarchical author-ity and have suppressed baronial feuds and highway brigandage. Monks at the same time have given an example of living in accord with a different scale of values, renouncing much of that for which men fight. One is tempted to say with Luther that God operates in history with a left hand and a right. The first is the consolidation of power, the second is the relinquishment of power. Note that on the frontier the achievement of orderly government was not so much the work of the vigilantes as of men who came to see that the only way to end disorder was voluntarily to remove the gun from the chimney piece and the revolver from the holster. Those in recent years who have argued that the only way to win world government was first to defeat all of the opponents of world government may come to see that a surer way is the voluntary renunciation of the means of self-defense.

When we turn from the view of man and God to a consideration of morals we may spell out the ethical implications of these assumptions, but our position cannot well be deemed Christian if it leave out of account the teaching of the New Testament. There are those today, even among Christians theologians, who are averse to an appeal either to its precepts or principles. The ethical teaching of Jesus is considered inapplicable because it was conditioned by the expectation of the speedy end of the age. This point has already been considered. Again an appeal to the sayings of the Master is excluded because we cannot be sure of what he said. If this be granted we may still turn to Paul, who also had the mind of Christ. The deepest source of reluctance arises from an aversion to all legalism so that even principles are rejected in favor of inspired hunches, and the Christian ethic comes to be devoid not only of predictability but even of coherence. By way of comment let it be said that one finds it difficult to call an ethic Christian which takes no account of the ethical precepts and principles of the New Testament. To be Christian an ethic must posit and seek to implement in proper balance love, justice, the integrity of the self, and the integrity of the other person—even should he be the enemy.

The Critique of the Tradition as to the Crusade

In the light of these assumptions we may now turn to an appraisal of the traditional positions. A beginning may be made with the crusade which is not simply to be brushed aside—as it so often is today by those whose primary objection is to enthusiasm of any sort. Such chastened sobriety precludes a crusade for peace as well as a crusading war! After all, there is something to ponder in the remark of R. H. Tawney, "War is either a crime or a crusade." It ought to be so overwhelmingly right as to be manifestly the will of God or else not right at all. One can think of wars which might fit the formula. Had there been a war for the sole purpose of saving the Jews, undertaken without reference to any national advantage for the participants, such a war, if any, might have been called holy. Had there been a war to save the Hungarians from suppression by Russia and only for that, one might have felt that the condition was fulfilled. But the Second World War was not undertaken to save the Jews, and the war for Hungary was never undertaken at all. One is thinking here in any case only of the intention, because in fact modern war could not have saved either. The Hungarians would have been incinerated in the explosion ignited by their defenders.

The crusade suffers from the assurance not to say the arrogance of all elitism. It is the war of a theocratically minded community which seeks to impose the pattern of the Church upon the world. The saints are to rule. They are the elite. One difficulty is to determine with any surety who are the elite—and to be sure that they will remain elite after having become elect. The crusade is furthermore dangerous because it breaks down such restraint as can be placed upon the carnage of war. The enemy being beyond the pale, the code of humanity collapses. The crusade is dangerous again because it impedes the making of a magnanimous peace. Those who have fought in a frenzy of righteousness against the enemies of God—or of the democratic way of life—are disposed to demand unconditional surrender, thus prolonging resistance by their refusal to state terms. The crusader is severely tempted to arbitrariness in the final settlement, for the mood of holiness leads to the punishment of war criminals by the victors under the fictitious trappings of impartial justice. At Nuremberg Field Marshall Keitel, Chief of the German staff, was hanged for carrying out the orders of a civilian government. That among those executed some had been guilty of violating the traditional code of war cannot be gainsaid, but why were not the Russians punished for the murder of some fifteen thousand Polish officers in the Katan Forest? Why was no action taken against Churchill for unleashing an aerial bombardment against Hamburg; or against Truman for use of atomic bombs without warning on Hiroshima and Nagasaki? This is not to say that they should all have been hanged, but rather that it were better had none been hanged. The victors in war cannot administer disinterested justice, and least of all is this possible in the case of a crusade.[18]

The point need not, however, be labored further because since the First World War there has been a revulsion against crusading. Christians who undertake to justify modern war do so through an attenuated version of the doctrine of the just war, which requires therefore a lengthier consideration.

As to the Just War

The first stipulation of the just-war theory is that the war must be conducted under the auspices of the state. As we have frequently seen, this theory confronts great difficulty when applied to a revolution, but this defect is not troublesome in the United States where revolution is relegated to the cult of the ancestors—except in the case of a revolt against our rivals, for we abet abroad what we suppress at home. Under the totalitarian states, however, the morality of tyrannicide has again become acute. Certainly one cannot withhold respect and admiration from those idealists who risked and gave their lives in the attempt to eliminate Hitler. Particularly tragic was the figure of Goerdeler who, while working with the conspirators, constantly exhorted them to avoid violence, hoping that Hitler might yet be open to persuasion. When the plot failed and the conspirators were caught, Goerdeler took full responsibility for the course from which he had sought to dissuade his associates. For months prior to his execution he ruminated in solitary confinement, with mingled feelings of regret and remorse over the plans which had failed and the method which should never have been attempted.[19] One finds it hard to pronounce any word of condemnation against those who acted in such complete self-effacement, but one may wonder whether, had they succeeded, they might not also have failed.

One of the prime requisites of the just-war theory is that the war shall be just on one side only. The determination of this point calls for an impartial court of judicature which does not and never has existed. Without it not even the information essential for a judgment is available. The intervention of the United Nations in the Korean conflict is frequently cited as an exception. Yet a decade later dispute continued as to whether the North or the South Koreans first crossed the line.[20] If ten years afterward the very facts are controverted how could they at the time have been self-evident?

Most Christian adherents of the just-war theory have given up the claim to exclusive justice, and now maintain only an edge of justice. One would not be disposed to confute this claim. In any war, victory for one side may be preferable to that of the other, but whether modern war can vindicate that edge of justice is another question and one of very great moment.

The protection of small states is the least contestable form of the edge of justice, provided of course that the protector is disinterested. We do well to remind ourselves that protection often imperils the protected. A historian of the Second World War made this statement: "An astonishing and ironic revelation regarding the campaign in Greece has been made since the war by the Greek Commander in Chief, General Papagos. The Greeks actually asked Britain not to send help, feeling that it would be too small to be effective but enough to attract Germans like a magnet. Britain insisted in order not to lose face." [21]

Again, any good which may be accomplished by intervention needs to be set over against the damage inflicted. In the case of Korea, here is the account of an eyewitness:

Some of these villages seemed to us of pure enchantment, the tiles of the roofs upcurled at eaves and corners like the toes of oriental slippers, while the poorer cottages lay under heavy grey thatches which seemed to embrace them. And in these villages, too, the women wore bright colours, crimson and the pale pink of watermelon flesh, and vivid emerald green, their bodies wrapped tightly to give them a tubular appearance, while mothers suckled their young from full breasts swinging free beneath a kind of apron, giving them a most curious appearance.

In the early hours of the following day, the airfield of Kimpo was captured, and when I came this way again, an infantry division had moved up to take over from the marines and had fanned out south and east. The brief respite had ended in death. The bright colors were gone from field and female under dust and pall. No longer the scarlet of pimentos, no longer the vivid green and crimson of silken clothes. Now the villages smoldered in the hollows and old men sat at the roadsides with the knowledge that the deluge of war, which had seemed for the moment to have passed them by, might now overwhelm them.[22]

When one turns to the conduct of this and of every modern war, the gravest ethical difficulties are encountered, for the more war has improved at the point of technology, the more has it deteriorated at the point of moral discrimination. The code of the just war calls for the sparing of noncombatants. Today not even children are immune. At the time of Mussolini's Abyssinian adventure a speaker in the United States defended resort to military sanctions. An inquirer put to him a question, "Would you then bomb Rome and kill women and children?" "Why not?" he retorted. "Is life any more sacred because it is young?" The answer must, of course, be no. Life is not more sacred because it is young, but it is less responsible. Civil law has developed to the point of making a distinction between the juvenile and the mature offender, between the sane and the insane. War obliterates all such distinctions. Modern war certainly cannot be squared with the code of the just war.

For the Christian the most uncompromising demand of his traditional ethic is that a war to be just must be fought in the spirit of love. The question then arises whether this is possible, whether it is actual. It is not impossible. There are those who fight in a spirit of inner desolation combining a sense of guilt with a sense of duty. They entertain only pity, not rancor, for the foe whom they must repel using the weapons which this age has imposed. Those who fight in this spirit are to be found, but they are few.

Again, there are those who fight without emotion, particularly if they never see the foe—if their task is to pull the levers of remote controls, to release bombs in darkness, or to fire rockets over the horizon. These lads have a job to do and they are out to get it done without griping and without hate.

There are again those who do see the enemy, as in the trenches during the First World War. They see that he, too, is in the rain, the mud, and the gore and there arises a fellow feeling for "old Fritz." The attitude is fatalistic. The poor dogs on both sides have been impressed into a service which they loathe and from which they cannot escape, but they will just have to go on killing and being killed till the bloody mess is over.

The possibility of killing in love is remote in the frenzy of battle when passions are unleashed and hate becomes the slogan. The so-called "beasts" at West Point are trained to work themselves up to maniacal combativeness. What happens in combat was described by an American soldier who had seen forty months of active warfare culminating in Iwo Jima and Okinawa.

What kind of war do civilians suppose we fought, anyway? We shot prisoners in cold blood, wiped out hospitals, strafed lifeboats, killed or mistreated enemy civilians, finished off the enemy wounded, tossed the dying into a hole with the dead, and in the Pacific boiled the flesh off enemy skulls to make table ornaments for sweethearts, or carved their bones into letter openers. We topped off our saturation bombing and burning of enemy civilians by dropping atomic bombs on two nearly defenseless cities, thereby setting an alltime record for instantaneous mass slaughter.

As victors we are privileged to try our defeated opponents for their crimes against humanity; but we should be realistic enough to appreciate that if we were on trial for breaking international laws, we should be found guilty on a dozen counts. We fought a dishonorable war, because morality had a low priority in battle. The tougher the fighting, the less room for decency; and in the Pacific contests we saw mankind reach the blackest depths of bestiality.

Not every American soldier, or even one per cent of our troops, deliberately committed unwarranted atrocities, and the same might be said for the Germans and Japanese. The exigencies of war necessitated many so-called crimes, and the bulk of the rest could be blamed on the mental distortion which war produced. But we publicized every inhuman act of our opponents and censored any recognition of our own moral frailty in moments of desperation.[23]

Lord John Fisher very well took care of love in war when he said:

The humanizing of War! You might as well talk of the humanizing of Hell! When a silly ass at the Hague got up and talked about the amenities of civilized warfare and putting your prisoners' feet in hot water and giving them gruel, my reply, I regret to say, was considered totally unfit for publication. As if war could be civilized! If I'm in command when war breaks out I shall issue my order:—

"The essense of war is violence.

"Moderation in war is imbecility.

"Hit first, hit hard, and hit everywhere." [24]

There are Christians who concede all of this, yet contend that battle frenzy is not really hate and that soldiers who have so behaved can be decent as an army of occupation. The point has some validity, but one should not exaggerate the benevolence of an army of occupation. Since the days of the Assyrians, it has never been a charitable institution, and the fraternization tends to be too largely directed to the female population.

One may conclude that although a war may be fought in sorrowful love, it can never be won in this mood. Those who entertain such a disposition are few, and wars are the affairs of the masses. To beat the enemy one must use the scum of one's own population. The Christian in war cannot win without the aid of obnoxious allies. He does not endorse their behavior but he cannot dispense with their assistance and he becomes therefore in a measure guilty of their crimes.

As to Pacifism

If the crusade and the just war are rejected as Christian positions, pacifism alone remains. The writer takes this view. A distinction must here be made between varieties of pacifism. There is a Christian pacifism of renunciation and a secularist pacifism of prudence. The Christian pacifism is not a strategy but a witness. Conscientious objectors have never been numerous enough to stop a war. Between the two wars the hope appeared not unrealistic that they might attain sufficient strength to apply an effective brake. They failed and there appears to be even less likelihood of success in our own day. The churches are certainly not disposed to commit themselves as churches to war resistance. Moreover a much more extensive movement would be necessary now than formerly to impede a war because at present twenty-five men possessed of modern weapons could launch an attack and all nonparticipants would wake up to find themselves either dead or in it. As for the impact of martyrdom on public opinion, one never knows. The scaffold may sway the future, but it may also be buried in oblivion.

At the same time there is the possibility of a new variety of pacifism which may attain large proportions, and that is a pacifism of prudence, based on the desire for survival. Such a movement may start not from Christians addicted to the Sermon on the Mount but from generals averse to futility. The two types of pacifism would largely coalesce as to their program. Their day is not yet, however, and in the meantime we have the questions, shall small groups of Christians espouse a pacifist view, and by so doing would they render themselves irrelevant?

The indictment of the pacifist is summed up in the charge that he is motivated by the desire to preserve his personal purity and fails to see that the price of purity is irrelevance as the price of relevance is corruption. We shall discuss first the claim that he is motivated by a concern to appear before God with clean hands and a pure heart. Personal purity is not the point, but rather the purity of the cause. The pacifist is fearful that, if in withstanding the beast he descend to the methods of the beast, he will himself become the beast, and though the field be won the cause will be lost.

The charge continues that by seeking to be pure the pacifist becomes irrelevant and this indictment is thought to hold whether the purity in question be that of the person or the cause. The assumption is that involvement entails corruption, particularly political involvement because power necessarily corrupts. Yet the exercise of power is essential to the attainment of justice. Consequently to ensure justice one will have to be corrupted. Therefore let one regard corruption as the supreme sacrifice, the sacrifice of one's virtue for the common good. Such an analysis requires scrutiny. It is faulty at the outset in the unqualified assertion that power corrupts. As a matter of fact the wielders of power have not infrequently been men of high integrity. If power corrupts, so also does weakness. Existence corrupts. Life in association with other human beings corrupts. That was why the monks went to the desert. There they discovered that solitude corrupts and returned. In every aspect of our living we are sinners before God, but not therefore criminals before men. It will not do from the divine perspective to reduce all human behavior to a uniform level of sinfulness and then to say that the purity of the ideal should be abandoned because we must sin that justice may abound. Nor is it true to say that we do sin in doing that which must be done that justice may abound. We may sin in the doing of it, but that which must necessarily be done is not of itself sinful. It may be distasteful; it may be revolting. To be bound to see it through in that case is not sin but tragedy.

The indictment continues that the pacifist by his abstention, whatever his motive, actually makes himself irrelevant. Justice requires action. In every circumstance something has to be done. What can be done may be far from the ideal but under the circumstances it is the best alternative. To hold out for the absolute means to forfeit the relative good. To this the reply may be that to elect the relative may be to forfeit the absolute. There are circumstances in which the highest relevance is irrelevance. During the Nazi period, for example, in Germany a school superintendent joined the party because by thus securing his position he could protect his subordinates from party interference and might also be able to mitigate the rigors of the regime. The motives of such a man are not lightly to be impugned. His discernment and his relevance may be questioned. He who adopted this course did not succeed in protecting subordinates, did not mitigate the behavior of the party, and after the war was excluded from the reconstruction. In the sequel he made himself irrelevant.

To dissociate oneself from the course of action adopted by the party or the nation is not irresponsible or craven. Americans are perhaps less ready than other peoples to recognize this point because of the system of government in which the president is expected not to resign but to finish his term, even though he may have lost the support of Congress and the country. If he remain in office he must then either stymie legislation or stifle his conscience and implement the public will. In Britain this dilemma cannot arise because a government which has lost the confidence of the House must resign, and the resignation of a cabinet member who dissents from his colleagues is deemed honorable.

The final and most telling criticism against the pacifist is that by his refusal to destroy the oppressor he abandons the oppressed, because there are circumstances in which military intervention may terminate tyranny. One answer to this reproach is pragmatic, that military intervention by the nation-state without due process of law normally impedes rather than aids the vindication of justice. The other answer is the admission of circumstances in which the refusal to employ violence may bring hurt to others and even to one's own family. Yet the protection even of one's own family cannot be an ultimate. The principle is recognized in war that if a civilian to protect his family shoots a soldier he will thereby unleash reprisals against an entire population. If the resister to tyranny, in order to protect his family, ceases to resist, all resistance may fold up, because the tyrant well knows how to exploit the love of family to quell resistance. The choices which confront the pacifist are almost as grim as those which confront the soldier, and he is not to delude himself by supposing that by his stand he can avoid inflicting all hurt. Yet, if he dissociates himself from the use of war to advance a cause however noble he is not for that reason irresponsible, and he may not be irrelevant.

Chapter 15

What Then?

THE pacifist must dissociate himself from war. He need not therefore dissociate himself from all political life. The Quakers have not done so. Pacifists agitate for legislation looking toward the elimination or mitigation of war. Critics claim that they have no business to do so. If they would be pacifists, let them be pacifists, but let them not presume to give advice to statesmen operating on nonpacifist principles. This word of the modern critic is a revival of the gibe of Celsus that the Christian must either participate fully in political life to the point of war or else give up marriage and parenthood and retire to the desert. Thus the only valid pacifism is monasticism. No middle ground can be found or conceded. Until recently the Mennonites have agreed to political abstention, but not the Quakers.

The line lies between politics and war, and it is not an easy line to draw because politics is so involved in war, and peace itself may be waged with an eye to war. John Bright located his middle ground by serving in Parliament but not on the cabinet, but the Quakers in Pennsylvania found themselves constrained to resign from the legislature. They were guided by two principles. One was opposition to war, and the other was respect for the consciences of those who did not renounce war. The element of fair play was and is involved. If a nation is committed to war as an ultimate recourse it must at all times be ready for war, and it is hardly fair for those who do not approve of war so to impede the preparation that, if it comes, those who do believe in it will be so ill prepared as to suffer defeat. If then a military appropriation is to be voted in time of peace the pacifist in a legislative assembly, if he does not resign, should at any rate abstain from voting.

This does not mean that he cannot oppose any military appropriation or that he cannot vote against involvement in any particular war. John Bright opposed every war in which England was engaged during his lifetime, not on Quaker principles but on grounds of public policy. There are wars that are indefensible on every count, and there are military appropriations so excessive as to imperil the peace through the fear and counter measures which they inspire in the enemy state. A nonpacifist liberal will oppose such appropriations and a pacifist may legitimately join him in so doing. A pacifist, then, may participate in politics as a liberal rather than as a pacifist.

Natural Law and a Program for Peace

At the present juncture there is more need for peace than there is for pacifism. If peace is preserved it will be through the efforts not of pacifists, but of peace-minded nonpacifists, who do not renounce war absolutely, but who oppose war in our time on grounds of the humanitarian and the pragmatic. The question then comes to be, what are the lineaments of a peace program on which those with differing presuppositions can make common cause? This will depend of course upon the ethic espoused by the national state and by the world community. The highest ethic which one can expect for the state is the ethic of natural law. For the Church one has a right to assume the ethic of the gospel, however interpreted. The two in large measure will coincide, but they may also clash; natural law recognizes the principle that force may be repelled by force, whereas the gospel, if not entirely excluding this principle, certainly inculcates a spirit of concession and even of renunciation.

The great natural-law tradition rests on the premise of rationality in man. This is not a popular doctrine in our day when reasonableness is decried alike in philosophy, theology, and ethics. Yet the irrational is a counsel of humanicide, and if we do not as intelligent beings appraise our situation and act with sanity in applying controls, we shall not be capable much longer of acting even irrationally. In any case, however men behave, the Christian in addressing his fellows and especially statesmen, must proclaim sanity, even though again he be only a John the Baptist raving to the ravens.

The second ingredient in the natural-law tradition is universality. The law of nature is intelligible to all men and binding upon all peoples. It must have regard to the welfare of all and is therefore incompatible with any ethic conceived in terms of national self-interest. Yet there are today many among us who assume that self-interest is and should be the primary concern of the state. This judgment rests on the distinction between private and public morality. Man, we are told, is moral; society is immoral. This is, of course, a pedagogical exaggeration. Some men—criminals, for example—are vastly less moral than society. The point is that society includes everybody and the morality of society must therefore be average. It is not so low as that of the scoundrel, nor so high as that of the saint.

There is, however, another and more valid distinction which is not exactly that of public and private. It is the distinction between the way in which one may legitimately act when involved for oneself alone and the course to be taken when one is responsible for others. A man can be more reckless in sacrifice if only he will suffer. This means that all those who by their acts involve others must behave soberly—including not only statesmen, but also business executives, college presidents, and fathers of families. Luther at this point classified fathers with magistrates and placed both in the category of public life. Still there is a difference between the statesman and the father. The statesman simply cannot commit his people to sacrifices which they are not ready to undertake. If for himself he must take another course, then as statesman he must resign. But a father cannot resign from being a father. If for himself alone he should refuse military service or resist a dictator or a totalitarian regime, not only may he be crushed, but his family may suffer reprisals. The ethical dilemmas of what we call private life are thus even greater than in the public domain, but our concern here is with the public. The point is simply to indicate that any sharp demarcation between private and public is excluded. Each has its own particular problems and neither is exempt from moral restraints.

In the realm of public affairs we are frequently told today that a nation does act and should act only in its own interest.[1] This view is being taken not only by secularists but also by Christian theologians. Their attitude results from a reaction against the pretentious altruism, the lofty do-goodism, the unctious moralism, which prompted us to commit Japan and Germany to the renunciation of arms and then in short order to force upon them rearmament. When their military assistance was necessary for our own security, we jettisoned the commitments which we had imposed upon them. We should have been less hypocritical had we never exacted what we were not prepared to adopt. The point is well taken that candor is to be preferred to cant, but candor can be achieved in either of two ways—by speaking as badly as we behave or by acting as finely as we pretend.

The pursuit of self-interest is highly precarious. Some assume that if it be sought by all, out of the ensuing clash a balance will emerge and an approximation to justice. This outcome is by no means self-evident. The two great rivals of the moment could easily divide the world into spheres for exploitation. A variant justification for the pursuit of self-interest is that we do not know enough as to the genuine interest of other peoples to take them into account. If this word is intended as a censure of our attempts to impose our culture[2] upon others the point is well taken. If it means that we are to act entirely without regard to the welfare of others, the statement is not true and the conclusion is not wise. Surely we know that it is not to the interest of others to suffer the expropriation of their territory, to be excluded from waterways and access to raw materials, to have their commerce wrecked by prohibitive tariffs, and the like. Already we are so interlocked with others that a tremor at the Pentagon causes a quiver at the Kremlin. We can no more pursue our national interest in isolation than Pan-American Airlines can plot their courses without regard to the routes of the Scandinavian, British, French, Italian,

German, and Swiss lines. Nothing is more to the interest of us all than the elimination of war.

Ways to Peace

The first, the most obvious, and the most imperative step in that direction is world disarmament. One could wish that our nation would disarm unilaterally. One could wish that the churches would urge such a course. There seems to be little likelihood that our nation will do so or that the churches will ask it. We shall probably muddle and spar precariously until the tensions are eased, provided in the meantime someone does not inadvertently pull the wrong lever. In urging disarmament one must, however, not forget that it would entail perils and drastic rearrangements in our way of life. Were we to strip ourselves of all defense the Communists might extend their sway. On the other hand they might with sincere relief turn their efforts to industrial production and relax their grip on the satellite countries. However that may be, the dismantling or conversion of armament plants would cause a huge dislocation of industry among ourselves and extensive preparations would need to be made in advance for new industries by way of replacement.[3]

World government is most heartily to be desired, and it does not exist. The United Nations is "a debating society with wide reverberations."[4] It serves also as a fact finding body and affords an opportunity for informal exchanges between diplomats. We are not to labor under the illusion that it is immune from the power struggle; nor, on the other hand, are we to belittle its influence, which would be greatly enhanced if all *de facto* governments were included.[5]

In the United States foreign aid is frequently regarded as a device for winning friends and averting war. Its effectiveness as an expedient for making friends is not to be exaggerated. It may also make enemies. We cannot give to all and if the chosen are grateful, the rejected may be resentful. Again a gift long continued comes to be assumed and withdrawal may be considered a grievance. The recipients again will not be impressed by our altruism if we employ foreign aid as a device for disposing of the surplus products of an economy of waste and will be suspicious if we attach to our gifts any political commitments. The real function of foreign aid is to assist global economic stability, which is conducive to peace.[6]

Cultural exchange is often regarded as a way to promote understanding and diminish tensions. It is certainly not to be despised, discouraged, or diminished, but neither are we to expect too much from it. There was cultural exchange in abundance between the nations of Europe during the nineteenth century but this did not prevent the First World War. A common language and a common culture have not prevented civil wars in England, the United States, and Spain. Let us by all means seek to know our neighbors, remembering however that the more we get together the happier we shall not necessarily be.

Some—especially pacifists—look to "nonviolence" as a way to combat injustice and to provide a substitute for war. Here we must bear in mind that nonviolent resistance has two objectives. The first is to coerce the opponent into compliance through pressures mainly economic. Gandhi's boycott of British cotton goods was of this order. It differed no whit in principle from any other boycott and resembled also the strike as a weapon. Nonviolent resistance of this sort is preferable to war because more amenable to moral control, and less likely to produce those passions which impede and preclude a generous peace. The other object is to persuade. Gandhi's fasts sought to persuade his followers to be disciplined and his opponents to yield. This method sometimes succeeds, sometimes fails. The British allowed the Irishman Sweeney to starve himself to death in prison and did not give in, at least not at the time. Vinoba Bhave's program of sharing the land operates only by persuasion and is not resistance, save to human nature. He has had an astonishing success in inducing landlords voluntarily to divide their holdings. Whether their motive is philanthropy or sagacity in forestalling an otherwise inevitable expropriation, the success of the effort is an eloquent proof that men are amenable either to sanity or benevolence and perhaps to both. Nonviolence in Africa presents a varied pattern. A report in 1957 declared that in South Africa, where it had been used, the feeling was better but the concessions less than in Kenya with terrorization. Since then Kenya verges on independence and violence has broken out in South Africa. In the French resistance movement the issue was complicated since the common cause, to save the Jews, was made by Christian nonresisters and the Maquis. In the United States the Negroes, who successfully boycotted the busses, combined economic pressure with persuasion and won.[7]

Nothing can be more important, and nothing can more properly engage the attention of all those interested in peace than a statesman-like grappling and a flexible handling of all the social changes which we shall have to confront and are not in a position to predict. The dislocations which such changes occasion provide fertile ground for wars. There is the problem of overproduction, to which our industry is geared. In order to keep going at all we have to make more than we can use. For a time foreign markets and foreign aid may absorb the surplus but this process cannot be continued indefinitely after all peoples come to be industrialized. The problem may be solved by an increase in population, but an increase in population may exhaust the food supply.[8] If new sources of food are discovered there will still be the question of space. In this whole picture there are many unpredictables. The upward trend in population may arrest itself. The food supply may be incapable of large increases. Natural resources of oil, steel, and rubber may be exhausted. Substitutes may or may not be found. These changes are all pertinent to our problem and demand a high degree of competence, imagination, flexibility, and genuine concern—not only for ourselves but for all the peoples of the earth. Since these matters cannot be settled by one nation in isolation they necessitate operations on a world scale, and since the solutions cannot be left to *laissez faire* they point to some measure of government control. This indicates a planned economy under a world government, a goal obviously remote and fraught with perils of its own.

In the meantime there is the problem of whether a nation committed to an ethic of natural law can find any common ground for dealing with a nation which frankly is acting partly in its own interest and partly in the interest of a world movement which aspires to the establishment of a classless society and an economic equality, but for the present achieves classlessness to a degree and equality in a measure by liquidating resisters within and without. In other words can we deal with the Russians?

One who has had a great deal of experience in dealing with them makes some pertinent suggestions. Our approach, he says, must be one of courtesy and patience because there is a heritage of suspicion from the days when the United States joined in the effort to restore czarism. In debate we must work from their premises and to that end must be versed in their scriptures. If we can show that their conduct is not consistent with the teachings of Marx and Lenin, they may reconsider. The most important point is that we should not present a plan with the claim that it is to their advantage. They will immediately look for the catch. We should say that it is to our advantage and leave them then to see whether it is also to theirs.[9]

What this adds up to is that we should talk only of our interests—otherwise we shall not be believed—but we should act as much in their interest as our own, because otherwise our proposals will not be accepted.

The Will to Peace

All of the devices thus far considered for the elimination of war will be futile without the will to peace. The desire for peace is universal; less so, the will to peace. The line between desire and will is not the line between non-Christians and Christians. The nontheists and the theists, the secularists and the Christians, can once more make common cause. The wisdom of the Greeks is again uttered in our day by a number of voices. Lewis Mumford touches the horror of it all in his article with the title "Kindling for Global Gehenna." [10] Norman Cousins stresses the pity of it all in his book *Who Speaks for Man?* Bertrand Russell points to the folly of it all when he inquires whether the sublimity of feeling which makes the species worth preserving is all to end in trivial horror because so few are able to think of Man rather than of this or that group of men? Is our race so destitute of wisdom, so incapable of impartial love, so blind even to the simplest dictates of self-preservation, that the last proof of its silly cleverness is to be the extermination of all life on our planet?—for it will be not only men who will perish, but also the animals and plants, whom no one can accuse of Communism or anti-Communism." [11]

In the voicing of such pleas, are Christians to be behind humanists? The churches as churches have not come out with unequivocal repudiations of modern war because their constituencies are divided and they wish to leave the individual conscience free. In that case there is all the more reason why individuals should declare their convictions. Some have done so. Attention may be called to two significant pronouncements from Christian laymen: the first, a German theoretical physicist, Karl Friedrich von Weizsäcker of the University of Hamburg; the second an American diplomat, George F. Kennan. The German physicist has this to say:

Christianity has differentiated between righteous and unrighteous wars, between a righteous and unrighteous manner of waging them. It has differentiated between the individual ethic which inclined towards the Sermon on the Mount and the ethic of political responsibility which dictated the protection of fellow men by means of weapons.

All this inspires respect where the effort is serious. I do not challenge it. But if I ask myself whether, after reading the New Testament, I can throw a hydrogen bomb, then I know that the answer is "No." And if I may not throw it, then I cannot make it for another to throw. And if I cannot make it in order that it may be thrown, can I then make it in order that it may be used to threaten? . . . I cannot believe that the Church can say "Yes" to the use of the H-bomb. If she is not able to say "No" she will have to acknowledge her perplexity either openly or else by complete silence. Yet I believe that members of the Church can do themselves and the whole world service if upon quite definite presuppositions they openly say "No." [12]

George Kennan refuses to condone atomic warfare. He writes:

In taking responsibility for the bombing of Dresden and Hamburg, to say nothing of Nagasaki and Hiroshima, Americans went beyond what it seems to me the dictates of Christian conscience should have allowed.

I regret, as an American and as a Christian, that these things were done. I think it should be our aim to do nothing of the sort in any future military encounter. If we must defend our homes, let us defend them as well as we can in the direct sense, but let us have no part in making millions of women and children and non-combatants hostages for the behavior of their own governments.

It will be said to me: This means defeat. To this I can only reply: I am skeptical of the meaning of "victory" and "defeat" in their relation to modern war between great countries. To my mind the defeat is war itself. In any case it seems to me there are times when we have no choice but to follow the dictates of our conscience, to throw ourselves on God's mercy, and not to ask too many questions.

He goes on to justify his stand by the wrongfulness of encroaching on the domain of the Creator. God has given us a natural environment which we did not create and have no right to destroy.

In the political process, says Kennan, we shall unavoidably find "much that is ambiguous in the Christian sense," but in our diplomacy "decency and humanity of spirit can never fail to serve the Christian cause."

Beyond that there loom the truly apocalyptic dangers of our time, the ones that threaten to put an end to the very community of history outside which we would have no identity, no face, either in civilization, in culture, or in morals. These dangers represent for us not only political questions but stupendous moral problems, to which we cannot deny the courageous Christian answer. Here our main concern must be to see that man, whose own folly once drove him from the Garden of Eden, does not now commit the blasphemous act of destroying, whether in fear or in anger or in greed, the great and lovely world in which, even in his fallen state, he has been permitted by the grace of God to live.[18]

The Spirit of Peace

The Christian must do more than say "no" to war. His vocation is to be, in the words of George Fox, "in that spirit which is above all war and contention." Those who in our day reinterpret the Judaeo-

Christian tradition in terms of political realism forget that in the New Testament the only appeal to political realism is to warn would-be disciples that they should count the cost for "what king, going to make war against another king, sitteth not down first, and consulteth whether he be able with ten thousand to meet him that cometh against him with twenty thousand?" [14] The New Testament is not concerned with the power struggle—"The kings of the Gentiles exercise lordship . . . ye shall not be so." [15] The New Testament is redolent of the gentler virtues; the fruits of the spirit, declared the apostle Paul, are "love, joy, peace, longsuffering, gentleness, goodness, faith, meekness, temperance." [16] He did not include massive retaliation.

Throughout the centuries the Christian ethic has always impressed outsiders as pacific to the point of weakness. Celsus in the second century brought the reproach that if all men were as the Christians, the empire would be overrun by lawless barbarians. Julian the Apostate in the fourth century mockingly asked the men of Alexandria whether their city owed its greatness to the precepts of the Galilean and not rather to the prowess of its founder Alexander the Great. In the Renaissance Machiavelli attributed the decadence of his times to the "feebleness of our religion." In the nineteenth century Friedrich Nietzsche thought that the sign by which Christianity conquered should be labeled "decadence." In our own time Alfred Loisy, having repudiated Christianity, interpreted its ethic in Tolstoyan terms. Rabbi Klausner believed that the ethic of Jesus would disintegrate the state.

These examples are not cited to contend that all of the above judgments are correct, and one may legitimately query whether unbelievers are at any point the best exegetes. Yet perchance they may be, because those who reject an exacting ethic may better keep it intact than those who, having accepted it, are then under the temptation to pare it down to the level of the attainable. Not vengeance, not retaliation, but compassion and reconciliation are the Christian notes.

Pope Pius XII spoke as a Christian when he reviewed what is entailed in atomic warfare and sought to turn men to a nobler way. In his Easter message in 1954 he said:

Thus, before the eyes of a terrified world there is presented a preview of gigantic destruction, of extensive territories uninhabitable and unfit for human use over and above the biological consequence that can result, either by the changes brought about by germs and microorganisms, or through the uncertain effect which a prolonged radioactive stimulus can have upon greater organisms, including man, and upon their future offspring.

At the same time, we ask: For how long will men insist on turning their backs on the salutary light of the Resurrection, seeking security instead in the deadly blasts of new weapons of war? For how long will they oppose their designs of hatred and of death to the Divine Saviour's precepts of love and His promises of life? When will the rulers of nations realize that peace cannot consist in an exasperating and costly relationship of reciprocal terror, but in the Christian rule of universal charity, and particularly in justice voluntarily applied rather than extorted and in confidence that is inspired rather than exacted?

The Christian must seek to exemplify the self-effacement of the Saviour, and he must remember that the concern of the gospel is for individual persons. There is not a word of advice in the New Testament about mass communication. When Paul wrote to the Romans he was not thinking of the Roman Empire, but of the local congregation at Rome, and his letter concludes with nearly a chapter of greetings to persons named—Apelles, Herodion, Tryphena, Tryphosa, Asyncritus, Phlegon, Julia, Nereus, and the rest. One of the ingredients in the degradation of modern war is that it has become so completely depersonalized that justice cannot be administered on a basis of individual responsibility, nor can punishment be made to fit the crime. Perhaps even worse, the revulsion against war is diminished because of the failure to realize that people are involved. We talk about power relations as if China, Korea, Iran, and Kenya were the pieces in a cardboard puzzle, and not nations of human beings. The participants in war may hate each other less because they do not see one another, but by the same token, they are less struck by the inhumanity of what they are doing when they know the enemy only as a target.

At the close of the Second World War two veterans met in the home of an American professor; one was a German, the other an American. Both were theology students. The German had been on a submarine, the American in an airplane. They compared notes. The German related that on a given day in a given month in a particular year he had been in a submarine off a Baltic port, dodging the bombs from an American plane. The American said that on the same day of the same month and the same year off that same Baltic port he had been in a plane dropping bombs in an effort to bag a German submarine. For the first time each of them felt the monstrous incongruity on the part of two men training to be ministers of Jesus Christ.

Grounds for Hope

Is there any possibility that a Christian word will be heard? We do not know, but we make a mistake to underestimate man's capacity for idealism. Professor Spykman made a very significant observation in the following passage:

In man's idealism lies both his strength and his weakness as a fire. He can be made to fight for his personal and social survival, but it is easier to inspire him with a call to service for abstract values than with a promise of material gain. In terms of interest men divide, only in terms of the defense of the moral order can they unite. Because man loves peace, it is always the opponent who is the aggressor, and, because he prefers decency it is always the enemy who fights unfairly and with cruel and dastardly means. National struggles inevitably become struggles between good and evil, crusades against sin and the devil. Modern wars can be fought successfully only in an atmosphere of unreality and make-believe." [17]

Such a statement embodies the ultimate irony, if it be true that nations are bound to fight, that they never do fight save in their own interest, but that they cannot induce their subjects to fight without pretending to wage war disinterestedly for an ideal. Whether or not all these assumptions are valid we need not here decide. The point is that men do respond more readily to an ideal than to a material goal. What an enormous potential lies here, if only this idealism might be channeled toward the ideal!

The bellicosity of soldiers is not innate. The frenzy of battle has to be induced by training which eradicates inhibitions. Brigadier General S. L. Marshall announces that enough soldiers do not fire to constitute a military problem. In the Second World War only 12-25 per cent of all the combat soldiers actually pulled the trigger. A sergeant testified, "Time and time again I had to expose myself and crawl from foxhole to foxhole to get half of the platoon to fire. Sometimes I'd practically have to sight the rifle and pull the trigger for the guy." General Marshall explains this behavior on the ground that, "All his life, the boy's mind works unconsciously to suppress any desire to kill. Then, abruptly, he is put into a soldier suit and told to shoot fellow human beings. One man in two loses the resulting struggle to break down the lifelong inhibition." He goes on to say that the Russians had an advantage over us because their men had fewer inhibitions against killing. The General despairs of obtaining 100 per cent firing from our men. If we could raise the proportion to 75 per cent, "That is the best we can possibly expect." The way to do it is to induce a mob psychology which overrides individual inhibitions. "The most dramatic innovation has been talking it up— the yelling in combat which has accompanied many of our most heroic actions in Korea." [18]

If aversion to killing is actually the normal response of our young men, to build out from that base toward peace should be easier than to reverse all of their previous training in favor of war.

Let us suppose that our nation should disarm unilaterally. What would happen? We do not know. Such an unparalleled renunciation might have an amazing effect. Weakness as such has no power; the Jews were helpless, and their helplessness did not soften Hitler. If a nation possessed of strength should voluntarily renounce its advantage, however, the enemy might respond with alacrity and relief. No proof of this can be offered because no nation has ever tried, but there are cases on a more personal level which point to hope. Hans deBoer, a German pacifist, went to Kenya, resolved to talk to the leaders of the Mau Mau. Everyone told him that if he went into the Mau Mau country, he would never come back with his head on. He consulted an American Quaker who had been in the land for some twenty years. The advice was, "Young man, I wouldn't do it if I were you. One should not tempt God."

DeBoer nevertheless went and entirely unarmed. After some two hours of walking, as he was approaching the first settlement, two natives in remnants of European dress accosted him in English, asking, "Are you Mr. DeBoer?" The Quaker friend who had counseled him not to go had in fact contacted the Mau Mau. DeBoer was able to have a conference with one of the leaders to whom he deplored alike the violence of the Mau Mau and of the whites, urging instead negotiation. The Negro replied that if the whites would come unarmed to talk, no blood would flow. The Negroes desired only freedom and the right to own their own land, and they were not lusting to murder all of the whites.[19]

This incident is significant for two reasons: first, because the Quakers throughout the whole conflict had been able to keep open the lines of trustful communication, and second, that a man voluntarily walking unarmed into the nest of the Mau Mau so impressed them that they gave him every courtesy. Disarmament and nonviolence might revolutionize the world's behavior.

But If Not

"But if not . . ." These words were spoken by the three Jewish youths who were commanded by Nebuchadnezzar to worship his image on pain of being cast into a fiery furnace. They answered that their God was able to deliver them from the hand of the king and from his burning fiery furnace. "But if not, be it known unto thee, O king, that we will not serve thy gods, nor worship the golden image which thou hast set up." [20]

"But if not . . ." If the threat of massive retaliation were removed, there is the possibility that tyranny might expand. The contemplation is the more grievous for American Christians because the first blow would be felt not by ourselves but by West Germany. The young of that land would be subject to propaganda and penalization under such pressures that their humanitarian ideals and Christian faith might crumble. The prospect is grim, but our sense of guilt for not affording them military defense is diminished by the fact that to defend them would spell their annihilation. If they and later we were subjected to an expanding Communism, what would emerge after a century is difficult to foresee. This only we know, that the spirit of man is resurgent, and that more than once in history the descendants of conquerors have looked upon themselves as spiritually the sons of the conquered.

"But if not . . ." and if by defenselessness we forfeit survival, the Christian answer can only be that survival is not the chief end of man. Survival is not lightly to be relinquished. Life is a precious boon, but life is not to be had at any price. That point surely need not be labored among those who will not have peace at any price. During the war British churchmen well stated the principle. Principal Cairns of the Scottish Church declared with reference to reprisals that there are some things which no nation ought ever to do, even at the risk of destruction. The Archbishop of Canterbury affirmed that there must be limitations to reprisals "below which, at whatever cost, honor will forbid us to fall." The British *Church Times* wrote: "The reason why, even to win the war or to win it quickly, this country cannot adopt methods of the jungle is simply that it does not wish the world to be a jungle when the war is finished." [21]

Father Ford, after branding as immoral the use of atomic weapons, concluded that if the alternative were subjugation to an atheist regime or the extinction of the human race "the followers of Christ should abandon themselves to divine Providence rather than forsake these [Christian moral] imperatives." [22]

Once again the realists tell us that if we renounce power, we shall be at a disadvantage. Of course we shall. When were the scrupulous not at a disadvantage in dealing with the unscrupulous?

267

Shall the scrupulous then become unscrupulous in order to survive? Are we to renounce honor, shame, mercy, and compassion in order to live? The ancient pagans would not have said so. Did not Socrates declare that to suffer injustice is better than to inflict it? Shall we allow this pagan to take over the virtues which we have been wont to call Christian, while we invoke Christ to justify nuclear annihilation?

Notes

Chapter 1

1. Ps. 122:7.

2. Ps. 128.

3. On the concept of peace in the Old Testament consult: The article *eirené* in Gerhard Kittel, *Theologisches Wörterbuch* (1935); Wilhelm Caspari, "Vorstellung und Wort Friede im Alten Testament," *Beiträge zur Förderung Christlicher Theologie*, XIV, 4 (1910); Caspari, "Der biblische Friedensgedanke nach dem Alten Testament," *Biblische Zeit-und Streitfragen*, X (1916); Martin Noth, "Die israelitischen Personennamen . . . ," *Beiträge zur Wissenschaft vom Alten und Neuen Testament*, III, 10 (1928).

4. John L. Myres, *The Political Ideas of the Greeks* (New York, 1927), p. 142.

5. Fragment 71 in *Comicorum Atticorum Fragmenta*, ed. Koch (1884).

6. On concepts of peace in classical antiquity: Wallace E. Caldwell, *Hellenic Concepts of Peace* (New York, 1919); Wilhelm Nestle, "Der Friedensgedanke in der antiken Welt," *Philologus*, Suppl. Bd. XXXI, 1 (1938); articles by Bruno Keil and Karl Brugmann in *Berichte sächs. Gesellschaft der Wissenschaften*, Philol. hist. Kl., LXVIII (1916); fuller bibliography in Michael Rostovtzeff, *The Social and Economic History of the Hellenistic World*, III (Oxford, 1941), pp. 1358-59.

7. Lev. 26:5-6.

8. Denyse Le Lasseur, *Les Déesses Armées dans l'art classique* (Paris, 1919); André Baudrillart, *Les Divinités de la Victoire en Grèce et en Italie* (Paris, 1894).

9. Heinrich Gross, "Die Idee des ewigen und allgemeinen Weltfriedens im Alten Orient und im Alten Testament," *Trier Theol. St.*, VII (1956); Michael Rostovtzeff, *A History of the Ancient World. The Orient and Greece*, Vol. 1 (Oxford, 1930), pp. 119-21.

10. William S. Ferguson, "Economic Causes of International Rivalries and Wars in Ancient Greece," *Annual Report American Historical Association.* (1915), pp. 111-21.

11. A. W. Gomme, *A Historical Commentary on Thucydides*, I (Oxford, 1945), p. 14.

12. Hesiod, *Erga*, lines 109-20 and 276 ff.

13. Aratus, *Phaenomena* II, 7:96-136. Cf. Arthur O. Lovejoy and George Boas, *Primitivism and Related Ideas in Antiquity* (Baltimore, 1935), pp. 34-35.

14. Plutarch, *De Stoicorum Repugnantiis*, XXXII, 2.

15. Ovid, *Metamorphoses*, I, 98. Cf. *Fasti*, I, 719 ff. *Epistolae ex Ponto* II, Ep., IX, 39, 40. Lovejoy, *op. cit.*, pp. 44-46.

16. The biblical citations in this section are in the following order: Isa. 9:6-7; 11:3-4; 2:4; Mic. 4:3; Hos. 2:18; Ps. 46:9; Isa. 9:5; Ezek. 38:11.

17. The biblical citations are: Isa. 51:3; 11:6-9; Hos. 2:18.

18. Polybius, *Historia*, VI, Loeb Library ed., pp. 438-39.

19. *Iliad*, XIII, 635-39.

20. *Ibid.*, II, 290-94. Cf. *Odyssey*, XXIV, 486.
21. *Agamemnon*, lines 399-449.
22. Lines 764-70.
23. *Persians*, lines 845-51.
24. *Naturales Quaestiones*, III, *Praef.*
25. *Satire*, X, 168-73.
26. *Res Gestae Alexandri*, VII, 8, 15.
27. Julius Caesar, *De Bello Gallico*, VII, 77.
28. Tacitus, *Agricola*, 30.
29. *Seven Books*, VI, 1.
30. Justinus, *Epit. Pompei Trogi*, XXVIII, 2.
31. *Epode*, VII.
32. *Catilina*, ch. I-X, fragments 11-12.
33. Tacitus, *Historia*, III, 25, 81.
34. Stobaeus, *Anthology*, III, 40, 9.
35. Fragment 110.
36. Aeschylus, *Seven Against Thebes*, trans. Gilbert Murray (London: George Allen & Unwin Ltd.) , lines 345-51.
37. *Pythian Odes*, 4, 272-74.
38. *Historia*, I, 87.
39. I, 594, trans. Benjamin B. Rogers (Loeb Classical Library ed.; Cambridge, Mass.: Harvard University Press) , p. 63. Used by permission.
40. Dio Chrysostom, *Orat.* XL, 35.
41. *Nicomachean Ethics*, VIII, 1155A, I, 18.
42. *Satire*, XV, 159-70.
43. Karl von der Lieck, *Die Xenophontische Schrift von den Einkünften* (Diss. Köln, 1933) .
44. Philostratus, *Vita Apollonii*, II, 26.
45. Gen. 21:32-34.
46. Gen. 13.
47. Diodorus Siculus, *Historia*, XIII, 20-27.
48. Nestle, *op. cit.*, p. 36.
49. Diogenes Laertius, *Lives*, II, 98.
50. *Epicurea*, ed. Hermann Usener (Leipzig, 1887) , p. 329, No. 560.
51. *De Rerum Natura*, I, 30-43.
52. *Enneades*, III, 4, 2, and 1, 5, 10.
53. *Vita*, 12.
54. Lovejoy, *op. cit.*, ch. on the Cynics.
55. Seneca, *Ep.*, XC.
56. *Ep.*, CVIII, 17.
57. Fragment 28.
58. Jamblichus, *De Vita Pythagorica*, XXX, 186.
59. Seneca, *Ep.*, XCV and *Naturales Quaestiones*, 5, 18.
60. *Meditations*, X, 10.
61. The biblical citations are: Isa. 59:7-8; 48:22; 57:21; 32:17; Ps. 85:8-10.
62. The biblical citations are: Isa. 39; 30-31; 30:15; and Hos. 7:11.
63. Jer. 29:5-7.
64. Isa. 53.
65. *Aeneid*, VI, 790 ff. and IV, 559, VI, 847-53.
66. *Georgics*, II, 490 ff.
67. *Eleg.*, II, 1, 20, and 5, 105 ff.
68. *Eleg.*, IV, iii, 20, and III, v.
69. *Laus Romae*, lines 214-16.
70. *De Consulatu Stilichonis* III, 150.

Chapter 2

1. *History* VII, 9, 1.
2. Hermann Diels, *Die Fragmente der Vorsokratiker* (3 vols.; Berlin, 1952), II, 87, 44.
3. Diogenes Laertius, *Lives*, VI, 63.
4. W. W. Tarn, "Alexander the Great and the Unity of Mankind," *Proceedings of the British Academy*, XIX (1933).
5. *De Alexandri Magni Fortuna*, I, 6.
6. *Meleagri Gadareni Fragmenta*, ed. Friedrich Graefe (Leipzig, 1811), No. CXXVII, condensed and freely translated.
7. Amos 9:7.
8. Isa. 19:24-25.
9. Isa. 9:2.
10. A. Raeder, "L'Arbitrage International chez les Hellenes," *Publications de l'Institut Nobel International*, I (1932); Marcus Niebuhr Tod, *International Arbitration Among the Greeks* (Oxford, 1913).
11. F. Laurent, *Études sur l'historie de l'Humanité*, II, *La Grèce* (Paris, 1880), pp. 97-105.
12. Coleman Phillipson, *The International Law and Custom of Ancient Greece and Rome*, II (London, 1911), pp. 5-11 and 219-20.
13. *Laws*, 628, *Republic*, 471.
14. *Republic*, 469 ff.
15. Xenophon, *Hellenica*, II, ii, 3-23.
16. Matthias Gelzer, "Nasicas Widerspruch gegen die Zerstörung Carthagos," *Philologus*, LXXXVI (1930-31), pp. 261-99.
17. *Republic*, 469-71.
18. Myres, *op. cit.*, pp. 167 ff.
19. *Politics*, I, 1256, B., 23-26.
20. *Gorgias*, 489, AB.
21. Auguste Bill, "La Morale et la Loi dans la Philosophie Antique," *Études d'Histoire et de Philosophie religieuse . . . l'Université de Strassbourg*, XVIII (Paris 1928), p. 172.
22. The rules for the just war are mainly in *De Officiis* I, 34-40, 83; II, 27; III, 46, 107.
23. *De Republica*, III, 34.
24. *De Officiis*, I, 36; *De Republica*, II, 31; *De Legibus*, II, 9, 21.
25. *De Republica*, III, 35.
26. Rudolf Pfeiffer, "Humanitas Erasmiana," *Studien zur Bibliothek Warburg*, XXII (1931); Richard Harder, "Nachträgliches zu Humanitas," *Hermes*, LXIX (1934), pp. 64-74; Max Pohlens, "Antikes Führertum, Cicero de Officiis und das Lebensideal des Panaitios," *Neue Wege zur Antike*, II, 3 (1934), pp. 137 ff.
27. The biblical citations are: Jer. 11:10, Hos. 2:18, Jer. 33:20-25, I Enoch 69:10 ff., Jer. 31:31-34.
28. I Macc. 2:38 and Josephus, *Antiquities*, XII, 6 and XIV, 4.

Chapter 3

1. Num. 10:35.
2. Judg. 5, Cf. Gerhard von Rad, *Der heilige Krieg im Alten Israel* (Zürich, 1951).
3. Edward Meyer, "Kritik der Berichte über die Eroberung Palästinas" and Bernhard Stade, "Nachwort des Herausgebers," *Zeitschrift für alttestamentliche Wissenschaft*, I (1881), pp. 117-50. There has been much discussion since with Noth attacking and Albrecht defending the tradition in substance.

4. I Sam. 22:6.
5. I Sam. 22:13; II Sam. 15:18; I Kings 1:8.
6. I Kings 10:26.
7. I Sam. 8:11-18. Cf. Rudolf Kittel, *Geschichte des Volkes Israel*, II (Gotha, 1925), pp. 174-75.
8. I Sam. 24.
9. Judg. 3:1-4.
10. Judg. 3:5.
11. II Sam. 21:2.
12. I Kings 18.
13. II Kings 10:28.
14. II Sam. 21:3-9.
15. Hos. 1:4.
16. Deut. 7:1-2; 13:15-16.
17. Exod. 14:26-29; Num. 16:31; Josh. 10:12-14; Judg. 5:20.
18. Deut. 32:41-42.
19. Judg. 7.
20. Judg. 4:21.
21. Josh. 6.
22. Num. 21:2.
23. Josh. 7.
24. I Sam. 15:10-33.
25. Josh. 6:21.
26. Josh. 10:40. Cf. Num. 31 and the many passages collected by Maurice Davies, *The Evolution of War* (New Haven, 1929), pp. 312, 318-19, 321, 327, 338-39.
27. Ehrhard Junge, "Der Wiederaufbau des Heerwesens des Reiches Juda unter Josia," *Beiträge zur Wissenschaft vom Alten und Neuen Testament*, IV, 23 (1937).
28. II Kings 23:30.
29. The references in the above paragraphs are to the following passages: Ps. 137:8-9; Isa. 13:17-22; Nah. 3:7; Isa. 14:12-17.
30. I Macc. 1:11.
31. Elias Bickermann, *Die Makkabäer* (Berlin, 1935), and *Der Gott der Makkabäer* (Berlin, 1937).

Chapter 4

1. *De Clementia* II, 5, 4-5.
2. *Meditations* 7, 22.
3. *Satire* 15.
4. I John 5:4.
5. I Macc. 4:10.
6. I Cor. 11:25.
7. Matt. 25:31-46.
8. Rom. 14:17.
9. Rom. 16:20.
10. Eph. 4:1-3.
11. Only in Acts 12:20 and 24:2.
12. Ps. 85:8, Isa. 57:21.
13. Rom. 5:1.
14. Eph. 2:11-23.
15. Phil. 4:7.
16. Matt. 10:13.
17. Rom. 15:13.

18. Matt. 5:9.
19. John 2:15.
20. Matt. 10:34.
21. Luke 12:51.
22. Luke 22:35-38.
23. Matt. 26:52.
24. Mark 12:17.
25. Ethelbert Stauffer, "Die Geschichte vom Zinsgroschen," *Christus und die Caesaren* (Hamburg, 1948). English: *Christ and the Caesars* (Philadelphia, 1955).
26. Matt. 17:24-25.
27. Rom. 13:1-6. Cf. I Pet. 2:13-17; I Tim. 2:2.
28. Gal. 6:16.
29. I Pet. 2:9.
30. Rev. 5:10. Cf. 1:6.
31. Col. 1:6.
32. I Cor. 15:29.
33. Eph. 1:23.
34. Phil. 3:20.
35. See II Cor. 6:14-18.
36. Heb. 11:10, 13; 13:14; I Pet. 1:17; 2:11.
37. *Meditations*, VII, 9.
38. Eph. 4:5.
39. Jas. 4:1.
40. Luke 2:1.
41. Luke 3:1.
42. Luke 3:12-14.
43. Luke 14:31-33.
44. Matt. 26:52.
45. Luke 22:25-38.
46. Matt. 5 and Luke 6.
47. James Moffatt, *Love in the New Testament* (New York, 1930), pp. 113-19.
48. Lev. 19:2.
49. Hans Windisch, *Der Messianische Krieg und das Urchristentum* (Tübingen, 1909).
50. Rom. 13:11-14.
51. Luke 6:36; Rom. 12:19.
52. Hans Windisch, "Friedensbringer-Gottessöhne . . .", *Zeitschrift für die Neutestamentliche Wissenschaft*, XXIII (1924), pp. 240-60
53. Eph. 6:10 Moffatt.
54. II Cor. 10:5 Moffatt.
55. I Thess. 5:8.
56. Eph. 6:16-17.
57. I Tim. 6:12.
58. James Moffatt, article "War" in *Dictionary of the Apostolic Church.*

Chapter 5

Abbreviations: *CSEL*   Corpus Scriptorum Ecclesiasticorum Latinorum
                PG   Patralogia Graeca
                PL   Patrologia Latina

1. For examples see my article "The Early Church and War," *Harvard Theological Review*, XXXIX, 3 (July, 1946), pp. 189-212, portions of which are incorporated into this chapter. Substantially in agreement is Hans Freiherr von Campenhausen, "Der

Kriegsdienst der Christen in der Kirche des Altertums," *Offener Horizont* (Jasper's Festschrift, München, 1953) , pp. 255-64. The usual Catholic attempt to discover non-pacifist motives for the rejection of military service reappears in Edward A. Ryan, "The Rejection of Military Service by the Early Christians," *Theological Studies*, XIII (1952) , pp. 1-32.

2. *Contra Celsum*, VIII, 68-69.

3. *Apologeticus*, XXXVII, cf. XLII, 5. (Abbr.: *Apol.*)

4. *De Corona Militis*, XI. (Abbr.: *Cor.*)

5. *Epistolae*, XXXIX (XXXIII) , 3.

6. Eusebius, *Historia Ecclesiastica*, VIII, app. (Abbr.: *HE*) .

7. *Ibid.*, VIII, 1, 8.

8. Adolf Harnack, *Militia Christi*. (Tübingen, 1905) , pp. 117-21.

9. C. J. Cadoux, *The Early Church and the World* (Edinburgh, 1925) , p. 580.

10. Nos. 12, 21, 22, 24, 29, 47.

11. Cadoux, *op. cit.*, p. 421.

12. *Contra Celsum*, VIII, 73.

13. W. M. Ramsay, *Cities and Bishoprics of Phrygia* (2 vols.; Oxford, 1895) , p. 717, no. 651.

14. *Cor.* XI.

15. Ruinart, *Acta Martyrum* (Ratisbon, 1859) , pp. 340-42.

16. Eusebius, *HE*, IX, 8, 2-4.

17. *Ibid.*, VII, 30, 8.

18. Theodoret, *HE*, II, 26.

19. F. C. Burkitt, *Early Eastern Christianity* (London, 1904) .

20. *Oratio ad Graecos*, XI.

21. *Ante-Nicene Fathers*, VIII, 730. (Abbr.: *ANF*) .

22. *Acts of Archelaus and Mani*, 1, *ANF*, VI, 179.

23. *Legatio pro Christianis*, XI.

24. *Trypho*, CX.

25. I *Apol.*, XXXIX.

26. *Stromata*, IV, 8. (Abbr.: *Str.*)

27. *Paedagogus*, I, 12. (Abbr.: *Paed.*)

28. *Ibid.*, II, 4, Cf. II, 2.

29. *Protrepticus*, XI, 116. (Abbr.: *Protr.*)

30. *Adversus Haereses*, IV, 34, 4. (Abbr.: *Haer.*)

31. *De Idolotria*, XIX. (Abbr.: *Idol.*)

32. *Apol.*, XXXVII.

33. *Cor.*, XI.

34. *Octavius*, XXX, 6. (Abbr.: *Oct.*)

35. *Ad Donatum*, VI, 10. (Abbr.: *Don.*)

36. *De Habitu Virginum*, XI.

37. *Adversus Nationes*, I, 6. (Abbr.: *Nat.*)

38. *Divinae Institutiones*, VI, xx, 15-16. (Abbr.: *Inst.*)

39. Leclercq, article "Militarisme" in Cabrol's *Dictionnaire d'Archéologie Chrétienne;* II, pp. 1107-81; on this point pp. 1116-19.

40. Passage from Cramer, *Catena in I Cor. V*, p. 98. Cited in Adolf Harnack, "Der kirchengeschichtliche Ertrag der exegetischen Arbeiten des Origenes," *Texte und Untersuchungen*, XLII, 3 (1918) , p. 117, note 2.

41. *Idol.*, XIX.

42. "Carmina," *Corpus Scriptorum Ecclesiasticorum Latinorum*, XV. Abbreviated hereafter *CSEL*. On the date see my article listed above note 77.

43. Eusebius, *Historia Ecclesiastica*, IV, xxvi, 7.

44. Igino Giordani, *The Social Message of the Early Church Fathers* (Paterson, N. J.,

1944), p. 149, associates with Melito two other Asiatic bishops, namely Theophilus and Abercius.

45. On Rome as the power that restrains: Tertullian, *De Resurrectione Carnis*, XXIV; Origen, *Com. in Joh.* 6:3; Lactantius, *Inst.*, VII, 25; Hippolytus, *In Danielem* IV, 21, 5.

46. Harold Fuchs, *Der geistige Widerstand gegen Rom in der antiken Welt* (Berlin, 1938).

47. Tertullian, *Ad Nationes*, IX. Minucius, *Octavius*, XXV.

48. *Inst.*, VII, 15.

49. *Apol.*, XXV.

50. *Inst.*, VI, 9.

51. Wilhelm Bousset, *The Antichrist Legend* (London, 1896), p. 126.

52. *Haer.*, IV, 30, 3.

53. *De Pallio*, I.

54. *Contra Celsum*, II, 30. Cf. C. J. Cadoux, *The Early Church and the World* (Edinburgh, 1925), pp. 378, 386.

55. II Pet. 3:4.

56. Adolf Harnack, *Die Chronologie der altchristlichen Literatur . . .* , II (Leipzig, 1904), p. 273, and my discussion in the article listed in note 1.

57. Robert Frick, "Die Geschichte des Reich Gottes-Gedankens in der alten Kirche bis zu Origenes und Augustin," Beihefte z. Zt. f. d. neutestamentliche Wissenschaft, VI (1928), and Cadoux, *op. cit.*, pp. 305 ff., 347, 379.

58. *Apol.*, XXXII, XXXIX, *Ad Scapulum* III. But a speedy coming desired in *De Oratione V*. On the *mora finis:* cf. Cyprian, *Ad Donatum*, XX. On Hippolytus: Karl J. Neumann, *Hippolytus von Rom in seiner Stellung zu Staat und Welt* (Leipzig, 1902), pp. 56-57.

59. The Epistle of Diognetus contains the classic statement. For parallels consult Luigi Salvatorelli, "Il pensiero del Cristianismo antico intorno allo stato dagli Apologeti ad Origene," *Bilychnis*, XVI (1920), pp. 264-79, 333-52, and Wilhelm Wagner, *Der Christ und die Welt nach Clemens von Alexandrien* (Göttingen, 1903).

60. Cyprian, *Ad Demetrianum*, XVII, and Tertullian, *De Spectaculis*.

61. *Apol.*, XXXVII. Cf. Justin, I *Apol.*, XIV.

62. *Protrepticus* X.

63. Cyprian, *De Patientia*, XV-XVI.

64. *Ep.*, XIV.

65. Tertullian, *De Patientia*, VI.

66. I *Apol.*, XV.

67. Acts 15:29.

68. *De Pudicitia*, XII.

69. This and many other citations in Gotthold Resch, "Das Aposteldekret nach ausserkanonischer Textgestalt," *Texte und Untersuchungen*, XXVIII, N.F. XIII, 3 (1905), p. 12, No. 21, cf. p. 43.

70. *Apol.*, XXXVII.

71. *Oct.*, XXX, 6.

72. *Ad Donatum*, VI, 10.

73. *Nationes*, I, 6.

74. *Inst.*, VI, 20.

75. Paulini Nol. *Ep.* XVIII, 7, Migne PL, LXI, 240 C.

76. *Legatio*, XXXV.

77. *Contra Celsum*, III, 7.

78. Canon, XVI.

79. *Ep. Cl.*, II, 188, 13. Migne, PG, XXXII, 682.

80. *ANF*, VIII, 728. A thorough study has been made of the aversion of the early Christians to the taking of life by Bernhard Schopf, *Das Tötungsrecht bei den frühchristlichen Schriftstellern* (Regensburg, 1958).

81. P. K. Baillie Reynolds, *The Vigiles of Imperial Rome* (Oxford, 1926).

82. On their functions see Theodor Mommsen, *Ephemeris Epigraphica*, IV (1881), pp. 529-30.

83. *Dist. d'Archéologie Chrétienne*, II, p. 1160, no. 24.

84. *De Fuga*, XIII.

85. *Dict. d'Archéologie Chrétienne*, II, pp. 1172-73.

86. E.—Ch. Babut, "La guarde impériale et les officiers de l'armée romaine," *Rev. Hist.*, CXIV (1913), pp. 225-60; CXVI (1914), pp. 225-93. Cf. Ernst Stein, *Geschichte des spätröm. Reiches* (1928), p. 82.

87. Eusebius, *HE*, VIII, IX, 7.

88. Burton Scott Easton, *The Apostolic Tradition of Hippolytus* (New York, 1934), Pt. II, Canon 16, p. 42.

89. *Idol.*, XIX.

90. *Protrepticus*, X, 100.

91. Gustave Combès, *La Doctrine Politique de Saint Augustin* (Paris, 1927), p. 261.

92. John Eppstein, *The Catholic Tradition of the Law of Nations* (Washington, D.C., 1935), p. 40.

93. *Paedagogus*, I, viii, 65, 1.

94. Adolf Harnack, *Militia Christi*, p. 87 f.

95. Sulpicius Severus, *Vita Martini*, I. 1-4.

96. *Idol.*, XIX and *Corona* XI.

97. Adolf Harnack "Marcion," *Texte und Untersuchungen*, XLV (1921), p. 105, cf. pp. 88 and 161.

98. Tertullian, *Idol.*, XIX.

99. Tertullian, *Adversus Marcionem*, IV, 16.

100. Origen, *Contra Celsum*, VII, 26.

101. Origen, *Hom. in Jesu Nave*, XV, 1.

102. Tertullian, *Adversus Marcionem*, I, 24, and I, 14.

103. *Ibid.*, I, 29.

104. Origen, *Contra Celsum*, VIII, 55.

105. *Ibid.*, VIII, 73.

106. "Comm. Ser. 37 in Mt. 24:7-8" *Die griechischen christlichen Schriftsteller*, XXXVIII, p. 69.

107. Origen, *Contra Celsum*, VIII, 72.

108. *Haer.*, V, 20. Cf. Wolfgang Schmidt, *Die Kirche bei Irenaeus* (Helsingfors, 1934).

109. II *Apol.*, VII.

110. *Contra Celsum*, VIII, 75. Cf. Heinrich Weinel, *Die Stellung des Urchristentums zum Staat* (Tübingen, 1908).

111. *Apol.*, XXXVIII.

112. *Contra Celsum* IV, 70. Cf. Guglielmo Massart, *Società e stato nel cristianesimo primitivo: la concezione di Origene* (Padua, 1932).

113. *Apol.*, XXX.

114. *Stromata*, II, 18.

115. *Contra Celsum* IV, 82.

116. *Ibid.*, VIII, 73.

117. *Demonstratio Evangelica*, I, viii, 29b-30b; cf. Cadoux, *op. cit.*, 469 note and 578.

Chapter 6

1. Lactantius, *De Mortibus Persecutorum*, IX. Cf. René Pichon, *Lactance* (Paris, 1909), p. 404.

2. Felix Rütten, "Die Victorverehrung im christlichen Altertum," *Studien zur Geschichte und Kultur des Altertums* XX, I (1936), p. 42.

3. Eusebius, *Oratio Constantini*, XVI, 3-8. GCS, VII, 249-50. *Praeparatio Ev.*, I, iv. Migne *PG*, XXI, 35-42. cf. Erik Peterson, *Monotheismus als politisches Problem* (Leipzig, 1935).

4. Karl Staab, "Pauluskommentare aus der griechischen Kirche," *Neutestamentliche Abh.*, XV (1933), p. 107.

5. *Expos. in Ps. XLV*, Migne, *PG*, LV, 207.

6. On Micah 4:2. Migne, *PL*, XXV, 1187-88.

7. *En. in Ps. XLV*. Migne, *PL*, XIV, 1142-44.

8. *Historiarum Libri VII*, VII, 3, 4. *CSEL*, V, 438.

9. *Contra Symmachum*, II, 586 ff. Migne, *PL*, LX, 227-30.

10. *Theodosiani Libri XVI*, XVI, 10, 21, Dec. 7, 416.

11. *Supra.*

12. *Letters of Synesius of Cyrene*, trans. A. Fitzgerald (Oxford, 1926), letters 104, 122, 125, 132. Greek in Migne, *PG*, LXVI, 1479, 1501-05, 1517.

13. James Franklin Bethune-Baker, *The Influence of Christianity on War* (Cambridge, 1888).

14. Sulpicius Severus, *Vita Martini*, I, i-v. Migne, *PL*, XX, 161-63.

15. *Ep.*, XVIII, 7-10, Migne, *PL*, LXI, 240-44.

16. John T. McNeill, "Asceticism versus militarism in the Middle Ages," *Church History*, V (1936), 3-28.

17. Origen, *Contra Celsum*, VIII, 55.

18. Orosius, *Historiarum Lib. VII*, XXXIII, *CSEL*, V, 516.

19. Migne, *PG*, XLVII, 389, sec. 2.

20. Julian, *Ep.*, 51.

21. *De Fide Christiana*, II, 16. Migne, *PL*, XVI, 587-90.

22. *De Officiis*, the Latin in Migne, *PL*, XVI, English PNF 2d, X.

23. *Sermo Dom.*, I, iv, 12, Migne, *PL*, XXXIV, 1235.

24. *Retract.* I, xix, 1.

25. *De Civitate Dei*, XVII, 13.

26. *In Joan. Ep.*, XXXIV, 10, Migne *PL*, XXXV, 1656.

27. *De Civitate Dei*, XIX, 28.

28. *En. Ps. CXLVII*, 20 Migne, *PL*, XXXVII, 1930. Many passages are collected by Harald Fuchs, "Augustin und der antike Friedensgedanke," *Neue philol. Unters.* No. 3 (Berlin, 1926), p. 47 f.

29. *Sermo Dom.* I, xx, 64, Migne, *PL*, XXXIV, 1262.

30. Gustave Combès, *La charité d'après Saint Augustin* (c. 1934).

31. Roland H. Bainton, "The Parable of the Tares," *Church History*, I (1932), 67-89.

32. *De Civitate Dei*, I, 35.

33. *Epist.* 99, *CSEL*, XXIV, 533-34; *Epist.*, 111, *ibid.*, 653-54; *Epist.*, 228, *ibid.*, LVII, 484-98; *Epist.*, 189, *ibid.*, LVII, 134-35.

34. *Epist.*, 138, 16 and *De Civitate Dei*, V, 15.

35. *De Civitate Dei*, II, 18.

36. *Ibid.*, XIX, 24 and IV, 4.

37. *Ibid.*, XVI, 43.

38. *Ibid.*, XV, 5; II, 17-18. Cf. Walter Rehm, "Der Untergang Roms in abendländischem Denken," *Das Erbe der Alten*, XVIII (Leipzig, 1930).

39. *De Civitate Dei*, III, 21.

40. P. Gerosa, "S. Agostino e l'imperialismo Romano," *Miscellanea Agostiniana* II (Rome, 1931), pp. 977-1040.

41. *En. in Ps. XLV*, Migne, *PL*, XXXV, 522.

42. *De Civitate Dei*, XIX, 7; V, 17; III, 14; III, 3; IV, 6.

43. *Ibid.*, III, 3; V, 19, 25, 26.

44. *Sermo CVI*, vii-viii, Migne, *PL*, XXXIV, 623-25.

45. *De Civitate Dei*, I, 10-19.

46. *Epist.*, 189, 6, and 209, 2.
47. Rom. 12:18. *De Civitate Dei*, XIX, 12-13.
48. *Quaest. Hept.*, VI, 10, *CSEL*, XXVIII, 2, p. 428.
49. *De Civitate Dei*, XXII, 6.
50. *De Libero Arbitrio*, V, 12. Migne, *PL*, XXXXII, 1227.
51. *Quaest. Hept.*, IV, 44, *CSEL*, XXVIII, 2, p. 353.
52. *Contra Faustum*, XXII, 76 and 79.
53. *Epist.*, 138, ii, 14.
54. *Sermo Dom.*, I, xx, 63 and 70. Migne, *PL*, XXXIV, 1261 ff.
55. *Epist.*, 138, ii ,15.
56. *Contra Faustum*, XXII, 70 and 75.
57. *En. Ps. CXXIV*, 7, Migne, *PL*, XXXVII, 1654.
58. Passages collected by Gustave Combès, *La doctrine politique de Saint Augustin* (Paris, 1927).
59. *De Civitate Dei*, I, 6-7.
60. *De Libero Arbitrio*, V, ii, Migne, PL, XXXII, 1227.
61. *Epist.*, 47, 5.
62. Ps. 25:7. *De Civitate Dei*, XIX, 6.
63. Robert Grosse, *Römische Militärgeschichte von Gallienus bis zum Beginn der byzantinischen Themenverfassung* (Berlin, 1920), p. 264.
64. E. Homes Dudden, *The Life and Times of St. Ambrose* (2 vols.; Oxford, 1935), I, 164-76.

Chapter 7

1. *History of the Franks*, II, 30.
2. *Heliand*, German trans. K. L. Kannegiesser (1847), pp. 145-46.
3. Edgar Nathaniel Johnson, *The Secular Activities of the German Episcopate 919-1024* (University of Nebraska Studies, 1932).
4. Albrecht von Stade, *Chronicon Alberti Abbatis Stadenis* (Helmestadii, 1587), for the year A.D. 1172.
5. Lina Eckenstein, *Woman under Monasticism* (Cambridge, Eng., 1896), pp. 65-67.
6. Alfred Vanderpol, *La Doctrine scholastique du Droit de Guerre* (Paris, 1919), pp. 77-84.
7. Bede Jarrett, *Social Theories of the Middle Ages* (1926, reprinted 1942), p. 192.
8. Vanderpol, *op. cit.*, p. 51.
9. Martin Grabmann, "Das Naturrecht der Scholastik von Gratian bis Thomas von Aquino," *Archiv für Rechts- und Wirtschaftsphilosophie*, XVI (1922-23); Odon Lottin, *Le Droit naturel chez Saint Thomas d'Aquin et ses predecesseurs* (Bruges, 1931); Friedrich Wagner, *Das natürliche Sittengesetz nach der Lehre des hl. Thomas von Aquino* (Breslau, 1910).
10. Thomas Aquinas, *De Regno*.
11. Vanderpol, *op. cit.*, and Heinrich Finke, "Das Problem des gerechten Krieges in der mittelalterlichen theologischen Literatur," *Beiträge zur Geschichte der Philosophie*, Suppl. III (1935), pp. 1426-34. On this point p. 1430.
12. The idea but not the proverb is classical. Cf. E. Wölfflin, "Krieg und Frieden im Sprichworte der Römer," *Sitzungsberichte der bayr. Ak. der Wiss.*, phil.-hist. Kl. (1888).
13. Vanderpol, *op. cit.*, p. 29.
14. Emanuel Hirsch, *Luther Studien*, Bd. 1, *Drei Kapitel zu Luthers Lehre vom Gewissen* (Gütersloh, 1954); Michael Wittmann, *Die Ethik des hl. Thomas von Aquino* (1933), pp. 176-78; Oskar Renz, "Die Synteresis nach dem hl. Thomas von Aquino," *Beiträge zur Geschichte der Philosophie des Mittelalters*, X, 1-2 (1911), p. 137.
15. Ferdinand Geldner, *Die Staatsauffassung und Fürstenlehre des Erasmus von Rotterdam* (Berlin, 1930), p. 14 note 12.

16. Fritz Kern, "Gottesgnadentum und Widerstandsrecht," *Mittelalterliche Studien I*, 2 (Leipzig, 1914).

Max Lossen, *Die Lehre vom Tyrannenmord in der christlichen Zeit* (München, 1894).

17. Vanderpol, *op. cit.*, pp. 119-24.

18. *Ibid.*, p. 117.

19. Ludwig Huberti, *Studien zur Rechtsgeschichte der Gottesfrieden und Landfrieden*, I (all that appeared, Ausbach, 1892), pp. 314-15.

20. *Ibid.*, p. 165.

21. *Ibid.*, p. 211 ff.

22. Bede Jarrett, *op. cit.*, p. 187.

23. Passages are here combined from several versions translated in Dana Carlton Munro, "Urban and the Crusaders," *Translations and Reprints* (University of Pennsylvania, 1901).

24. Carl Erdmann, *Die Entstehung des Kreuzzugsgedankens* (Stuttgart, 1935), p. 164.

25. Historia Francorum, trans. Frederick Duncalf and August C. Krey, *Parallel Source Problems in Medieval History* (New York: Harper & Brothers, 1912). Used by permission.

26. Anna Comnena, *The Alexiad*, trans. Elizabeth Dawes (London: Routledge & Kegan Paul Ltd., 1928), pp. 255-57. Used by permission.

27. Migne *PL*, 182, 921 ff. Cf. Steven Runciman, *A History of the Crusades*, vol. I, ch. I, "Holy Peace and Holy War" (Cambridge, Eng., 1951).

28. Hoffman Nickerson, *The Inquisition* (London, 1923), p. 115; Jean C. L. Simonde de Sismondi, *History of the Crusades Against the Albigenses* (London, 1826), pp. 35, 77-78.

29. Richard Wallach, "Das abendländische Gemeinschaftsbewusstsein im Mittelalter," *Beiträge zur Kulturgeschichte des Mittelalters und der Renaissance*, Bd. 34 (Leipzig, 1928).

30. Mileto Novacovitch, *Les Compromis et les Arbitrages Internationaux du XII au XVe Siècle* (Paris, 1905). The examples are mostly from northern Europe. A summary and bibliography of works covering also southern Europe is given in M. de Taube, "Les Origines de l'Arbitrage International. Antiquité et Moyen Age," *Receuil des cours de l'Academie de droit international* IV, Tome 42 (1932).

31. Helen Jenkins, *Papal Efforts for Peace under Benedict XII*, 1334-1342 (University of Pennsylvania Diss., Philadelphia, 1933).

John Gruber, "Peace Negotiations of the Avignonese Popes," *Catholic Historical Review*, XIX (1933-34), pp. 190-99; Clemens Bauer, "Epochen der Papstfinanz," *Historische Zeitschrift*, CXXXVIII (1928), pp. 457-504.

32. George B. Flaliff, "Deus non vult," *Medieval Studies*, IX (1947), pp. 162-88.

33. Palmer Throop, *Criticism of the Crusade* (Amsterdam, 1940), especially p. 58.

34. Ellen Scott Davison, *Forerunners of St. Francis* (Boston 1927), pp. 257, 271.

35. *Der Christ in der Welt*, III, 3 (1952-53), p. 82.

36. Herbert E. Winn, *Wyclif, Select English Writings* (Oxford, 1929), p. 113; cf. Geoffry F. Nuttall, *Christian Pacifism in History* (Oxford, 1958).

37. Peter Brock, *The Political and Social Doctrines of the Unity of Czech Brethren* (Gravenhage, 1957); Frederick Heymann, *John Zizka and the Hussite Revolution* (Princeton, 1955).

38. Werner Fritzemeyer, "Christenheit und Europa," *Historische Zeitschrift*, Beiheft 23 (München, 1931), expecially pages 7-13.

Chapter 8

1. *Istorie Fiorentine*, IV, 6; V, 33; VII, 20. Cf. Felix Gilbert on Machiavelli in *Makers of Modern Strategy*, ed., Edward M. Earle (1943), pp. 12-13. A full treatment of warfare in this period is given by Piero Pieri, *Il Rinascimento e la crisi militare italiana*

(1952). On Machiavelli and his political thought consult Frederico Chabod, *Machiavelli and the Renaissance* (London, 1958). On the international community of the Italian city-states see Angelo Sereni, *The Italian Conception of International Law* (New York, 1943), ch. VI.

2. *Discorsi*, II, 2.

3. *Principe*, XVIII.

4. *Ibid.*, XVII.

5. *Istorie Fiorentine*, V, I.

6. Thomas Fenne, *Fennes Frutes* (1590), fol. 53, cited in Paul A. Jorgensen, *Shakespeare's Military World* (Berkeley, 1956), p. 192.

7. Paracelsus, *Sozialethische und sozialpolitische Schriften*, hrsg. Kurt Goldammer (Tübingen, 1952), pp. 310-16.

8. Sebastian Franck, *Kriegbüchlein des Friedens*, excerpts and commentary in Kurt von Raumer, *Ewiger Friede* (Freiburg i. Br., 1953).

9. William J. Bouwsma, *Concordia Mundi. The Career and Thought of Guillaume Postel* (Cambridge, Mass., 1957).

10. *Gargantua*, XXV. Cf. Paul Stapfer, "Les Idées de Rabelais sur la Guerre," *Bibliothèque Univ. et Rev. Suisse*, XL (1888), pp. 367-79.

11. Montaigne, *Essais*, II, xii.

12. J. Clichtovuis, *De Bello et Pace* (1523), photocopy ed. Olivart (Madrid, 1914).

13. Ludovicus Vives, *Opera Omnia* (Basel, 1555), *De Bello Turcico*, II, 947-59.

14. Thomas More, *Utopia*, VIII, tr. 1551 (Oxford, 1895).

15. Erasmus, *Vita Coleti*.

16. Agrippa of Nettesheim, *On the Vanity of the Arts and Sciences* (English, London, 1676), pp. 254-55.

17. Lester K. Born, "The Education of the Christian Prince," *Records of Civilization*, XXVIII (New York, 1936).

18. R. H. Bainton, "The Classical and Christian Sources of Erasmus' *Querela Pacis*," *Archiv für Reformationsgeschichte*, 42 (1951), pp. 32-48, for full literature.

Chapter 9

1. The most important writings of Luther on this subject are the following arranged in chronological order and with references to the Weimar edition:

1523 *Von weltlicher Oberkeit*, II, 245-81.

1525 *Ermahnung zum Frieden*, XVIII, 291-334.

Wider die räuberischen und mörderischen Rotten der Bauern, XVIII, 357-61.

Sendbrief von dem harten Büchlein wider die Bauern, XVIII, 384-401.

1527 *Ob Kriegsleute*, XIX, 623-62.

1529 *Vom Kriege wider die Türken*, XXX, II, 107-48.

Heerpredigt wider den Türken, XXX, II, 160-97.

1534 *Zwo Predigten von Zorn*, XLI, 748 ff.

The following literature covers Luther's political theory and his views as to war against the peasants, the Turk and the emperor:

Paul Althaus, "Luthers Haltung im Bauernkrieg," *Jahrbuch der Luthergesellschaft*, VII (1925), 1-39.

Heinrich Bornkamm, "Luthers Lehre von den zwei Reichen . . ." *Archiv für Reformationsgeschichte*, 49 (1958), pp. 26-49.

Harvey Buchanan, "Luther and the Turks," *Archiv für Reformationsgeschichte*, 47 (1956), pp. 145-60.

Harald Diem, *Luthers Lehre von den zwei Reichen* (München, 1938).

Johannes Heckel, "Im Irrgarten der Zwei-Reichen-Lehre," *Theologische Existenz Heute*, Heft 55 (1957).

Fritz Kern, "Luther und der Widerstand," *Zeitschrift der Savingy-Stiftung für Rechtsgeschichte*, Kanonistische Abt. VI (1916).

Kurt Mathes, "Luther und die Obrigkeit," *Aus der Welt christlicher Frömmigkeit*, XII (1937).

Karl Müller, "Luthers Äusserungen über das Recht des bewaffneten Widerstands gegen den Kaiser," *Sitzungsberichte der kön. Bayr. Akad.* philos.-philol. Kl., VIII (1915).

Gustaf Törnvall, *Andligt och världsligt regemente hos Luther* (1940), German, *Geistliches und weltliches Regiment bei Luther* (1947).

Oscar Waldeck, "Die Publizistik des Schmalkaldischen Krieges," *Archiv für Reformationsgeschichte*, 7 (1909-10), pp. 1-55.

2. Weimarer Ausgabe, I, 535. (Abbr. *WA*).

3. *WA*, XIV, 553.

4. *WA*, LII, 26.

5. Especially *Von weltlicher Oberkeit*.

6. *WA*, XLI, 748 ff.

7. *WA*, VI, 267.

8. *WA*, XXX, I, 202.

9. The saying comes from Suetonius, *Vita Octavii*, XXV. In Luther *WA*, VI, 261. It is quoted sometimes as a golden hook and sometimes as a golden net.

10. LII, 189 and XXXVII, 319.

11. On Zwingli consult Walter Koehler, "Ulrich Zwingli und der Krieg," *Christliche Welt* 29, No. 34 (1915), pp. 675-82. The same theme is handled by Oskar Farner in *Zwingliana*, III (1914), pp. 78-80.

12. Oskar Farner, *Huldreich Zwingli* (2 vols.; 1943, 1946), II, 194.

13. *Huldreich Zwinglis Sämtliche Werke*, 1 (*CR*. LXXXVIII), pp. 175-76.

14. On Calvin and Calvinism consult:

J. W. Allen, *A History of Political Thought in the Sixteenth Century* (New York, 1928).

R. H. Bainton, "Castellio Concerning Heretics," *Records of Civilization*, XXII (New York, 1935), the section on Calvin.

——*The Age of the Reformation* (Anvil Original, 1956), documents on the right of revolution.

Robert Kingdon, *Geneva and the Coming of the Wars of Religion in France* (Geneva, 1956).

——"The First expression of Theodore Beza's Political Ideas," *Archiv für Reformationsgeschichte*, 46 (1955), pp. 88-100.

Richard Nürnberger, *Die Politisierung des Französischen Protestantismus* (Tübingen, 1948).

15. *Calvini Opera, Corpus Reformatorum*, VIII, 476; XXIV, 360; XLIV, 346.

16. *Ibid.*, XVIII, 425-26.

17. I Kings 11:11.

18. Henry White, *The Massacre of St. Bartholomew* (London, 1868), pp. 238, 248.

19. Chanon. *Trois Verités*. Cited in Geoffrey Atkinson, *Les Nouveaux Horizons* (Paris, 1935), p. 396.

20. See R. H. Bainton, "Congregationalism: from the Just War to the Crusade in the Puritan Revolution," *Andover Newton Theological School Bulletin*, Southworth Lecture (April, 1943).

21. Thomas Carlyle, *The Letters and Speeches of Oliver Cromwell*, ed. S. C. Lomas (3 vols.; London, 1904), I, 396.

22. London, 1643.

23. *A Sermon Preached Before the Commons*, May 27, 1646 (London, 1646), p. 8.

24. *Fovre Speeches* (London, 1646), p. 21.

25. *Ibid.*, pp. 15-16.

26. John Redingstone, *Plain English* (London, 1649), p. 3, on Ps. 149.

27. *A Sermon*, Jan. 29, 1644 (London, 1645).

28. Carlyle, *op. cit.*, II, 100.

29. *A Great Victory God hath vouchsafed by the Lord Generall Cromwels Forces against the Scots* (London, 1651), p. 5.

30. *A full RELATION of the Great Victory* (London, 1648), p. 7.

31. Carlyle, *op. cit.*, I, 511.

32. *THE WORKES of Ephesus Explained*, April 27, 1642 (London, 1642), p. 50.

33. *A WARNING-PEECE to WARRE* (London, 1642).

34. T. B. Howell, *A Complete Collection of State Trials* (London, 1816), V, pp. 1116-18.

35. Robert S. Paul, *The Lord Protector* (London, 1955), p. 210.

36. C. V. Wedgewood, *The Thirty Years' War* (New Haven, 1939).

Chapter 10

1. On the Anabaptists consult:

Franklin Littell, *The Anabaptist View of the Church* (new ed., Boston, 1958).

Hans J. Hillerbrand, "The Anabaptist View of the State," *Mennonite Quarterly Review* XXXII, 2 (1958), pp. 83-111.

—— "An Early Anabaptist Treatise on the Christian and the State," XXXII, 1 (1958), pp. 28-48.

Harold Bender, "The Pacifism of the Sixteenth Century Anabaptists," *Mennonite Quarterly Review*, XXX, 1 (1956), pp. 5-19.

John Horsch, *The Principle of Nonresistance as held by the Mennonite Church* (Scottsdale, Pa., 1927).

Guy F. Hershberger, ed., *The Recovery of the Anabaptist Vision* (Scottsdale, Pa., 1957).

—— *War, Peace and Nonresistance* (Scottsdale, Pa., 1944).

Stanislas Kot, *Socinianism in Poland* (Boston, 1957).

On the Brethren:

Rufus Bowman, *The Church of the Brethren and War* (Elgin, Ill., 1944).

On the Quakers:

Margaret E. Hirst, *The Quakers in Peace and War* (London: George Allen & Unwin Ltd., 1923).

Geoffrey F. Nuttall, *Christian Pacifism in History* (Oxford, 1958).

2. Rom. 13.

3. Lydia Müller, "Glaubenszeugnisse oberdeutscher Taufgesinnte," *Quellen und Forschungen zur Reformationsgeschichte*, XX (1938), p. 249.

4. Cited by Horsch, *op. cit.*

5. R. H. Bainton, "The Immoralities of the Patriarchs . . ." *Harvard Theological Review*, XXIII, 1 (January, 1930).

6. A. J. F. Zieglschmid, ed., *Die älteste Chronik der Hutterischen Brüder* (Ithaca, 1943), p. 307.

7. *Op. cit.*, note 3, p. 199.

8. *Op. cit.*, note 5, pp. 54, 87-88.

9. Hirst, *op. cit.*, p. 43. Used by permission of George Allen & Unwin Ltd.

10. *Ibid.*, p. 46.

11. *Ibid.*, pp. 118-19.

12. Robert Barclay, *An Apology* (Philadelphia, 1805), pp. 582-83.

13. Hirst, *op. cit.*, p. 124.

14. *Ibid.*, p. 57.

15. *Ibid.*, p. 59.

16. Isaac Sharpless, *A History of Quaker Government in Pennsylvania* (2 vols.; Philadelphia, 1899), I, 190, condensed.

17. Robert Barclay, *Apology*, pp. 584-85.

18. Hirst, *op. cit.*, p. 213.

19. Waldo Beach, *The Meaning and Authority of Conscience in Protestant Thought of Seventeenth Century England* (Unpublished dissertation, Yale University, 1944).

20. *Oeuvres diverses de Mr. Pierre Bayle* (The Hague, 1727), II, 432-33.

21. *Boswell's Life of Johnson* (London, 1904), I, 511 under the year 1773.

22. Leonard T. Hobhouse, *The Metaphysical Theory of the State* (London, 1918), pp. 91-94.

23. Hirst, *op. cit.,* p. 125.

24. *Ibid.,* p. 130.

25. Bowman, *op. cit.,* p. 43.

26. Thomas Lurting, *The Fighting Sailor* (London, 1770's).

27. On the Spanish conquest consult:
Lewis K. Hanke, *The Spanish Struggle for Justice in the Conquest of America* (Philadelphia, 1949). The statements below refer to the following pages: 7, 71, 6, 7, 34, and 2 in this order.

—— *Aristotle and the American Indians* (London, 1959).

28. Franciscus de Vittoria, *Classics of International Law,* ed. J. B. Scott (1917), pp. 129, 250, 163-87.

29. Hanke, *Aristotle,* p. 26.

30. Cotton Mather, *Souldiers Counselled and Comforted, a Discourse Delivered Unto Some Part of the Forces Engaged in the Just War of New England Against the Northern and Eastern Indians. September 1, 1689.* (Boston, 1689).

31. George Leon Walker, *Thomas Hooker* (New York, 1891), p. 100.

32. Jer. 46:10. Henry Gibbs, *The Right Method of Safety or, The Just Concern of the People of God . . .* (Boston, 1704).

33. Samuel Phillips, *Souldiers Counselled and Encouraged* (Boston, 1742).

34. Thomas Bridge, *The Knowledge of God Securing from Flattery, and Strengthening to the Most Noble Exploits* (Boston, 1705), pp. 46, 50.

35. James Cogswell, *God, the Pious Soldier's Strength and Instructor: A Sermon Deliver'd at Brooklyn . . . to the Military Company, under the Command of Capt. Israel Putnam . . .* (Boston, 1757), pp. 7, 26.

36. Thomas Prince, *Extraordinary Events the Doings of God, and Marvellous in Pious Eyes* (Boston, 1745), pp. 18-20.

37. Samuel Woodward, *A Sermon Preached October 9, 1760. Being a Day of Public Thanksgiving on Occasion of the Reduction of Montreal and the Entire Conquest of Canada, by the troops of His Britannic Majesty . . .* (Boston, 1760), p. 26.

38. Nathaniel Appleton, *A Sermon Preached October 9, being a day of Public Thanksgiving, Ocassioned by the Surrender of Montreal, and all Canada, September 8, 1760. to His Britannic Majesty* (Boston, 1760), pp. 7 and 29.

39. *Records of Plymouth Colony,* IX, p. 7, art. IX and X, pp. 26 and 56. On this period compare Arthur H. Buffinton, "The Puritan View of War," *Publications of the Colonial Society of Massachusetts,* XXVIII (April, 1931), pp. 67-86.

40. Robert L. D. Davidson, *War Comes to Quaker Pennsylvania 1682-1756* (New York, 1957).

41. Deut. 7:2.

Chapter 11

1. George Norman Clark, *War and Society in the Seventeenth Century* (Cambridge, Eng., 1958).

2. Jorgenson, *op. cit.*

3. Palace of Peace, The Hague, *Bibliography of the Peace Movement Before 1899* (1936). Lists twenty-eight editions during the seventeenth century and six during the eighteenth exclusive of the *Opera.*

4. Eymeric Crucé. *Le Nouveau Cynée,* ed. Thomas W. Balch (Philadelphia, 1909), pp. 30, 84-85.

5. *Oeuvres* (54 vols., Paris, 1829-30), 11, 357.

6. Elizabeth V. Souleyman, *The Vision of World Peace in 17th and 18th Century France* (New York, 1941), especially pp. 11, 13, 113; Kurt von Raumer, *Ewiger Friede* (München, 1953), analizes the peace plans beginning with Erasmus. The smaller are printed in full, the longer in excerpts.

7. *De Ivre Belli ac Pacis* (Amsterdam, 1642), Prolog. XX.

8. T. S. K. Scott-Craig, *Christian Attitudes to War and Peace* (New York, 1938); Joachim von Elbe, "The Evolution of the Concept of the Just War in International Law," *American Journal of International Law*, XXXIII, 4 (October, 1939), pp. 665-88.

9. William Penn, *An Essay towards the Present and Future Peace of Europe*, reprinted by the Peace and Service Committee, Friends General Conference (1944).

10. Compare note 4 above.

11. Comenius, *The Angel of Peace,* ed. M. Safranek (Pantheon, New York, n.d.).

12. Immanuel Kant, *Perpetual Peace,* reprinted from the translation of 1796 (Columbia University, New York, 1939).

13. On the background see:

Michael Roberts, *The Military Revolution 1560-1660* (University of Belfast, 1956).

B. H. Liddell Hart, *The Revolution in Warfare* (London, 1946).

George Clark, *War and Society in the Seventeenth Century* (Cambridge, 1958).

Fritz Redlich, "De Praeda Militari, Looting and Booty 1500-1815," *Vierteljahrschrift für Sozial- und Wirtschaftsgeschichte*, Beiheft, 39 (1956), especially p. 72.

14. John V. Nef. *War and Human Progress* (Cambridge, Mass., 1950), p. 233.

15. *Ibid.,* p. 162.

16. Denis de Rougement, *Love in the Western World* (1939), p. 239.

17. Emmerich de Vattel, *Le Droit des Gens* (Neuchatel, 1773), III, pp. 110-11, 94-96.

18. Charles L. Montesquieu, "L'Esprit des Lois," Bk. X, iv, *Bibliothèque de la Pleiade*, 81 (1949), p. 381.

19. Nef, *op. cit.,* pp. 118, 122, 252, 260.

20. Elise Constantinescu-Bagdat, *Études d'histoire Pacifique*, II *De Vaughban à Voltaire* (Paris, 1925), p. 252.

21. Thomas Hobbes, *Leviathan* (reprint Oxford, 1909), pp. 457-69.

22. Charles F. Mullett, *Fundamental Law and the American Revolution 1770-1776* (New York, 1933).

23. Alice Baldwin, *The New England Clergy and the American Revolution* (Durham, N.C., 1928).

24. Dagobert De Levie, "Patriotic Activity of Calvinistic and Lutheran Clergymen during the American Revolution," *Lutheran Church Quarterly*, VIII, 4 (November, 1956).

Chapter 12

1. Harry Rudin, "Diplomacy, Democracy, Security: Two Centuries in Contrast," *Political Science Quarterly*, LXXI, No. 2 (June, 1956), pp. 161-81 and "The Problem of Security," in *God and the Nations*, ed. Paul Poling (New York, 1952).

2. Werner Fritzmeyer, "Christenheit und Europa," *Historische Zeitschrift*, Beiheft, 23 (1931).

3. W. Freeman Galpin, *Pioneering for Peace* (Syracuse, 1933); Merle Curti, *Peace or War, the American Struggle* (New York, 1936).

4. Ralph Waldo Emerson, *Works* (12 vols. Boston, 1909), XI, 201.

5. Curti, *The American Peace Crusade 1815-60* (Durham, N.C., 1929), p. 53.

6. Galpin, *op, cit.,* p. 113.

7. Adin Ballou, *Christian Non-resistance* (Philadelphia, 1842), p. 163.

8. Galpin, *op, cit.,* pp. 77 and 25 ff.

9. Cited in Ralph Barton Perry, *Puritanism and Democracy* (New York, 1944), p. 608.

10. Bertha von Suttner, *Lay Down Your Arms*, trans. T. Holmes (London, 1894), pp. 236-37 and 203.

11. J. F. C. Wright, *Slava Bohu* (New York, 1940).

12. Pauline V. Young, *The Pilgrims of Russian Town* (Chicago, 1932).

13. George P. Fedotov, *The Russian Religous Mind* (Cambridge, Mass., 1946), and "The Religious Sources of Russian Populism," *Russian Review* (April, 1942), pp. 27-39, Nadijda Gorodetzky, *The Humiliated Christ in Russian Thought* (New York, 1938).

14. Leo Tolstoy, *My Religion* (Crowell edition, 1899).

15. H. C. G. J. Mandere, *De Vredesbeweging in hare Geschiedenis* (Leiden, 1928) p. 114.

16. Curti, *Peace or War*, pp. 222-26.

17. Merze Tate, *The Disarmament Illusion* (New York, 1942), pp. 167 ff.

18. Chester Forrester Dunham, *The Attitude of the Northern Clergy Toward the South 1860-65* (Toledo, Ohio, 1942).

19. C. S. Ellsworth, "American Churches and the Mexican War," *American Historical Review*, XLV, 2 (January, 1940), pp. 301-26.

20. Julius W. Pratt, *The Expansionists of 1812* (New York, 1925).

21. William Archibald Karraker, *The American Churches and the Spanish-American War* (Unpublished dissertation, University of Chicago).

22. Hirst, *op. cit.*, p. 275. Used by permission of George Allen & Unwin Ltd.

23. *Ibid.*, p. 286.

24. George B. Smith, *The Life and Speeches of . . . John Bright* (New York, 1881, pp. 219, 231, 237.

25. John Morley, *Recollections* (2 vols.; London: Macmillan & Company Ltd. 1917), II, 86. Used by permission.

26. Raoul Allier, *Les Églises de Réforme et le Problème de la Paix au cours du XIXe siècle* (Paris, 1931).

27. *Literary Digest, XXIX*, nos. 4, 5 (January, 1904), pp. 115-16, 141.

28. Ernst Troeltsch, *The Ideas of Natural Law and Humanity in World Politics;* appendix in Gierke, *Natural Law* (English, Boston, 1957).

29. Georg Wilhelm Hegel, *Werke* (18 vols.; Berlin, 1832-45), VIII *Philosophie des Rechts*, sections 259, 333-39.

30. Joseph Mausbach, *Vom gerechten Kriege . . .* (Münster, 1914).

31. Karl Holl, *Gesammelte Aufsätze*, III (1928), section 7, pp. 147-70. This address was delivered in 1917.

32. Bishop A. F. Winnington-Ingram, *The Potter and the Clay* (London, 1917), pp. 41-42.

33. George K. A. Bell, *Randall Davidson* (2 vols.; Oxford, 1935), II, 903.

34. Ray H. Abrams, *Preachers Present Arms* (New York, 1933).

35. H. C. Peterson and Gilbert C. Fite, *Opponents of War 1917-18* (Madison, Wis., 1957), p. 134.

36. Maurice Baring, "In Memoriam A. H.," from *Collected Poems* (London: The Bodley Head, 1925), pp. 3-4. Used by permission.

Chapter 13

1. Herbert Hoover, *Shall We Send Our Youth to War?* (New York: Coward-McCann, Inc., 1939). Used by permission.

2. Vera Brittain, *The Testament of Youth* (New York, 1933); A. A. Milne, *Peace with Honor* (New York, 1934); Aldous Huxley, *Ends and Means* (New York, 1937); Charles E. Raven, *Is War Obsolete?* (1934), and *War and the Christian* (New York, 1938); Archibald MacLeish, *Air Raid* (New York, 1938); Harry Emerson Fosdick, *A Christian Conscience about War* (1925).

3. P. J. Noel Baker, *Disarmament* (New York, 1926); Mary Katherine Reely, *Select*

Documents on Disarmament (New York, 1921); Benjamin H. Williams, *The United States and Disarmament* (New York, 1931).

4. Statements not otherwise documented in this chapter are covered in my pamphlet, "The Churches and War: Historic Attitudes toward Christian Participation," *Social Action* (January, 1945).

5. Hajo Holborn, *The Political Collapse of Europe* (New York, 1951), p. 136.

6. John W. Wheeler-Bennett, *The Pipe Dream of Peace* (New York, 1935), pp. 116-18.

7. Arnold Wolfers, *Britain and France between Two Wars* (New York, 1940).

8. John A. Fisher, *Memories* (London, 1919), p. 274.

9. *New York Times*, January 23 and 27, 1941.
Christian Century (April 16, 1941), p. 523.

10. *Ibid.* (December 11, 1940), p. 1546; (July 17, 1940), p. 900; (February 5, 1941), p. 179.

11. Reinhold Niebuhr, *Christianity and Power Politics* (New York, 1940).

12. *Christianity and Crisis* (September 21, 1942), p. 6 and (April 19, 1943), p. 4.

13. *Christendom* (Autumn, 1943), p. 482.

14. *Christian Century* (November 1, 1939), p. 1347.

15. *Christianity and Crisis* (February 10, 1941), p. 6.

16. *Ibid.* (September 21, 1942), p. 1.

17. From "Fears in Solitude," composed 1798.

18. *Memoirs of Bertha von Suttner* (Boston, 1910), II, 408-9.

19. Liddell Hart, *The Revolution in Warfare* (London, 1946).

20. Patrick M. S. Blackett, *Fear, War and the Bomb* (New York, 1949), p. 15.

21. Cited by John C. Ford, "The Morality of Obliteration Bombing," *Theological Studies* (September, 1944), pp. 261-309. This citation p. 26.

22. Churchill's statements are cited in Vera Brittain, *Seed of Chaos* (London, 1944), p. 15.

23. Reprinted in *Fellowship* (March, 1944).

24. "Hiroshima—It must *Not* Happen Again," (London, 1955). Used by permission of the publisher, *Today and Tomorrow Publications*.

25. Herman Hagedorn, *The Bomb that Fell on America* (Santa Barbara, Cal., 1946), pp. 9, 14.

Chapter 14

1. On the possibility of defense against nuclear warfare consult:
Bernard Brodie in Quincy Wright, ed., *A Foreign Policy for the United States* (Chicago, 1947), pp. 92-94.
Patrick M. S. Blackett, *Fear, War and the Bomb* (New York, 1948), pp. 20-30, 36-38, 60.
Stanton A. Coblents, "H-Bombs; New Maginot Line," *Christian Century* (November 28, 1956), and his *From Arrow to Atom Bomb* (New York, 1953).
A number of articles in the *Bulletin of the Atomic Scientists* deal with the subject, e.g., McCleary (September, 1956), Kahn (January, 1959). Chisholm on bacteriological warfare (May, 1959); and Lapp (October, 1959), who discusses the obsolescence of massive retaliation.

2. *Committee of the World Council of Churches* (July, 1958), Article 79, 2.

3. Hanson W. Baldwin, "Limited War," *Atlantic Monthly* (May, 1959), pp. 35-43.

4. Henry A. Kissinger, *Nuclear Weapons and Foreign Policy* (New York, 1957), p. 189.

5. Compare C. F. von Weizsäcker, *Ethical and Political Problems of the Atomic Age* (London, 1958).

6. *Fellowship* (March, 1944).

7. *Christian Century* (March 22, 1944), p. 361.

8. See note 21, chap. 13.

9. Federal Council of Churches, *Atomic Warfare and the Christian Faith* (March, 1946).

10. Federal Council of Churches, *The Christian Conscience and Weapons of Mass Destruction* (1950), pp. 14, 23.

11. Wilfred Parsons, "Peace in the Atomic Age," *Catholic Association for International Peace* (1947).

12. Kaspar Mayr, *Der Andere Weg* (Nürnberg, 1957), p. 312.

13. Fifth World Order Study Conference, Cleveland, Ohio (November 18-21, 1958).

14. Hajo Holborn, *The Collapse of Europe* (New York, 1951), p. 149.

15. George F. Kennan, *American Diplomacy* (New York, 1951), p. 53.

16. P. A. Sorokin, *Social and Cultural Dynamics* (1 vol. ed.; Boston: Porter Sargent, 1957), p. 548.

17. Albert Schweitzer, *Civilization and Ethics* (London, 1923), p. 254.

18. F. J. P. Veale, *Advance to Barbarism* (Appleton, Wis., 1953), pp. 186-97.

19. Gerhard Ritter, *Carl Goerdeler* (Stuttgart, 1954). Cf. Oscar Jaszi and John D. Lewis, *Against the Tyrant* (Glenco, Ill., 1957).

20. Lothar Kotsch, "The Concept of War in Contemporary History and International Law," *Études d'Histoire èconomique, politique et sociale XVIII* (1956), p. 77, footnote 129.

21. Cyril Falls, *The Second World War* (London, 1948), p. 91. Cited in Blackett, *Fear, War and the Bomb* (1948), p. 19.

22. Reginald William Thompson, *Cry Korea* (London: Macdonald & Company, 1952). Used by permission.

23. Edgar L. Jones, "One War Is Enough," *Atlantic Monthly* (February, 1956), pp. 48-53. Used by permission.

24. Reginald Hugh Bacon, *Lord Fisher* (London, 1929), I, 120-21.

Chapter 15

1. The view that foreign policy should be directed primarily to national self-interest is espoused by:

Hans J. Morgenthau, *In Defense of the National Interest* (New York, 1951), p. 252; and "The Decline and Fall of American Foreign Policy," *New Republic* (December 10, 1956), p. 14.

Louis J. Halle, "A Touch of Nausea," *New Republic* (January 21, 1957), pp. 1-17.

Kenneth Thompson, *Christianity and Crisis* (January 7, 1957).

Ernest Lefever, *Ethics and United States Foreign Policy* (New York, 1957).

2. George F. Kennan, *American Diplomacy 1900-1950* (Mentor Paperback, 1952), p. 100.

3. Friends Committee on National Legislation (October, 1956).

4. André Philip, "What the UN Can and Cannot Do," *New Republic* (January 14, 1957), pp. 8-10.

5. John Foster Dulles, *War and Peace* (New York, 1950), pp. 190-91.

6. Vera Micheles Dean, "Anti-Westernism: Cause and Cure," *Christian Century* (May 9, 1956); George Meader, "Our Foreign Aid Program," *Reader's Digest* (April, 1957), p. 98; Bernard S. Van Rensselaer, "How Not to Handle Foreign Aid," *Reader's Digest* (February, 1957), pp. 25-30; Max F. Millikan and W. W. Rostow, *A Proposal for a United States Foreign Policy* (New York, 1957).

7. On various ventures in nonviolence consult: (Gandhi does not need documentation)

Barthelemy de Ligt, *The Conquest of Violence* (London, 1937).

Hallam Tennyson, *India's Walking Saint* (New York, 1955).

Vinoba Bhave, *Bhoodan Yajna* (land-gifts mission) (Ahmedabah, 1953).

Cecil E. Hinshaw, "Nonviolent Resistance," *Pendle Hill Pamphlet* 88 (1956).

André Trocmé, "Stages of Nonviolence," *Fellowship* (1953).

Leo Kuper, *Passive Resistance in South Africa* (New Haven, 1957).

Martin Luther King, Jr., "Nonviolence and Racial Justice," *Christian Century* (February 6, 1957).

8. On the population problem:

Information Service of the National Council of Churches (June 6, 1959), bibliography.

United Nations, *Population Studies,* especially *The Determinants and Consequences of Population Trends* (1953).

Richard M. Fagley, *The Population Explosion and Christian Responsibility* (New York, 1960), Cf. *Social Action* (December, 1958).

Population Bulletin (March, 1959). The prospects to A.D. 2000.

A. Myrdal and P. Vincent, "Are we too Many?" *Bureau of Current Affairs* (1949). Discriminating.

John Boyd Orr, *The White Man's Dilemma* (London, 1953). The cycle will run its course.

Daedalus (summer, 1959), articles by Hudson Hoaglund on the control of fertility and by John L. Thomas and John Bennett on the Catholic and Protestant approaches to the control of population.

9. John N. Hazard, "The United States and the Soviet Union," Quincy Wright, *A Foreign Policy for the United States* (Chicago, 1947).

10. Lewis Mumford, "Kindling for Global Gehenna," *Saturday Review of Literature* (June 26, 1948), p. 7, and "The Morals of Extermination," *Atlantic Monthly* (October, 1959), pp. 38-44.

11. Bertrand Russell, "Man's Peril from the Hydrogen Bomb," *The Listener* (December 30, 1954), reprinted by the *Friends Peace Committee, London.*

12. C. F. von Weizsäcker, *Ethical and Political Problems of the Atomic Age* (London: Student Christian Movement Press, 1958). Used by permission.

13. George F. Kennan, "Foreign Policy and Christian Conscience," *Atlantic Monthly* (May, 1959), pp. 44-49. Used by permission.

14. Luke 14:31.

15. Luke 22:25-26.

16. Gal. 5:22-23.

17. Nicholas Spykman, *America's Strategy in World Politics* (New York: Harcourt, Brace and Company, 1942), p. 37. Used by permission.

18. Bill Davidson, "Why Our Combat Soldiers Fail to Shoot," *Colliers* (Nov. 8, 1952); S. L. A. Marshall, *Men Against Fire* (New York, 1947).

19. Hans de Boer, *The Bridge is Love* (Grand Rapids, 1958).

20. Dan. 3:18.

21. *Christian Century* (July 5, 1939), p. 862; (January 31, 1940), p. 155; (November 6, 1940), p. 1365.

22. *Theology Digest* (Winter, 1957), p. 9. Two forthright Catholic statements have lately appeared: Francis M. Stratman, *War and Christianity Today* (Westminster, Md.: Newman Press, 1956).

Charles S. Thompson, ed., *Morals and Missiles* (London, 1959).

Guide to Literature

The literature on the problems and the ethic of war and peace is too voluminous for coverage in the notes or even in a separate bibliography which would itself comprise a volume. Space precludes more than a reference to bibliographical aids. Guides to literature have been issued by:

The Fellowship of Reconciliation, Box 271, Nyack, New York.

The Friends Peace Committee, 1520 Race St., Philadelphia 2, Pa. In December, 1956, and again in 1959.

The Puidoux Theological Conference, August, 1955. Apply to the secretary Pastor Dale Aukerman, Gluckstrasse 3, Becklinghoven bei Beuel, Germany. The compiler of this list, Walter Dignath, has provided bibliographies in his: "Kirche, Krieg und Kriegsdienst," *Theologische Forschung,* X (Hamburg, 1955) : and in his article: "Friedensbewegung," in the new edition of *Die Religion in Geschichte und Gegenwart.*

Ralph Luther Moellering covers the recent American scene in *Modern War and the American Churches* (New York, 1956).

Three journals are important for current material:

For the United States: *Fellowship,* published by the Fellowship of Reconciliation, Box 271, Nyack, New York.

For Britain: *Reconciliation,* 29 Great James St., London, England.

International: *Reconciliation Quarterly,* 3 Herndon Ave., Finchley, London N. 3, England (formerly *Christus Victor*).

For the continent: *Der Christ in der Welt,* ed., Kaspar Mayr, Nachreihengasse 48, Vienna 17, Austria.

For Catholic coverage see the publications of The Catholic Association for International Peace.

Index